Tea with Mr

100,000 MIL

THE LONGEST 'PROTEST MA

The Little Wonder: The Untold Story of Alfred Shrubb – World Champion Runner

'Today [5 November 2004] is the ideal opportunity to pay homage, exactly 100 years after the event, to one of the greatest individual runs from a British athlete. Chances are you have never heard of Alf Shrubb, but it is never too late to recognise sporting genius.' *Daily Telegraph*

'*The Little Wonder* tells the mysterious story of Alfred Shrubb ... It is a story that is richly evocative of the heyday of Edwardian athletics.' *The Guardian*

'The strongest contender for the greatest athlete never to have won an Olympic medal must surely be Alf Shrubb, who was the world's greatest distance runner 100 years ago. When he beat Olympic marathon champion Billy Sherring, Shrubb had time after finishing to return to the changing rooms, fetch his camera and take a picture of Sherring coming in second.' *Daily Mail*

Beer and Brine: The Making of Walter George – Athletics' First Superstar

'Rob Hadgraft has a penchant for uncovering athletes whose stories have been buried under layers of dust and neglect. Hadgraft's painstaking research reveals George was more than a one-race wonder; rather he was a lovable rascal with a destructive love of the ladies, alcohol and gambling.' *Daily Telegraph*

'This book is one of the finest sporting biographies you will ever read. Not only is the text illuminated with stirring reportage of the record-breaking races in which George took part, but it also provides the reader with as good a picture of mid- to late-Victorian England and the growth of sport as any book has ever done. Gripping from start to finish, it is meticulously researched and vividly encapsulates what sporting biography is all about. The story of George's early life in the idyllic Wiltshire countryside is beautifully told with plenty of social and political background, a feature which underpins the narrative throughout. This is a wonderful book, full of epic encounters, eccentric characters and unforgettable stories.' *Birmingham Post*

Deerfoot: Athletics' Noble Savage: From Indian Reservation to Champion of the World

'This absorbing account of Louis Bennett, known as Deerfoot, completes a trilogy by Rob Hadgraft, who has done athletics history a huge service in chronicling three great pioneering runners. These are meticulous, yet inspiring accounts, written with empathy for the athletes and an understanding of the times. It would be difficult to name the best of trilogy, but I can say for sure that Deerfoot's story entertained me the most.' *Trackstats Magazine*

'The first book-length biography of this extraordinary American athlete, who dominated English professional running from 1861-63, has been written by the assiduous Rob Hadgraft, the English enthusiast who already gave us fascinating books on Shrubb and George. Hadgraft's usual thoroughness brings to life the noisy, rough-edged vigour of 19th century running. It also gives insight into matters as important as racism, Victorian popular culture and the colourful early history of advertising and promotion. Hadgraft is commendably forthright about the prevalence of race-fixing and show-boating – Deerfoot often terrified the crowds with bloodcurdling war whoops as he crossed the finish line.' *Running Times (USA)*

Tea with Mr Newton

100,000 MILES:
The Longest 'Protest March' in History

Series Editor: Clive Leatherdale

Rob Hadgraft

Desert Island Books

First paperback edition published in2010
First hardback edition published in 2009
by
DESERT ISLAND BOOKS LIMITED
7 Clarence Road, Southend-on-Sea, Essex SS1 1AN
United Kingdom
www.desertislandbooks.com

© 2009, 2010 Rob Hadgraft

The right of Rob Hadgraft to be identified as author of this work has
been asserted under The Copyright Designs and Patents Act 1988

British Library Cataloguing-in-Publication Data
A catalogue record for this book is available from the British Library

ISBN 978-1-905328-85-7

Printed in Great Britain by
4edge Ltd, Hockley. www.4edge.co.uk

Contents

Author's Note

Taking up long-distance running at the grand old age of 38, as an anti-government publicity stunt, led to quintessential Englishman Arthur Newton becoming the unlikeliest of athletics champions. Newton was a loner, a man who lived and trained in splendid isolation, but who quickly became known across the globe as he began tearing up the long-distance record book.

Newton's story is of a struggling white farmer in South Africa, who travelled 100,000 miles by foot to end his days a wise old coaching guru, holding court in a suburban semi in West London.

Perhaps Newton's true achievement, topping even his world record runs, was the remarkable manner in which he carefully worked out for himself how to become a sporting champion from scratch in middle age, and then left a legacy of common-sense advice for the great ultra-distance men who followed in his wake. Modest to a fault, Newton always admitted he was a 'manufactured runner', and that his records would soon be broken by any man who set himself the task and trained properly. Newton had few worthy opponents during his golden years, for most ordinary working men of the era had neither the opportunity nor the motivation to train all day and every day as he could, under those clear blue African skies.

After he settled back in England in his fifties, champions and novice runners alike wrote to him and visited in vast numbers, eager to soak up his advice and anecdotes – encouraged to stay and talk by the unlimited supplies of tea and cake. Scalding hot tea was always Newton's fuel-of-choice during his long runs, and in his latter years he dispensed the stuff in copious amounts to his disciples.

'Tea With Mr Newton' became the highlight of many a Sunday afternoon for members of the distance-running fraternity. Some were casual callers who lived just around the corner, others travelled from the other side of the world. Newton's sitting room in Ruislip, West London, became a Mecca for marathon men.

Fifty years after his death in 1959 Newton remains widely regarded as the founding father of ultra-running (i.e. distances longer than the 26.2-mile marathon). He is particularly revered in South Africa, where he is known as 'Mantabeni' or 'Greatheart', the inspirational figure behind the annual 56-mile Comrades race, the world's leading 'ultra'.

In researching Arthur Newton's remarkable life, I was able to plunder a wide range of sources. This, of course, included his own quartet of books published around the time of the 1939-45 War, although much of the content of these books is coaching and training advice rather than pure autobiography. In the final 25 years of his life, Newton became a prolific writer, his books supplemented by scores of magazine and newspaper articles and countless lengthy letters, routinely bashed out daily on a battered typewriter as he recovered from his morning run. He established regular correspondence with runners, coaches and others from all around the globe, all eager for Newton's fatherly advice and opinions, and all of whom could expect a prompt and lengthy reply.

However, Newton was selective over what he revealed about himself in print. He wrote relatively little, for example, about his four eventful 100-mile runs between Wiltshire and London, presumably because of the frustration he felt over their outcomes (even though he set records, his perfectionist nature was dissatisfied by these performances).

Furthermore, as a modest Victorian gentleman of middle-class background, he saw no reason to share details of his private life with the world at large. Marriage, he once obliquely offered, was rather like a lobster salad – interesting if you're that way inclined, but otherwise best left alone. Perhaps typical of his generation, he was embarrassed and secretive when it came to discussing matters such as his health, or his financial situation. When his income dried up completely in 1925, for example, he felt so ashamed about his predicament that he set out to walk the 770 miles from Durban to Rhodesia under cover of darkness, rather than face friends only too willing to help out.

Nevertheless, despite his self-effacing traits, Newton did not write in a 'buttoned up' manner, and understood the value of being provocative and controversial in order to make a magazine article impactful. He was evidently a real Jekyll and Hyde character, for his natural shyness contrasted sharply with the campaign of self-publicity he launched in order to fight the stubborn Union government in 1922. He didn't take up running for fun, or even for the pleasure of victory, it was strictly a means to an end. The way he scuttled away from the crowds at the finish of his big races, desperate to sit somewhere quiet with his pipe, proved that being the centre of attention did not come easy to him.

Aside from Newton's own voracious scribblings, I consulted more recent athletics writing by other authors, a wide range of newspapers and periodicals from the last 125 years or so, and various Newton paraphernalia kindly passed my way by athletes and historians. I obtained interviews with a handful of people who met Newton in the 1950s and trawled nuggets of information from across the internet. An important additional source was the enthralling collection of letters, scrapbooks and assorted papers now held in the University of Birmingham's Special Collections archive. As I understand it, this treasure trove was rescued from Newton's personal belongings after he died in 1959, largely by his friends at the Road Runners Club. It was fascinating to be able to sift through yellowing gems such as original handwritten letters to Newton from leading politicians, various telegrams and race-day passes, and even Newton's well-thumbed contacts book.

In my three previous athletics biographies published by Desert Island Books (Alf Shrubb, Walter George and Deerfoot), I appended the manuscripts with a list of reference sources. But as Newton was from a more recent era, I was able to gather more material than on the other three runners, meaning most episodes in this book are written using a 'blend' of information and detail from many sources. It would have proved difficult to accurately attribute individual chunks of Newton information to one particular source. I hope athletics historians will therefore forgive the lack of a list of reference sources linked to the text in this book. Often, if information did come from one particular source, I have said so within the text anyway. The illustrations used in the book are either my own, or from private collections.

I am grateful to the following people and organisations (in no particular order) for their assistance during my research: Andy Milroy; Alexander Wilson; Jackie Mekler; Donald MacGregor; Ian Champion; Norman Harris; Harry Berry; Alan Firth; Kevin Kelly; Trevor Vincent; Ian Tempest; Richard Bond; Mike Sandford; Dave Terry; Peter Lovesey; Linden Porter; William Steynor; Dudley Steynor; Sally Galbraith (nee Newton); Caroline Howlett; Norrie Williamson; Wilf Morgan; Mike Bath; Bob Phillips; Helen Farquarson; Mel Watman; Tim Noakes; Beryl Gillies; the British Newspaper Library, Colindale; the British Library St Pancras; the University Of Birmingham Information Services (Special Collections); The Road Runners Club; The National Union of Track Statisticians (NUTS) Historical Group; Various Comrades runners; Weston-super-Mare Reference Library.

NEWSPAPERS AND PERIODICALS:
The Times, News of the World, News Chronicle, Weston Mercury, New York Times, Montreal Gazette, Natal Mercury, Natal Witness, Natal Advertiser, Times of Natal, Cape Argus, Johannesburg and Transvaal Sunday Times, Johannesburg Star, Kokstad Advertiser, Bulawayo Chronicle, Athletics, Athletics Weekly, The Scots Athlete, Runner's World, Athletics Review, Running Review, RRC Newsletter, Farmers Weekly (SA), Time, London Gazette, World Sports.

BIBLIOGRAPHY:

Running – Arthur F H Newton (Witherby, 1935); *Running In Three Continents* – Arthur F H Newton (Witherby, 1940); *Commonsense Athletics* – Arthur F H Newton (Berridge, 1947); *Races and Training* – Arthur F H Newton (Berridge, 1949); *Lore of Running* – Tim Noakes (Human Kinetics, 2003); *The Lonely Breed* – Ron Clarke & Norman Harris (Pelham) 1967; *From LA to New York, From New York to LA* – Harry Berry (self-published, 1990); *Bunion Derby* – Charles B Kastner (University of New Mexico, 2007); *C C Pyle's Amazing Foot Race* – Geoff Williams (Rodale, 2007); *The Great American Bunion Derby* – Molly Levite Griffis (Eakin, 2003); *The Comrades Marathon Story* – Morris Alexander (Juta, 1976); *The Comrades Marathon Yearbook* – Tom Cottrell (Southern, 1998); *Just Call Me Wally* – Bill Jamieson (Penprint, 1999); *Why Die?* – *The Extraordinary Percy Cerutty* – Graem Sims (Lothian, 2003); *A History of South Africa* – Frank Welsh (Harper Collins, 1998); *Oxford Dictionary of National Biography* – ed L Goldman (Oxford University Press, 2004); *A Selection of Victorian Athletic Clubs* – Warren Roe & Kevin Kelly (self-published, 2008); *Honour of Empire, Glory of Sport* – Bob Phillips (Parrs Wood, 2000); *Heroes and Sparrows* – Roger Robinson (Southwestern, 1986); *Great Moments in Athletics* – F A M Webster (Country Life, 1947); *Beer and Brine: The Making of Walter George, Athletics' First Superstar* – Rob Hadgraft (Desert Island Books, 2006); *The Little Wonder: The Untold Story of Alfred Shrubb, World Champion Runner* – Rob Hadgraft (Desert Island Books, 2004); *World History of Long Distance Running* – Roberto L Quercetani (SEP Editrice, 2002); *Eagle Sports Annual 2* (Hulton Ross, 1953); *In The Long Run* – Jim Peters & J Edmundson (Cassell, 1955); *Annals of the Thames Hare and Hounds* – J Ryan & I Fraser (self-published, 1968); *Around and About: Memoirs of a South African Newspaperman* – Michael Green (New Africa, 2004).

ROB HADGRAFT
Chelmsford, Essex
May 2009

Foreword

Why is it that the names of a select few echo down the corridors of time? What are the personal characteristics and the special circumstances that produce those whose contribution becomes iconic?

When the 38-year-old Arthur Newton first began to train as a distance runner on January 1st 1922, his motivations were specific. He wished to draw attention to recent decisions of the ruling government that, in his view, threatened his livelihood as a farmer in the South African province of Natal. He had happened on the eccentric idea that only by becoming a successful distance runner could he bring his desperate plight to the attention of the South African nation.

But why sport and why distance running? For there was no obvious historic precedent. Nor was there any reason to believe that a beyond middle-aged former school teacher, now farmer, with no previous history of even mediocre athletic prowess would ever do anything that would capture the notice of a nation of which he was not even a citizen. He did begin with one correct decision – his age precluded success at any of the Olympic running distances. But where possibly would he find a running race of the correct distance that could foster his ambition? For the world was recovering from the ravages of the Great War and such events were uncommon, most especially in the recently independent former British colony in which he then found himself.

But, by extraordinary co-incidence, just seven months earlier, a 56-mile race had recently been inaugurated in his home province, a few hours' drive from his farm. The race – the approximate distance of a 24-hour route march in the British Army – had been started to honour 'for one day' those Comrades who did not return from the bloody battlefields of the First World War. Somehow he decided that this race would be his focus. His first training run of two miles on January 1st 1922 – a run which he could not complete without a 'longish' stop after the first mile and which left him 'abominably stiff' and unable to run for the next four days – could not have filled him with great confidence. But he was not to be deterred.

Five months later he won the second running of the Comrades Marathon in a new record time. Through perseverance he had discovered the singular activity that would bring him national attention. But perhaps appropriately his running did not help his political advocacy. The government he wished to influence was voted out of office, leaving Newton without any future prospects as a farmer. Running, as this book details in fascinating detail, would have to become the focus of his middle-aged life. And his experience would be his gift to all those who have become runners in the past century.

For my conclusion is that Arthur Newton is the most important runner at any distance ever produced in Southern Africa. As faithfully recorded in this book, his contribution to the evolution of global ultra-distance running, might have been even more important. He made three profound contributions. First, he produced world-record setting performances that in some cases exceeded the performances of the pedestrians of the 1880s like Charles Rowell. Thus he was the link to a past that might have been forgotten but for his contribution. Unquestionably his record performances in the Comrades Marathon are the reason why that race became iconic and has survived to become what some regard as the greatest distance race in the world. After the First World War the lure of the Olympic Games would sustain races of marathon distance. But the disappearance of pedestrianism in the 1880s left a gap in ultra-distance running that might not have been filled but for the appearance of Arthur Newton and his incredible resolve.

Second, he was one of the first runners after the pedestrians to run prodigious distances in running. He developed in the 1920s the 100-mile-a-week training regime that New Zealand coach Arthur Lydiard would adopt with great success to middle-distance running in the 1960s. Third, he faithfully recorded all his ideas in four books published in the 1930s and 40s. Those books captured his training philosophies in a manner not previously reported. From his ideas I developed '15 Laws of Training' in my book *Lore of Running*.

It is appropriate that a carefully researched and complete biography of this extraordinary man should finally have been written 88 years after that decisive moment on January 1st 1921 when Arthur Newton laced on his running shoes for the first time. We are indebted to Rob Hadgraft for turning his prodigious writing talents and an unmatched passion for the history of running to the task of recording Newton's life in the appropriate detail.

And so Arthur Newton now joins the stable of the three other iconic runners of the past, Walter George, Alfred Shrubb and Deerfoot, who have also enjoyed the same privilege of Hadgraft's sharp focus. We are all enriched by his efforts.

TIMOTHY NOAKES OMS, MD, DSc
Professor in the Discovery Health Chair of Exercise and Sports Science
University of Cape Town, South Africa

Prologue

A Pipe, a Bath and a Pot of Tea

Friday, 20th July 1934. It is not yet three in the morning and in the little village of Box, deep in rural Wiltshire, something remarkable is afoot. Sunrise is still two hours away, yet bleary-eyed locals are pulling on their coats and flat caps and scurrying outside to grab their bicycles. Butchers, quarrymen and farmers, housewives and children, all chatter excitedly as they emerge from their humble homes to head up the hill where they will congregate outside an inn called The Bear.

For today the old runner with the pipe is back among them. The famous Arthur Newton, a maverick of 51 summers, is having a final crack at the world record for running 100 miles on the road. To the locals' delight, he has again chosen their village as his starting point as he tries to make history. And again he will be setting off in the dead of night.

It may be summer, but at this time of night it is decidedly chilly and as they gather on the main road outside The Bear, the crowd stamp their feet and rub their hands to keep warm in the breeze. There are no street lamps, and thick cloud obscures the moon, so there is little to see, even though Box nestles prominently on the southern slope of the By Brook Valley. The village is best known for Isambard Kingdom Brunel's famous railway tunnel, which burrows underground for nearly two miles, but today Box is set to make headlines for only sporting reasons.

The main road between Bath and London snakes eastwards out of the village, and in a short while Arthur Newton, honoured guest of the village, will head down the road like a modern day Pied Piper, villagers in his wake lighting the way with the lamps of their cars and bicycles. While they wait for the runner to appear from his upstairs bedroom at the inn, there is much excited chatter about how he is attempting to run from here to London in 14 hours. Some laugh and shake their heads, believing the old boy would be better off heading down the road the other way to the Kingsdown Lunatic Asylum, a place known locally as the Box Mad House.

Inside the inn, once a haunt of notorious highwaymen John Poulter and Tom Baxter, the quiet figure of Newton is sitting down to eat, his bright white running kit modestly veiled by an overcoat. He consumes a meat omelette, prepared by landlord Hatcher, who is clearing away quickly so that he too can accompany the run in his car and not miss the fun. There has been an inn at this spot for nearly 350 years now, providing refreshment and accommodation to all types of visitor, but Hatcher is fairly sure they've never before been asked to supply a meat omelette at 3.15 in the morning to help a guest run all the way to London.

By around 3.30, the crowd outside the main door has built to well over 100, and among them are Joe Binks, sports writer with the *News of the World*, and Walter George, former champion runner from nearby Calne, both of whom are carefully adjusting their stop-watches and positioning their car to accompany the run. They talk earnestly with a journalist who has come all the way from Johannesburg to ride with the run, and with another important-looking athletics official from London.

Suddenly cheers ring out. Newton is emerging through the white portico at the roadside door of the inn, under the bold advertisements welcoming commercial travellers and offering telephone and breakfast facilities. He nods acknowledgement, shyly dipping his head and smiling quietly. 'Good luck Newton' comes the cry, many of the crowd having performed this ritual before and treating the runner like an old friend, like one of their own. He may be wearing a white running shirt that proclaims 'Rhodesia and Natal', but deep down he's a west country lad, born not far away in Weston super-Mare.

The photographers bustle around, politely urging 'Mr Newton' to get into position and roughly arranging the crowd around him. As the flash bulbs go off, Newton's white running uniform dominates the scene, a splash of brightness in the dark road. The crowds press in eagerly, raising their arms and cheering at the photographer's signal, with even the bespectacled figure of journalist Binks joining in the ritual.

As usual, Newton looks calm and collected, moving around slowly to conserve energy and never outwardly betraying his desire to get away from this hubbub and begin his ordeal. He looks slim, tanned and fit, with neatly trimmed moustache and receding dark hair. He looks more like a diplomat or a bank manager, rather than an athlete who has run tens of thousands of miles on three continents in recent years. His white kit is neatly trimmed in black, he wears no socks and his canvas shoes with crepe rubber soles look far too lightweight for the gruelling task ahead. So, for that matter, do his slender, well-toned legs.

As 3.45 looms, the crowd is asked to step back and Newton is given some room. He takes a deep breath and at the signal sets off steadily along the A4 road towards Corsham. A huge cheer rings out and the shrieking continues as a motley procession follows him. The cyclists sing and whistle gaily, occasionally getting dangerously close to clipping Newton's heels and also hampering the official cars. Those Box residents hitherto asleep will surely have been roused by now. As they head out of the village, the cars edge up behind Newton and the beam from their lights help him find the smoothest part of the road.

Newton knows only too well that all the serious hills on the 100-mile trek are in the first 30 miles or so, and that it would be foolish to attack these with too much vigour. If things go according to plan he will be running for the next 14 hours without a break, so over-cooking things now while he is full of energy has to be guarded against. Settling into his well-known 'pit pat' stride, his feet not rising more than three inches from the ground, he makes smooth progress, many cars and bikes staying with him as they pass Chippenham (7.25 miles) in just under 50 minutes.

People come out to wave as he passes, despite the ungodly hour, and he feels good as he cruises past the 10-mile point in 67 minutes, a little faster than he needed to go, but seemingly with no effort whatsoever. As he enters Calne, the birthplace of Walter George, there is the expected large crowd to greet them. George hadn't been in good health lately, but was determined to join this run and he laps up the cheers and waves regally from inside a car crawling just behind Newton. As they pass through the small town, the sun is coming up on the horizon and it turns into a most gorgeous sunrise. As the cheers ring out and the sky begins to sparkle, Newton's spirits are lifted.

He can now see the road properly without the aid of car lights, and by now most of the loyal procession behind is dropping away, shouting their final good luck wishes as they go. There are some serious inclines ahead and Newton focuses his concentration on maintaining a steady pace, his experience enabling him to motor up and down the hills in economical fashion, barely breaking sweat. At 18 miles he reaches the highest point of the entire run – about 600 feet above sea level – and glances across at the imposing sight of Silbury Hill, the biggest artificial mound in Europe, which towers 130 feet above them. Beyond the hill and to the right, Newton glances across and tries to make out the famous white horse etched into the downs nearly 100 years earlier.

He passed the 20-mile point in 2hrs 12mins 15secs, considerably quicker than his previous runs on this road, but doesn't see the need to hold back, for so far the run is feeling 'like child's play.' The town of Marlborough represents a quarter of the task done, and he duly passes the 25-mile point near the well-known school, in exactly three hours. Hundreds of admirers lean from their windows, and gather in the street, cheering him on his way.

Leaving the town, he is faced with a severe climb though Savernake Forest, and at this point stops for his first drink, reporting to his helpers that he was feeling very well and confident about the task ahead. Up and over the hill at the 26-mile point and he knows now the worst of the hills are over. Over the next ten miles or so to Hungerford, his average pace begins to slip a little and a clocking of 4:18.00 at 35 miles means he is now slower than on past journeys, but still comfortably ahead of the record pace he needs overall.

A quiet stretch parallel to the River Kennett takes Newton towards Newbury where, as he'd correctly guessed, a large crowd awaited. The town's clock tower was positioned just after the 44-mile point and he passes in 5:20.15, at least 10 minutes ahead of target pace. Vast numbers have come out in the pleasant weather to watch him pass, and Newton smiles as they call his name. He hopes he is not appearing surly by not waving to them, but he is keen to heed George's instructions not to raise his arms as this would only waste energy that would be needed later on.

Newton would recall later that it was around here where serious tiredness began to set in, which was pretty much as anticipated, and as a result he decides it is time to take on some food. In his 1928 run he had stopped at Thatcham to wolf down some hot minced beef to fortify himself, but it had been a big mistake, upsetting his already grumbling stomach and seriously affecting his performance. This time he just takes thinly sliced sandwiches of cheese and honey from his helpers, and munches them slowly and thoroughly as he continues running. He said later: 'I had sandwiches only, eating them as I went along, [but even a] sandwich is a very difficult affair to masticate if it is in any way dry.'

At the halfway point he is still going well and reaches 50 miles near the village of Woolhampton in 6:09.30. The clocks strike 10 as he heads towards Reading and the weather is now noticeably warmer, and beginning to give Newton cause for concern. Through the centre of Reading he encounters more large crowds, which for several minutes at least, takes his mind off the increasing tiredness and heat that is beginning to unsettle him. His helpers pour iced water over him at regular intervals, as requested, but Newton deliberately resists the temptation to guzzle too much of his specially prepared drink, made up of lemonade, sugar and salt. This so-called 'magic drink' has worked well in the past when the going got hot, but last year he drank far more than normal and suffered badly with stomach pains as a result. It was a harsh lesson, and now he errs on the side of caution, even though feeling very thirsty.

The only crumb of comfort during this difficult stage is that last year he felt even worse than this, and was forced to stop several times to be sick. Although he now felt 'pretty badly done in', it was not evidently affecting the pace of his running. The 67-mile point, halfway between Reading and Maidenhead, was passed in 8:47.20, which was well under eight-minute-miling. This was a highly encouraging statistic to think about when Binks calls it out to him, although he knew the hardest parts of the trip were still to come and some slowing down would be inevitable.

Around the 70-mile mark he passes through the village of Twyford, choosing not to use the new by-pass, and past the spot at Hare Hatch where he'd been violently sick last year. Knowl Hill marks the 70-mile point and then it is into Maidenhead, where the sun is shining brightly and the crowds are out in their summer clothes. This is in sharp contrast, he thinks, to his 1928 winter run through here, when the place was flooded by melting snow and slush and the council had erected emergency walkways to allow people through. Among the crowds, Newton is pleased to pick out a small group of friends over from Rhodesia, who shriek their support enthusiastically as he trots by.

But there is no such boost for his spirits as he leaves Maidenhead and heads for Slough. This new town, with its 850 factories, presents a grim sight; it is a vista that less than three years on will prompt John Betjeman to pen his famous poem advocating bombing the place. Further on, Newton's exhaustion and depression wasn't helped by having to run past Slough Crematorium, whose four tall chimneys featured in Aldous Huxley's *Brave New World*, published two years earlier.

Joe Binks would recall that neither Slough nor Newton presented a pretty picture as they encountered each other on that sunny Friday morning: 'At Slough, Newton had his first really bad time. With the heat so oppressive I had some misgivings about him succeeding. He was going very groggy, but I know of his tremendous powers of recovery. Alternately he had some good and bad spells.'

The next major landmark for the struggling runner would be Colnbrook level crossing. Again the measured 100-mile route would mean they had to ignore a by-pass here, and the level crossing would mark the spot where Newton ground to a painful halt last year, before being reluctantly persuaded to give up altogether because of his dreadful condition. Today he clocks 11:33.00 at the crossing, which is actually nine minutes slower than the aborted run, but this time he is in slightly better shape.

Newton's main concern by now is to simply keep going, but his time-keepers have noticed that he is slowing quite dramatically and might soon drop behind the pace required for creating a 100-mile record. They calculate that in the last two hours he had effectively lost 30 minutes, and his time in hand on the record is slipping away. The pressure is really on and after a quick consultation George and Binks agree that Newton is unlikely to finish in under 14 hours, which had been his ambition, but could still beat his previous best of 14:22.10. From Colnbrook to the finish line, his task is to cover 15 miles in two hours and 49 minutes, which sounds easy by itself, but Newton's condition is deteriorating badly and he seems to be stopping more often.

He would reflect later: 'It was just about here that I became aware that the combination of damp heat and prolonged effort was bringing on stomach disorder again and that it was this, and not merely heavy perspiration, that was making me wilt. Yet I wasn't as bad as on the former occasion, when I had dropped out at 85 miles, and though the pace was reduced by all of a mile an hour, I reckoned I should get through. Indeed, knew that I must, since it was my last chance. It was a pretty near thing all the same.'

Three stops on the edge of West London cause huge anxiety among his helpers, but he somehow resumes each time and struggles on towards Kew Bridge, which marks the 94-mile point. He had decided to go into town by the Great West Road, despite the fact that it meant an extra 400 yards or so, because he is keen to avoid heavy traffic. Along the Chiswick High Road to Hammersmith Broadway he is cheered on enthusiastically but stops several times for glasses of his 'magic drink', which Binks and George hand over reluctantly, thinking it was probably doing his stomach more harm than good at this point. 'He jogged along looking far more dead than alive at this point,' recalled Binks.

Newton looks unsteady on his feet and decidedly groggy by Hammersmith Broadway, with 3.25 miles to go and 42 minutes left to crack the record.

Despite their own long careers as champion runners, Binks and George have never felt so nervous in all their lives. Having witnessed every inch of the struggle, and past struggles, they can't bear the thought of Newton not succeeding on this final attempt.

Binks tells Newton what is needed in the last three miles or so, and the runner gasps 'thanks' as he plods on. The 51-year-old Newton summons what strength he can and pulls himself together for the big final effort, the very last of his life as a competitive runner. Binks shakes his head in awe, scarcely believing the resilience and courage of the man after nearly 14 hours of running. Newton lengthens his stride and brutally forces himself to ignore the cries of his tormented body to end the misery. Binks then goes up ahead to fix the 100-mile post at the measured spot in Knightsbridge, so that it is clear to all. The run would formally end further on at Hyde Park Corner, 100 miles plus 880 yards from where they'd started in Box.

The crowds line the street in appreciation as he goes by and Newton seems surprised as he eases past the 100-mile post, perhaps not expecting to see the marker and his timekeepers there. Binks calls out that he has done the 100 miles in 14 hours and six minutes. His old record, the world's best on a road, had been beaten by 16 minutes. He felt relief rather than joy, somehow managing to push on up the final slope to Hyde Park Corner, where enormous crowds greeted him and roared him over the line. Within seconds the times are read out, the records confirmed, and the noise levels rise further.

Newton is in something of a daze and is desperate for time and space to recover himself. Head down, he slips across to the entrance to the park opposite, the crowds parting to let him through, and he goes inside and sits down on a chair where the crowds can't get at him. All he asks for is his pipe and coat. After being photographed and given 'three cheers' again, he is spirited away in a car to his home for a bath and a much-anticipated pot of tea. Some were probably disappointed at the lack of ceremony, and the way Newton slipped away after they'd waited all this time to see him. But this was typical: he appreciated their support very much, but really couldn't face too much fuss.

Binks is one of those who knows it is advisable to give Newton some space while he recovered. But the experienced newspaperman is left incredulous as he tries to analyse the performance just witnessed. He began filing his report for that weekend's *News of the World*: 'I am doubtful we shall ever see the like of this marvellous distance runner again. We have heard of our fast miles, flying sprints and huge shot puts, but do they really compare with Newton's magnificent record of running 100 miles on this road in tremendous heat, up and down hills, at just over seven miles per hour? Surely it is the running feat of the century?'

Newton had run his last race. Starting out when almost 40 years old, merely as a publicity stunt, he'd now covered more than 90,000 miles in 13 years, averaging an unprecedented 20 miles per day. His status had changed almost overnight from struggling farmer in South Africa to world athletics legend. But now the glory days were over. Soaking in the bath in the quiet of a Friday evening at his West London home, his thoughts no doubt centred on what he would do with his life next. They must also have drifted back to the extraordinary sequence of events that had brought him to this point.

Chapter 1

From Seaside to War-Zone

During his 76 years, Arthur Francis Hamilton Newton put one leg in front of the other more times than almost anyone you could care to mention. He ran, walked and shuffled thousands of miles across three different continents. This lifetime of self-generated motion began with a few faltering steps in the genteel seaside resort of Weston-super-Mare. Newton was born here during the town's Victorian-era pomp on Sunday, 20th May 1883, the fifth child of eight born to the Reverend Henry Newton and his wife Selina.

Weston-super-Mare at the time was a rare mix of the refined and the rowdy. The opening of Isambard Kingdom Brunel's railway permitted thousands of visitors to converge on the Somerset town via works outings and Bank Holiday jollies. To entertain them, Birnbeck Pier was built, offering amusement arcades, tea rooms and fun-fair rides. As they pottered around on the beach, the working-class hordes must have gazed across the bay in awe at the southern slopes of Worlebury Hill. Here there were scores of handsome detached villas, newly crafted from Bath stone and occupied by middle-class families like the Newtons.

Arthur Newton was born here at 7 Glentworth Terrace, a sweeping crescent of curving lines that was pleasing on the eye and positioned in the heart of a select area known as the Shrubbery Estate. An ornate water tower gave the denizens of this prestigious neighbourhood their own private water supply, and the lawns, foliage and ornamental footbridge spoke volumes about the class of person who could afford to live here.

Reverend Henry Newton was 36 years old when his third son Arthur was born, and was a man of some standing. By now forging a new career for himself as a clergyman, he'd earlier spent years as a senior civil engineer in India, the country of his birth. Rev Newton had been born when most of India was under the control of the British East India Company, but during his boyhood the first war of independence, the Sepoy Mutiny, led to an instability which led to direct rule by the British Crown. As a young adult, Henry Newton was a key figure in the creation of a major rail network of around 16,000 miles of track, mostly radiating inland from the three major port cities of Bombay, Madras, and Calcutta.

But, with middle-age approaching, Henry felt the pull of matters spiritual and decided the time was right to settle in England with his wife and expanding family, and to dedicate his life to the church. He and Selina

Elizabeth Saunders, a Bristol girl by origin, had married back in June 1872 at St Mary Magdalene church, close to London's Regent's Park, in a service carried out by Selina's brother, another man of the cloth. The wedding was formally announced in *The Times*, and some readers will have recognised the groom as the son of another Henry Newton, this one a senior figure of the Bombay Civil Service, who had in recent years served as a Judge of the High Court of Bombay.

The first ten years of their marriage saw Henry Jr and Selina produce four children in a period of travel and upheaval. Arthur's eldest brother Henry Clement Newton (known as 'Harry') was born in Ireland in 1874, to be followed less than two years later by Cyril Vaughan Newton. Hilda Ethelwyn Newton arrived in London in 1879, while Ursula Mildred Newton was born in 1881 in Ceylon (now Sri Lanka), where father Henry was by now working for the Church Missionary Society. In all, Henry spent five years with the CMS here, one of four men appointed to set up schools and work among the natives in this important trading post of the British Empire.

After the move to Somerset came the arrival of the Newtons' fifth child Arthur in May 1883. It meant life continued to get busier for Rev Newton and his wife, who employed domestic help to run their household, but nevertheless only got around to registering Arthur's birth some months after the event! Arthur's first birthday in May of 1884 coincided with him gaining a younger brother, Ambrose Edward Anselm, and before long the family was on the move again.

True to form, the Newtons failed to rest long in Weston-super-Mare, despite the attractive surroundings, and with Arthur still less than two years old, they moved to Brighton, where Rev Newton became curate of St Marks in the Kemp Town district. The family moved into St Marks Vicarage at 16 Church Place, Kemp Town. The beautiful chapel at St Marks would later achieve listed building status and be absorbed into the St Mary's Hall School Chapel & Arts Centre complex.

Soon after the family arrived in Brighton, a House of Lords privileges committee dealt with a lengthy and complicated case relating to ownership of the title of Lord Lovat. It seems likely this was the occasion when – according to Newton family lore – Rev Henry put himself forward as a claimant upon the Lovat peerage. He is said to have claimed connections via his mother's lineage. The title had earlier been the property of the notorious Simon 'The Fox' Fraser (the 11th Lord Lovat), who in 1747 became the last man beheaded in the Tower of London. Rev Newton clearly had no qualms about being associated with such a scoundrel, but as it turned out his claims were dismissed and after a court appearance to stake his claim, he had to let the matter drop. Later, however, members of the family, including Arthur, would name their homes 'Lovat'.

After the move to Brighton, Arthur gained two more siblings when Dorothy and Bernard were born at the Vicarage in 1887 and 1890, respectively. But perhaps the biggest upheaval of all in his young life came at the age of six when he became a day boy at the Lady Matron School at Eaton Place in Eaton Court, Brighton. The Newtons lived less than half-a-mile from this school, but within a year the decision was taken for Arthur to become a full-time boarder there. Thus, at the age of just seven, Arthur began a new phase of his life and never again would his main place of residence be with parents or family, apart from holidays or brief visits.

No doubt many a boy of his age and background was sent packing in similar fashion in Victorian England, but it cannot have been easy for Arthur to depart the bosom of the family in this way. We can only speculate over the reason: perhaps the Newtons' young governess Margaret Rummings couldn't cope with the number of children she had to teach, and with Arthur being such a bright spark, with a streak of independence to boot, he was the natural choice to be educated externally? Or perhaps a lack of space at the Vicarage was an issue. Census records show that eight adults and five children were living there after Arthur departed with his trunk to live round the corner in Eaton Place. This included the sisters Beatrice and Gertrude Fosberg, who were identified as 'visitors', plus the family's cook Mary Perks, the two housemaids Emily Webber and Emma South, and the above-mentioned governess.

The Lady Matron School, situated around 300 yards from the Marine Parade sea-front, was a 'dame school' typical of the era, a relatively small establishment run by women for the education of small children at a cost of a few pence per week per child. The school was run by five women, all of them single, with principal Catherine Roworth, in her early fifties, employing governesses Caroline Drake and Florence Powell, two elderly assistants in Ada Green and Catherine Phillips, three female servants plus a houseboy. The pupils numbered 26, all aged between 7 and 14, and hailing from all over southern England. Upon his arrival, little Arthur was the youngest of them all.

The young Newton settled into life at the Lady Matron School and would spend a total of six years here, switching to the fee-paying Bedford School in the mid-1890s once his teenage years were upon him. At Bedford he was a full boarder in Talbot's House, the largest of the school's boarding houses. As a generally quiet and self-contained boy he may not have enjoyed the School tradition of regular inter-house singing contests, but will have had the opportunity to develop his already considerable skills at the piano. He will also have enjoyed the many outdoor pursuits and the sporting atmosphere of the place. Bedford later gained a reputation over the years for producing sporting talent, including Olympic gold medallist Harold Abrahams, Test cricketer Alastair Cook and rugby stars Martin Bayfield and Andy Gomarsall. Newton would recall enjoying football, cricket and tennis during his schooldays but never took any particular interest in running.

After less than four years at Bedford, for reasons not entirely clear, Rev Newton arranged for his son to switch schools to complete his education. He was sent deep into the Norfolk countryside to attend a private grammar school in Banham, a bucolic outpost some 20 miles south-west of Norwich and a far cry from the urban settings of his previous schools. Following the recent death of his father William, the establishment was now being run by schoolmaster Fred Cole, locally born and a single man in his early thirties. Cole was popular with his pupils and particularly keen on sport and outdoor pursuits, which pleased Arthur no end. Cole had charge of around 17 pupils and for the day-to-day teaching was aided by assistant schoolmasters, Percy Shelford, Ernie Cracknell and Frank Long, none of whom had reached their mid-twenties. Also living on the premises were various members of Cole's family, including his mother Susannah, his sisters Edith and Mary and brother Frank. Five servants, all female, completed the list of occupants at the Church Green premises. The finishing touches to Arthur's education were added in this rural setting and during his final months here, he was at 17-years-old by some distance the oldest of the pupils, and the same age or older than at least one of his teachers and most of the servants.

Arthur's name is recorded in the 1901 census as 'Hamilton Newton', and during his youth he seems to have on occasion preferred to be known by this middle name. It is said that his youngest brother Bernard initially found it difficult to pronounce 'Hamilton' and came up with his own shortened version of 'Tom' – which then became established as Arthur's family nickname for the rest of his life.

By the time he was ready to leave Banham and make his way in the outside world, his parents had upped sticks yet again and had now made their home in the western suburbs of London, in Grange Park, Ealing. By now six of the eight Newton siblings had flown the nest, only Ursula and Dorothy remaining at home. At least two of the boys – Harry and Cyril – had left for foreign climes to seek their fortune, with Harry embarking on a career in business in South Africa. Accordingly, Rev Newton now only had need for two junior servants.

And so, in the autumn of 1901, Arthur arrived at a crossroads. Having remained a schoolboy beyond his 18th birthday, a decision on his future was long overdue. He was fit, intelligent and certainly no idler – but he would have struggled to deny a charge of being indecisive. His parents quizzed him over and over about what he wanted to do, and by his own admission he failed to come up with anything particularly constructive, apart from having vaguely considered teaching. His despairing father decided he should be put under the supervision of his two elder brothers in South Africa, who were by all accounts doing well in the business world, and would be able to point him in the right direction. Never mind that the second Boer War was currently in full swing, southern Africa it was to be!

The two main newsworthy events as far as Britain was concerned in 1901 were the death of Queen Victoria after 64 years on the throne, and the continuing conflict in South Africa. Newspapers covered the second Boer War in great detail, so the Newtons will have known all about the potential dangers. But Arthur was to be despatched to the Natal port of Durban which, compared to some areas, seemed relatively safe. Over the Christmas period of 1901, he packed his things and prepared for a daunting and lengthy journey south.

Perhaps Arthur's father felt sending another son to South Africa was his patriotic duty in order to help increase the number of British settlers in this trouble-torn region? As a man who had worked and travelled widely across the Empire himself, Rev Newton would certainly have echoed the views of diamond magnate and politician Cecil Rhodes, who famously pontificated: 'The settlement of our people on the soil of South Africa is the only method by which a lasting peace can be secured in that country.'

Curiously, there are a number of parallels between Cecil Rhodes and Arthur Newton. Both men were plucked out of grammar school in rural England and sent alone to Natal, South Africa, because their families thought it in their best interests. Both sailed to Durban to be put under the wing of elder brothers already settled in that country. And both were the fifth child of a Church of England vicar.

Rhodes, of course, gained huge riches after starting the De Beers mining company and founding the state of Rhodesia. He tried to use his money and power to overthrow the Boer government and supported an infamous attack on the Transvaal which sparked the start of the second Boer War in late 1899. As we shall see, Arthur Newton would soon have a war of his own to fight in South Africa – although not quite on the scale of the Rhodes-influenced conflict.

Chapter 2

An Englishman Abroad

In January of 1902, Newton disembarked at the bustling port of Durban, and gazed around at one of the world's largest harbours. He had little real idea what his new life in South Africa held in store or even how long he was likely to remain here.

After five years in the cosy world of a Norfolk private school, he now had to learn fast how to stand on his own two feet. He linked up with his brothers, who had been based hereabouts for several years, and they set about fixing him up. Newton recalled the episode ruefully: 'Business said my brothers, was what I ought to go in for and, as I had always been taught to defer to my elders, I settled down to an office job they found for me.'

The 18-year-old greenhorn's clerical position was the first of a series of jobs that would fail to stretch or inspire him, but would have to do while he got his bearings and adjusted to a life in the sun. Initially he was earning around £7 a month, and in a bid to increase this paltry income he soon began shifting from job to job, all of them proving rather dull affairs in city offices.

However, Arthur would soon grow to love the world outside this drab office environment. Natal was a colony which had been self-governed for some eight years by now, having been proclaimed British territory in 1843. In the Anglo-Zulu War of 1879 the British defeated the Zulu army, and Zululand was annexed to Natal in 1897.

A few months after Newton landed, the last of the Boers surrendered to the British and this saw the end of the second Boer War, with the South African Republic and Orange Free State quickly absorbed into the British Empire. The two-year war had cost around 75,000 lives, nearly a third of them British soldiers, most of them through disease. The scorched earth policy of the British had wreaked devastation among both Boer and black African populations and would have a lasting effect on the demography and quality of life in the region.

The post-war reconstruction administration saw British civil servants and municipal officials begin work in the heartland of the former Boer Republics helping to forge the new identities of 'British South Africans' and, later, 'white South Africans.'

Politics were a side issue as far as Newton was concerned, for he occupied his time by getting out and about to exploring the fascinating new world on his doorstep. He also loved to play the piano, he read voraciously (P.G.Wodehouse was a particular favourite) and he became deeply interested in philosophy and metaphysics. He found these wide-ranging interests offset the drudgery of his office job, and before long his search for excitement saw him take up the new pursuit of motor-cycling.

Motor-cycles were few and far between in Natal in those days, indeed the first one to be sold to the public anywhere in the world had only been produced a few years earlier. In 1902, the English firm Triumph produced its first motorcycle – a bicycle fitted with a Belgian-built engine. It was a big success and within a year the American company Harley-Davidson had followed suit. By now Newton had saved up and purchased his first machine.

Many of his pursuits were, and would be throughout his life, solitary affairs. However during early 1904 he linked up with like-minded young enthusiasts from the region and they decided to form the first Johannesburg Motorcycle Club. The club was formally launched at a gathering in the boardroom of the Permanent Mutual buildings in Harrison Street, which was packed for the evening with keen followers of the new pursuit. Their stated purpose was to arrange social rides to various parts of the Transvaal 'by this rapid and exhilarating mode of locomotion'. Newton was one of six young men who agreed to form a temporary committee to get things moving. They decided their club colours would be green and gold, and subscriptions would cost one guinea a year.

The first official run would be from the city's Market Square at 9.30 am on Sunday, 29th May 1904. They decided on a fairly modest trip, just a leisurely five-miler from the centre of the city, heading eastwards out to Rosherville Lake and back. The *Rand Daily Mail* reported the club's arrival with the headline: 'New club formed to scorch the Transvaal.'

Newton cut a dashing figure on his motorbike. A quiet but confident young Englishman, handsome and tanned with a neat moustache and tall, slim figure. He must have caught the eye of many a young woman. According to one report he did for a while establish a close relationship in Africa that saw him engaged to be married for a spell; exactly when this took place and why it would subsequently be broken off remains a mystery. He would later brush off such matters with the comment that marriage was rather like a lobster salad: 'Very interesting if you're that way inclined, but otherwise best left alone!'

Although he loved the fresh air and freedom he enjoyed on his motorbike, Newton became acutely aware of the need to carry out proper regular exercise to keep himself fit and strong. He felt a little guilty over the fact that he was at this time a regular smoker, and worried that his avid private studies of philosophy and metaphysics were preventing a balanced and active life. He said later: 'I was reading heavily, doing a lot more of it than was good for me, as I sacrificed the exercise necessary to a young man, in order to dive deeper into metaphysics and allied subjects. Common sense soon came to the rescue and I knew I should be able to make a better job of my mental work if I made certain of a healthy physique. So I started a daily walk, whether I liked it or not!'

He began leaving the bike at home more often, and his regular walking developed into occasional gentle jogging of distances up to five and six miles. He noticed that this activity refreshed his mind and helped his ability to think and work. Sometimes people would stare quizzically at the eccentric Englishman running down the road, and his acute self-consciousness saw him learn to do most of his exercise in the early hours after dawn when few people were about.

His logical and analytical nature saw him experiment with his own capabilities, and he gained great satisfaction from working out his own routines involving physical and spiritual stimulation. He developed an ability to select the 'best bits' from the accepted experts and from his own experiences and put them into action. It was a skill that would later serve him well.

At a time when it was not at all fashionable, he began studying yogi philosophy. He was also an admirer of the writings of Sir Oliver Lodge (1851-1940), the English physicist, spiritualist and writer. Another favourite became George Hackenschmidt (1878-1968), the man widely described as 'the finest physical specimen in the world', an Estonian wrestling and weight-lifting pioneer and philosopher, who later in life would become a close friend.

Hackenschmidt's 1908 book *The Way to Live* would go on to be published in 21 editions and become one of the best-selling books on physical culture of all time. It was part-autobiography and part-training manual and Newton was fascinated by its advice on nutrition, bathing and sleeping. He endorsed the sentiment of the so-called 'Russian Lion' who liked to tell people: 'If you don't find time to become and remain healthy, you will be obliged to find time to be ill.' Central to his theories was that health and strength derived from a cosmic energy which flows through all nature with rhythm, harmony, beauty and grace. He wrote: 'There are few plagues and pestilences these days, but there would appear to be an infinitely greater number of sickly, weedy, stunted people than there used to be. The reason isn't far to seek. There is a universal urban immigration, a vast increase in the numbers of those who are engaged in indoor and sedentary occupations.'

Reading this sort of thing might well have been behind Newton's bid in 1904 to strike out and find an occupation that would give more job satisfaction. Fed up with his lowly office job, he applied for a teaching position at Hilton College, near Pietermaritzburg. When news filtered back to Newton's parents in England, they were not best pleased, feeling that teaching was not Newton's best route to success and fulfilment. Meanwhile, Newton based himself in Hilton, a small town that lies on the brow of the escarpment above Natal's capital Pietermaritzburg. He found the college's recent owner and headmaster Henry Ellis had introduced the main characteristics of the public school system of England, modified to suit South African conditions. A group of Old Hiltonians had now formed a company to buy the school from him and around the same time as Newton's arrival as a junior master, William Falcon took over as head and led the college through halcyon days.

Over the ensuing years Newton would take on a number of different teaching jobs, as well as serving briefly in the armed forces when men were needed to quell a 1906 native rebellion. His teaching work included a private tutoring job on a remote farm, and a position at Blenheim College in Pietermaritzburg. He seemed to enjoy the lifestyle and made full use of the school holidays by travelling the region on bike or foot on lengthy sight-seeing trips. He would become remembered at Blenheim College for being a robust and energetic housemaster, with a penchant for excursions that often left the boys trailing wearily in his wake. His personal fitness and recently self-devised workouts meant he could show the boys a thing or two when it came to stamina.

A favourite trick was underwater swimming, at which he proved unbeatable. The boys would come up one by one gasping for air, while Newton glided effortlessly along under the water face down, apparently not requiring oxygen. He also developed impressive skills at fretwork and created some spectacular Chinese verandas at Blenheim, huge pieces of work that took hours of careful cutting to complete. He also made clocks, having stripped down other old clocks to put the parts together.

Although he mostly only played the piano for his own amusement, he was known to be an accomplished performer by now. When he became friendly with one particular pupil's family, he would visit their home and spend entire afternoons playing classical pieces on their fine piano. But it was noted that he preferred not to have an audience, and would modestly play down his efforts if congratulated. In early 1908 he was persuaded to give a rare public display of his skills, on the occasion of a concert for church funds held at the Argyle Arms hotel in the town of Mooi River. To a packed audience Newton played Beethoven's *Moonlight Sonata* and a write-up in the local paper described his efforts as 'extremely good' and 'high-class'.

But, best of all, Newton loved to organise long treks out of Pieter-maritzburg. One of his pupils later revealed how one particular excursion with Newton became indelibly printed in his memory. It involved a 300-mile round trip on bike and foot from the college up to Mont-Aux-Sources, near the border with Basutoland (now Lesotho), one of the highest parts of the Drakensberg mountain range. At 3,282 metres above sea level, it is close to the source of the Tugela and Orange Rivers and is an area of breathtaking beauty. It was an area that had captivated Newton, who was undaunted by its reputation for being a formidably dif-ficult area to reach.

The boy who accompanied him would later tell the story to the *Natal Mercury*, and his account reveals the extent of Newton's enthusiasm and spirit of adventure. The pair's camping equipment and other gear was loaded onto Newton's trusty bicycle, leaving it looking 'like a Christmas tree'. The odd couple then cycled out of Pietermaritzburg early in the morning, taking two days to get to the foot of the Gudu Pass. It was tough going with endless ascents and hilly all the way. They camped for the night at the humble home of the local Police boy, where they left their bikes and proceeded on foot, with Newton again generously carrying almost all the gear. On the strenuous climb the boy was left puffing and panting behind the fit Newton, wishing he'd stayed at home. They reached the summit by the afternoon and enjoyed the magnificent scenery while drinking cocoa made by melting snow and ice into a billy-can and heating it by burning bits of brush.

To get off the mountain top before dark they had to descend rapidly and then spend the night in a native hut, close to the bottom of the pass. Newton had no problems with the Spartan conditions, but for the boy it was the coldest he'd ever known. They had one thin blanket each, no fire, a hard floor, and the snoring of their hosts made sleep nearly impossible. The following morning they returned for their bikes and set off for home. Punctures meant they had to send to Pietermaritzburg for a new tyre to be sent up. This delayed them two days and they arrived in the town of Loskop with only a day to spare of their leave. This meant about 90 miles still left to cover, with only one day of their official leave remain-ing. Newton demanded they leave Loskop at 3am to beat their deadline, and after a miserable cold meal of Marie biscuits and marmalade, they plodded homeward along the dusty roads, the poor 14-year-old quietly cursing his teacher. 'We trailed into Pietermaritzburg weary, worn and sad,' he concluded. Newton's use of Yogi philosophy no doubt helped him to overcome fatigue on such occasions, and the boy added: 'I witnessed several astounding exhibitions of his powers in this cult, but perhaps I should be treading on forbidden ground were I to relate them.'

In view of his impressive stamina and keenness to try different sorts of athletic pursuits, it was not surprising that Newton soon decided to sample foot-racing. His first taste of the sport came at the age of 24 in February of 1908 when he put his name forward for what was described as a 'Go as You Please' race in the small town of Howick, just north of Pietermaritzburg. The race was 11 miles, from the Post Office in Howick to the Dargle Road and back again. It was staged under the rules of the Natal Amateur Athletic and Cycling Association and the first of its kind to be staged in the area.

It attracted interest from eight runners, with Newton being one of only three who came from outside the town. Newton was by now living in Kamberg, a relatively remote spot in the Drakensberg mountains, where he was tutoring privately at a large farm. 'Towns were all right, but a country life always appealed to me,' he said about this move.

A good crowd gathered on the hot summer's day and saw Newton finish the race in fourth place in a time of around 90 minutes, winning himself a prize of ten shillings, some seven minutes behind the winner Young, who pocketed three guineas. The race was the highlight of the day's events in Howick, which included a smoking concert in the Falls Hotel later on. The route of the run, incidentally, passed over the exact spot where Nelson Mandela would be arrested many years later in 1962.

Encouraged by his efforts at Howick, the following year saw Newton make the trip across Natal to the small town of Kokstad, which was hosting a foot-race of around 12 miles. In the shadow of Mount Currie, he won the race with a minimum of fuss but would later modestly play down his efforts, calling the standard 'deplorable'.

Alongside his growing interest in running, Newton decided the time had come to do something about his love of nicotine. Since moving to Africa his smoking habit had escalated from five or six cigarettes a day to a level that he admitted was now 'scandalous'. It would take a clever trick played by a friend to finally get him to cut down. The moment of truth occurred when Newton ventured again into the Drakensberg mountains to spend a holiday with this friend. He recalled later:

'During the first few days I exhausted my immediate supply of cigarettes and wanted to send for more. My friend had reckoned on this and unconcernedly produced a pipe and tobacco. Appeals were useless. It was a pipe or nothing. He had taken steps to ensure that. I knew he was only trying to do me a good turn, so I ventured with the pipe. A whole week went by, and by that time I was beginning to find out that although I greatly preferred cigarettes, a pipe was much better than nothing at all. With cigarettes I used to inhale, but this didn't work comfortably with a pipe, and no doubt it accentuated the difference. Anyhow, after a week's martyrdom I agreed to carry on for a few days more, not only because it pleased him, but also because I fancied the cure might possibly become permanent.'

Although he was by now 26 and enjoying an independent lifestyle, his parents back in London had become concerned about Newton's lack of a clear career path. They felt that teaching was not lucrative enough to make their son financially secure and Rev Newton decided the time had come to summon his son home and insist on some changes. A letter told Arthur his father had found him an assistant's job on a tea plantation in Ceylon, the country Newton Sr knew well, having been a civil engineer there before converting to the ministry.

And so, with mixed feelings, Arthur sailed from Durban in the autumn of 1909, tail firmly between legs, to face his father. The Newtons were now based in Kingston-upon-Thames in Surrey and all the siblings, bar 21-year-old Dorothy, had by now flown the nest. Harry and Cyril were making their way in successful careers that would lead them to Australia and the West Indies, respectively, Ambrose had embarked on a sea-faring path, Bernard was headed for India and Ursula was making her way as an accomplished musician.

But Arthur arrived home to find the job earmarked for him in Ceylon had fallen through. Undaunted, his father promised he would find him another job if he would remain patient and stay put in the London area for the time being. Arthur now had some thinking to do. He missed Natal and the sunshine quite badly, but was reluctant to flee straight back to Africa and cause a family rift in the process. So he hung around to appease his father and decided to keep himself fit in the mean time by joining a local running club.

It was by now October of 1909 and the English cross-country season was about to start. So Arthur travelled the short distance from the Newton family home in Kingston to sign up with the famous Thames Hare and Hounds. Based on Wimbledon Common, this was the oldest cross-country running club in the world and a real 'gentleman amateur' club. It had been started by Walter Rye, who got the idea of a cross country club from reading about 'the Barley Run' in *Tom Brown's Schooldays*. This was a club that had steadfastly refused to allow 'tradesmen' to join and election was by ballot, requiring members be gentleman by position and education. Newton's privileged background meant he had no trouble getting in, and in his first run with his new friends, he finished third in the club's short-distance Challenge Cup race.

It was an impressive start and the tanned visitor from South Africa was quickly welcomed into the TH&H team to face Oxford University in the annual cross-country match a week or so later. Haigh of TH&H looked the likely winner until he was injured crossing a field of stubble, and this allowed Chandler of Hertford College to romp home in just under 40 minutes. Oxford men filled all the leading positions and won the match comfortably. Newton came home in a highly respectable 42:45, the 13th man to finish, but awarded ninth place in the results as four ahead of him had not been part of the official race.

Newton seemed to enjoy the camaraderie of club life and would maintain his membership of TH&H for many years to come, subsequently wearing their distinctive kit in races all over the globe. The club shirt featured a distinctive black cross or 'saltire' on the chest. The club's annals, published years later, would record that Newton ran the two races in 1909 and then disappeared again, 'no-one suspecting his future greatness.'

Newton was not ready to settle back in England and later wrote about these unhappy weeks: 'Loafing around didn't please me at all and presently I summoned up courage to tell [my father] I was only too keen to get back to Africa. He said he guessed as much and I should go, but he wanted me to keep my eyes open to find some other profession than teaching at which he could help me [get started].'

Chapter 3

The White Man's Burden

Upon his return to Natal, Newton did some serious thinking. During 1910 he came to the decision that would shape his future: He would have a crack at farming. White settlers were obtaining land in South Africa and he was sure he could join them, and overcome his lack of experience in this line of work.

It was a radical change of direction and coincided with major events in his new homeland, for in May of that year the colony of Natal joined the Orange Free State, Transvaal and the Cape in forming the Union of South Africa. This was the climax to four years of negotiations and had come exactly eight years after the end of the Second Boer War. It meant South Africa was a self-governing dominion of the British Empire.

Back in England the news that Newton wanted to become a farmer and acquire some land in the newly formed South Africa was cautiously welcomed by his father, who had promised to support his son financially provided the plans made commercial sense. For Newton these were exciting times and he eagerly read up on what would be required and looked around for suitable land to acquire.

In the meantime, he kept up his running and in December of 1910 represented Harding, the small town that was now his home base, at the Scottsville Racecourse in Durban, where Natal's best runners gathered to compete for the Houghting Shield and the title of Natal 10-mile cross-country champion. Newton was the only competitor not representing either the Pietermaritzburg or Durban athletic clubs. Being relatively inexperienced and not a regular racer, the handicapper gave Newton a 125-second advantage but he surprised all and sundry by coming in fourth in a time of 61:30 and winning the sealed handicap. Winner was pre-race favourite Landers of Durban in 59:42 (off scratch), who was to date clearly the best runner produced by Natal, and he was rarely seriously threatened.

During 1911 Newton's plans came to fruition when he bought 1,350 acres of Crown lands from the Union government, partly funded by money from his father. His farm was some 15 miles from Harding and around 50 miles inland from Port Shepstone on the Indian Ocean. Positioned in a very remote area in the Mzimkulwana River valley, the nearest settlement to the farmhouse was the village of Ihluku a few miles away. It was such a wilderness that, were it not for the main N2 road and narrow-gauge railway to Port Shepstone passing through the area, Newton might have thought he'd landed on the moon.

Newton had acquaintances in Harding and would soon make more friends there once settled at his farm. Weekly visits there supplied his basic needs, including advice about the farm from more experienced folk. Harding had been established as a military outpost following Britain's annexation of East Griqualand in 1873 and was now the home of a number of British expats. Nevertheless, Newton found himself quite isolated while at the farm and accepted he'd taken on a job wholly unsuitable to anyone who was not physically fit or unprepared to live without regular company. There were native tenants grazing their cattle on his land, but his nearest white neighbour was at least five miles away. There would be tough times ahead, but he was determined to make a success of things, in part to prove himself, and to repay the faith of his father.

His choice of the name 'Lovat' for his farm may have been in recognition of the 16th Lord Lovat , who formed The Lovat Scouts during the Second Boer War who were active in this region, or it may have been more to do with his father's reported claim on the Lovat peerage a few years earlier.

The early days at the farm proved a struggle, but Newton was a quick learner and was hungry to succeed. The huge workload certainly kept him fit. He gave up any thoughts of competitive running in such circumstances, although did get into the habit of running to and from his mailbox, which was positioned several miles from his living quarters. His lifelong appetite for letter-writing meant the amount of mail coming in and out was frequent. His parents followed his progress closely by letter, and when times were at their worst, supplied further financial help.

The farm was some ten miles from the main road, with nothing but rough tracks to connect it. Newton took it upon himself to build a proper road capable of carrying motor vehicles to and from the farm. He used a Martin ditcher excavation tool and gelignite for the job, and also created four miles of new road within the farm itself. On top of this he cleared some 140 acres of thornveld bush land. He was proud of his efforts and told friends in Harding it proved his intentions were serious about remaining here, and it also 'opened up the country' by showing the possibilities for other white settlers.

The first few years as a farmer passed quickly and money remained tight as Newton entered his thirties. Then, just when the farm began paying its way and the prospect of success looked realistic, along came the first world war. In Newton's words: 'Germany saw fit to interrupt my designs.'

Keen to do his duty for King and country, Newton went to Pieter-maritzburg on September 1st 1914 and signed on as a trooper in the Natal Light Horse. He recalled: 'I offered to take my motorcycle at my own expense, as I realised I was far more likely to be useful as a dispatch rider than anything else, being a competent and experienced motorcyclist. [But] as there was no Corps of this description yet formed, I had to engage for the ordinary three shillings a day and take my chance of being transferred to the proper department later on. Six months afterwards, when we returned from the Orange River, I joined the Motor Despatch Riders.' His war service was mainly in south-weset Africa and in Transvaal at Potchefstroom.

During the four years of conflict, Newton's farm stood abandoned and neglected, but he remained confident he could soon knock things into shape when he got back. However, what greeted him in 1918 on his return shocked him to the core.

Grass-fires had destroyed around two-thirds of his grazing land, with the fires also destroying a shed containing all his farm implements. On top of this, 'East Coast [tick] fever' was rife among the cattle on the land. It was a major setback and to Newton it felt like he would have to start all over again. He was in no doubt who was responsible for the fires and for not disinfecting the cattle. It was the local native black population, including those who rented grazing land from him. Like most white farmers in the country, his relationship with them had been uneasy, at best, from day one. Before the war started, he had been furious with them for their steadfast refusal to dip their cattle to prevent the spread of fever. He reflected: 'When I began farming . . . I came across the theory of dip-ping cattle in tanks. So I built a tank and therewith started trouble with the [natives], trouble that was to go on for all the rest of my time in the district. Would they dip their cattle? Not if they knew it! If they could at any time avoid the process or hide animals away it was "one up" to them. They insisted that the white man was only trying to kill what stock they had left.'

The dipping row was the tip of the iceberg. Newton and his black ten-ants would come to disagree on just about everything. The normally mild-mannered Englishman was driven almost mad by what went on. In letters and articles written later he would use the term 'kaffirs' to describe these people. Nowadays this term is considered derogatory and racist, but back then was widely employed to describe all natives to the region and used officially without derogatory connotations (apart from the implicit generalisation). It appears in many historical accounts by anthropologists, missionaries and other observers, as well as in academic writings. And during Newton's first year as a farmer a newly published edition of *Encyclopaedia Britannica* made frequent use of the term, even to the extent of having an article of that title.

Friends from the Harding area came to Newton's aid when he returned from the war, lending him man-power and tools. After a week or two an uneasy truce settled over Lovat Farm and things began to settle down. After a while, desperate for a way to increase his meagre income, Newton thought about growing cotton and tobacco. Early in 1919 he travelled down to Durban to meet a local expert for advice.

He then single-handedly cleared four acres of overgrown bush to plant a trial cotton crop, which proved a big success. He extended this crop across a wider area of around 16 acres and the expert paid him a visit and praised his efforts. Two individual plants, bearing what was declared a world record number of 550 bolls each, were photographed during the visit. The Department of Agriculture certified he had produced the finest 'King Upland' plants in the world and his 'Bancroft Improved' crop promised to be a thorough success. He also won prizes at a local show for the tobacco plants he was cultivating, but it was cotton that looked to be the way ahead.

Before long he had cleared more and more land for the cotton, amounting to around 80 acres. His problem was recruiting local labour to pick the crop. The natives seemed unhelpful and unreliable and to compound matters a number of them already owed him rent for the 30 or so 'kraals' (cattle enclosure and homesteads) on his land. Even with the help of a local official, Newton struggled to collect his rent, and one kraal in particular failed to pay up for at least three years. His frustration and anger at the local black population's attitudes grew to breaking point over this period and his letters and other writings were full of accusations about their alleged laziness, heavy drinking and distaste for hard work. He said they even complained about his road-building, refusing to believe he was adding value to the area. On one occasion they ploughed up his marker pegs and it needed court action to allow work to continue.

Newton reflected ruefully: 'The white man's work could go to Timbuktu before they would turn out and help – unless a famine happened to come along. Sure enough a mealie [maize] famine arrived and the women swarmed up asking for assistance. I went out of my way to make work for them so as to see them through, but . . . there is no word in their language to denote anything in the nature of gratitude – the majority of them are not sufficiently civilised to understand the virtue. Their reasoning was after this fashion: their landlord was a white man, one of the race who had access to all sorts of luxuries, moreover one who was obviously and admittedly there to help them when required, therefore it was no more than his duty to feed them when they couldn't manage the business for themselves.'

As his plans for cotton growing began to take shape, Newton took on a white former soldier as his assistant, who was sent round the kraals to offer a deal. In return for six months' work a year in his cotton fields, with pay of 10 shillings per month, the natives would not have to pay rent. The majority refused point-blank to provide any labour under these terms and were told it would now be a case of 'work or quit the land'. Most took this as a blatant attempt to drive them away, but after a magistrate intervened to confirm that working in lieu of rent was the custom on most local farms, a number did quit.

Newton's next ploy to recruit cotton workers was to offer to cleanse local people's cattle in his dip, in exchange for their labour. This offer went down better, and for a spell his fields contained around 30 busy women and children, working one day a week in return for a midday meal and free cattle cleansing. Slowly but surely the cotton proved a success and with 10,000 acres lying idle nearby, Newton and his local Farmers' Association urged the Government to throw open these Crown Lands for ex-servicemen to take over for cotton growing, just as he had at Lovat Farm. But not only did the Government reject this idea but their Native Affairs Department began re-populating the whole area with natives from the Cape colony. Newton was 'safe' in that he couldn't be turned off his farm as he held freehold rights, but he was dismayed at the prospect of being completely surrounded by a five-mile belt of what he called black squatters. He and his white friends protested to their Member of Parliament, but got nowhere.

During these struggles Newton, by now in his mid-thirties, was appointed a local Justice of the Peace. In the immediate post-war years his standing in the local white community and his initial success with cotton suggested that he had found his vocation and would be settling here in Natal for many years to come – but he hadn't bargained for the extent of the trouble he would experience involving the local workers and the intransigent authorities.

A long-running dispute over cattle dipping took many twists and turns and began to sap his energy, not to mention his resources. During the height of his frustrations, he wrote: 'All the way through I seem to have been kept as much in the dark as possible, lest I should give an untimely exposure to the designs of the [departmental] officials who, without authority from Parliament, were going to make [this] a black area, a place where only [natives] might own land or reside.'

Eventually his cotton crop began to suffer through lack of man-power to care for it, and Newton was fighting a losing battle to save it. Partly through bad luck, and partly his own lack of experience, he now faced financial ruin. He had invested large sums in the farm and looked unlikely to get a decent return. Before long the sad day arrived when he had to reluctantly tell his trusty assistant that he would have to let him go: 'I felt this very keenly, for he was a sound and conscientious man and had been with me for more than two years.'

Newton abandoned all other crops in a desperate bid to save the valuable cotton. His efforts were largely in vain. He was in despair. Years of hard work and improvements to the farm seemed completely wasted. With funds desperately low he was forced into bonding his farm to the Land Bank in order to release funds to allow him to carry on farming while he tried to plead with the Government to step in and help.

As a hard-working farmer he felt he had suffered unfairly and that the Government had a duty to help him. He applied to exchange his farm for land in a 'white area' so that he could move and start all over again. They refused. He then urged them to purchase his farm so they could hand it over to the native people they were re-settling in the area. They again refused, adding the unwelcome rider that if they were to purchase the freehold from him in future he should only expect a basic price for the land and no recompense for the many improvements or equipment at the farm.

It was a shattering blow but Newton, now nearly 40 and facing financial meltdown, was in no mood to give in. He was generally a polite and mild-mannered fellow, but the injustice and unfairness he felt galvanised him into a very uncharacteristic raging fury. He wrote: 'All right! If they were content to put a premium on retrogression, I wasn't. No one but an idiot would continue to put in improvements [to the farm] after they had been officially informed that such were, and always would be, of no great moment. There was only one sensible course left. If I wanted to progress I must get to another place where my work would not be thrown away. The responsible Department was determined to ignore the matter, and probably felt all the safer because I was quite unknown and therefore likely to be helpless.'

Newton was convinced he was being badly treated because he was a 'nobody' and they would not dare deal with somebody well known in this fashion. Therefore, he concluded, if he were to make himself famous, they would have to take notice because the public would demand it. Playing the role of a celebrity or public figure was contrary to his nature, but he was a pragmatist and had to do whatever was necessary. He even admitted to being basically a shy man who hated any form of limelight, but accepted that present circumstances demanded a well organised 'publicity stunt' – otherwise he would simply go under.

He recalled the momentous day that he hatched his new plan: 'Evidently I should have to make my name and the circumstances known to the public. I should then be in a position to show my fellow citizens how settlers should be safeguarded. It took careful and protracted deliberation to arrive at a promising solution, and one that could be relied on to be fairly speedy, for worthy reputations are not built up in a week.'

His idea was simple: To get attention and support for his cause he would need to make himself famous. To become famous he would turn himself into a star athlete. And to become a star athlete he would go and win the annual 54-mile Comrades Marathon from Durban to Pietermaritzburg!

He'd heard all about the first Comrades run, staged just recently, and had been fascinated to note that it was won by a fellow white farmer. The race was to become an annual event, organised by the League of Comrades, to which he was already associated, and was fundamentally aimed at returned infantrymen like himself. To train for the event would be cheap, easy and without reliance on others. To Newton it made perfect sense – but to friends and family must have seemed a crazy scheme for a man approaching middle age who had not run for years, and even back then nothing like the distance involved in the gruelling Comrades. And, of course, it wasn't a case of simply finishing the race, Newton would surely need to win to achieve his goal.

Looking back all these years later, Newton's plan was akin to a 21st century out-of-condition former fun-runner, fond of a cigarette or two, who expected to win the London Marathon on less than five months' preparation. It was mission impossible, surely?

Chapter 4

A Couple of Swigs of Brandy

Newton's plan defied logic. He seriously thought he could win the 54-mile Comrades Marathon as a 39-year-old novice, on less than five months' training. Yet he hadn't run properly for at least ten years – and even back then had only entered a handful of shorter races and never won anything of note. All he'd managed in recent times was a few long walks to collect his mail, or to pick up supplies from the nearest village.

He attempted to explain the thinking behind his scheme: 'Genuine amateur athletics were about as wholesome as anything was on this earth. Any man who made a really notable name [in athletics] would always be given a hearing by the public. Knowing through my studies that any average man could do as well as other average men if he were really determined and was in possession of an average physique – and with the Comrades Marathon already in existence – I decided that what with my age, it would be quicker and probably easier to achieve publicity through long-distance running than by any other methods.'

The first annual 54-mile Comrades Marathon had taken place in Natal on Empire Day in May 1921 and the press coverage back then had piqued Newton's interest. However, at the time he'd been so embroiled in the trials and tribulations at Lovat Farm that he quickly forgot all about it. Now, a few months on, the race returned to his thoughts in a big way.

Undaunted by the approach of his fifth decade, Newton began planning how to get into prime shape so that he could not only finish the gruelling 54-mile event, but give himself a good chance of winning it. If he could pull it off, he reasoned, the publicity would be enormous and would embarrass the Union government into helping him out. He pointed out:

'Through study and reading I had long been convinced that any man-in-the-street could do what any other man had done, provided handicaps were not too severe, and I was determined to have a shot at proving it. I had to allow for age. Real long-distance stuff was about the only thing where I might hope to compete with a reasonable chance. So I got what literature I could on the subject and wired in with training.'

He pencilled January 1st 1922 into his diary as the first day of his training programme. The race was on May 24th, meaning he had 20 weeks to prepare. The winner of the inaugural race – also a farmer, albeit a much younger one – had covered the dusty, hilly and largely unmade road from Pietermaritzburg to Durban in less than nine hours. That meant Newton's task was to train himself from scratch to be capable of running 54 miles without stopping at roughly nine minutes per mile. Any slower and he probably wouldn't win – and victory was essential to get the maximum publicity he needed.

It was a daunting task, and certainly a New Year's resolution with a difference. And to make matters even tougher, this year's race was to be run in the opposite direction – starting at sea level in Durban – meaning the runners would face much stiffer hills.

Thanks to his brief flirtation with distance-running many years earlier, Newton knew he was capable of jogging along for around an hour without undue distress – if properly prepared. And in more recent times he had happily walked distances of up to 20 miles without a problem. But, of course, 54 miles of competitive running was a very different matter, and he worried that his ageing body might struggle with the unfamiliar stresses it would face. Nevertheless it was a challenge that filled him with a grim determination, fuelled in no small part by his burning sense of injustice over the farming issues. Moreover, now that his farm was rendered virtually redundant, he could devote all his waking hours to whatever training and preparation was needed.

The Pietermaritzburg Comrades Marathon was the brainchild of Vic Clapham, an engine driver on the South African Railways, who had been inspired when reading tales of the 50-mile 'Stock Exchange Walk' from London to Brighton. Clapham felt that if infantrymen, drafted straight into the armed forces from sedentary occupations, could cope with long marches, then trained athletes should certainly be capable of covering the 54 miles between Pietermaritzburg and Durban. At the end of the 1914-18 War, Clapham, with other troops who served in East Africa, asked the ex-soldiers association, the Comrades of the Great War, to allow him to organise the race using their name. But he was laughed at, and told such a long race would be far too strenuous.

Clapham had been a member of the pre-war Mountain Harriers club in Cape Town, but had no competitive athletic experience himself. Nevertheless, he was convinced the doubters were wrong and he applied twice more, in 1919 and 1920 to stage his race, but again was refused. At the fourth attempt in 1921, permission was rather reluctantly granted and he was given a returnable advance of just £1 (two rand) to cover his expenses. He was told he could set up the race under the auspices of the Comrades of the Great War, as long as it didn't cost them anything.

So Clapham publicised his first event during the early months of 1921 and many of the men who came forward were ex-infantrymen. Nearly 50 registered for the race, although only 34 made it to the start-line shortly after dawn on May 24th to await the Mayor of Pietermaritzburg's starting pistol. To attempt to get from here to Durban on foot seemed an act of great optimism and many observers believed few would make it to the finish. And those who did would surely never get there by nightfall.

The pioneering runners had other ideas, of course, and set off briskly, many of them followed by friends and helpers on bicycles and in cars. Farmers set up refreshment stalls at the roadside en route, and householders joined the fun by holding picnic parties and giving food to the passing runners. Later that day Bill Rowan, a 26-year-old Transvaal farmer, trotted into central Durban just after four that afternoon, covered in dust and exhausted. He finished within a single minute of his predicted finish time of nine hours to become the first Comrades champion.

It had been a fascinating struggle of man against the elements and the interest generated and the wide press coverage exceeded even organiser Clapham's expectations. It ensured that when the time came round for the second staging of the race in 1922, twice as many men – well over 100 – put their names forward to take part. The list included all types, from all walks of life. Some were experienced runners, some had a modicum of running in their backgrounds, and others were complete novices. The list included the highly motivated Arthur Newton.

Newton had heard how the inaugural champion, Bill Rowan, had prepared, doing regular 20-mile cross-country runs at his Koster farm, supplemented by daily stints of prolonged skipping. Newton pondered long and hard how he could emulate Rowan's achievement, while overcoming the handicap of possessing a much older and less experienced body to get him there. He ignored sceptics who condemned the 54-mile struggle as too strenuous for the vast majority of men. He was confident he could devise and maintain a personal training schedule that would get him to the finish line, and having noted the times of the 1921 finishers, reckoned he could even be a serious contender for victory. The situation at his farm meant he had all the spare time needed to do the running and conditioning work necessary – albeit in a period of less than five months.

And so, on New Year's day, with the sun rising behind the hills to the east of his remote farm, Newton set out slowly on his first proper run in years. Sensibly, he planned a modest jaunt of no more than two miles. He felt slightly nervous and moved rather stiffly, but it felt good to be taking the first positive steps in his fight against the injustice and ill-luck that had plagued him recently.

Underfoot the terrain was rough and dusty and the hills in the area were relentless and cruel. Newton's enthusiasm for the task meant he pushed himself too hard, too soon, and before long he was suffering badly. Gasping loudly, he had to stop after barely a mile, his chest heaving as he bent forward with hands on knees. He was 38 and hadn't run for a decade, but still he never expected it to be this hard. He wrote afterwards: 'My condition was quite reasonably good. I could walk 15 or 20 miles in a day over rough country without becoming really exhausted, so I was surprised to find that two miles of running were altogether beyond me. Before I had gone a mile I was obliged to stop for want of wind. Having recovered somewhat I started off again, once more being pulled up by the same symptoms. After that I was so abominably stiff that I cut out running for a day or two and walked instead. Then I had another shot at it and found things were getting better.'

A month or so into his training, Newton reluctantly accepted he would have to do something about his smoking habit, otherwise his chances of success would be seriously compromised. He read up on the subject and found that all the experts condemned smoking as totally unsuitable for athletes. With heavy heart he hid the tobacco away and embarked on an experimental period of ten days during which he didn't touch a cigarette, pipe or cigar. Having indulged daily for 20 years or so, it proved more than a little difficult.

At the end of the period he concluded he could survive without the weed if really necessary, although the constant craving did pose 'a temporary menace to my mental health'. He felt the 'sustained mental disquietude' was hampering his training, and decided that cutting back gradually would be much easier than trying to give up entirely in one go. He allowed himself two pipes a day, both to come only after his daily running was over. Sure enough, the pleasure from being able to light up again lifted his spirits and consequently his overall performance too. It gave him something to look forward to during the difficult runs, and before long he decided a post-run pipe could become a permanent part of his routine, although cigarettes were pretty much banished for ever.

By the time February 1922 had dawned, the running was proving a little easier, interspersed with walks, and one morning he set out to run ten miles in two laps. He was delighted to survive the task with only the briefest of stops: 'This was very encouraging and I settled down to work at it harder than ever.' Heeding the rather limited coaching advice of the time, he timed all his runs carefully and tried to improve the clocking slightly every time he did a particular route.

During early March, encouraged by his progress and aware the big race was now only around ten weeks away, Newton decided a long run under race conditions was necessary. Suitable human opponents were non-existent in such a remote area, so his choice of rival was out of necessity an unusual one. He would race the local train. Man against machine seemed a fascinating challenge to Newton at the time, but what he never expected was that the effort would – in his own words – nearly kill him.

The narrow-gauge railway from Harding to the coast at Port Shepstone 50 miles away wound around the local hills for about 35 miles, with several stops, before arriving at Izingolweni. Newton reckoned he could beat the train to Izingolweni if he took the shorter road route. He recalled the episode:

'Taking it easier for a day or two, I then walked 17 miles into Harding and spent the night at a friend's house. Early next morning I started off from the station at the same time as the train, though I followed the road, a course much shorter and hillier than the rail line. The route was mountainous and I had very long hills to climb and even longer ones to go down. By the time I had gone a dozen miles I realised I was quite badly tired, but my watch told me I was going so well that I should have no difficulty at all in beating the train if I kept going at about the same rate. So I went on, getting more desperately tired with every mile, till I came to a 500 feet climb a mile or two from the station where I was to finish.

'All went well till I got to a hundred feet from the top – the steepest bit of the lot – and then something mighty near tragedy occurred. I was actually forcing myself to run up a gradient of about 1-in-6 when quite suddenly I was pulled up with an abominable ache around my heart, so distressing an experience that I knew, without any expert advice, that I had in some way damaged the organ. Even walking was out of the question for a time and I sat down on a rock and waited in the hope that I might recover. After a quarter of an hour I got up and, walking ever so slowly and unsteadily, managed to reach the top, where I took another rest. From there on I continued in the same manner for rather more than a mile till I got to the hotel near the station; the pain seemed to get no worse provided I travelled at about a mile an hour and, as I did not want a search party sent out to look for me, I decided to get there under my own steam.'

It was a frightening episode and, needless to say, Newton did not beat the train on this occasion. Attempting to run hard at altitude had put his respiratory system into serious oxygen debt, having no doubt ignored earlier warning signals. It would be a mistake he could not make twice. Shaken and deeply worried over what to do next, he wrote:

'I was driven back to my farm and sat down to think the position out. Evidently my training had not been on the right lines, and I decided to ignore practically everything I had read and start all over again with sound common-sense methods as soon as I had recovered sufficiently.'

He refused to go to a doctor, convinced he would only be told to give up altogether. He revised his training completely, dropping all time-trials and relying far less on his watch. In his own words, he would from now on travel 'ever so casually and quietly', concerning himself only with distance and not speed.

The enforced rest and slowing down evidently did him a power of good and by April he was running consistently again, if a lot slower than originally planned. He now worked hard on developing an economic running 'style' that would allow him to travel for long periods while expending a minimum of energy. Almost by accident, he thus discovered the benefits of 'LSD' running (long slow distance) that in later years would become a staple of all marathon runners' training programmes.

Newton's solid progress reassured him his unusual decision to take up running 'seriously' in his late thirties had not been a horrendous mistake. This was an era when too much exercise was deemed unhealthy for middle-aged men, but Newton was encouraged by the views of champion wrestler and fitness guru George Hackenschmidt who firmly believed the male body could withstand far greater stresses than polite society imagined, and reckoned the benefits and feelings of well-being which resulted from vigorous exercise were inestimable.

Newton learned, by experimenting with his own gait and posture, that economy of effort was imperative in long-distance work. He found he could shuffle along easily for many miles if he employed little knee-lift, a short stride and allowed his arms to dangle freely while keeping his shoulders and body still. This style allowed him to make good progress while saving energy. Expending too much effort early in a long race usually proved fatal, he concluded, and he had no intention of repeating the mistakes made by many men in the first Comrades Marathon.

He kept a meticulous training log and analysed the statistics carefully. He wrote: 'March and April in Natal are distinctly hot as a rule, in the daytime anyhow. The road I ran on was mountainous and contained no level going at all. On March 6th, 1922, I ran 25 miles, on April 15th, 26 miles. On the first occasion I dropped from 141¾ lbs to 134½ lbs, a matter of over seven pounds, on the other from 138 to 132lbs. With only a month to go to the great race I tried my luck at a 40-mile run, a very much greater distance than anything I had dared try before. It went through without a hitch and I knew at once that I was well away on improved lines. All along I had realised that as an athlete I was probably well behind the average of the men I should be competing against, but being fully aware that mentality counted for a great deal more than mere physical strength, I relied chiefly on this to bring me to the top.'

Filled with confidence now that he had recovered and learned from his first race with the local train, he went back to Harding station to try again. On one particular day he ran the main road towards Port Shepstone to the small town of Paddock, some 40 odd miles away, and was drinking his second cup of coffee at Paddock station's refreshment room by the time the train came in. This would be his longest run during the build-up and it went so well that he knew things were back on track. A week before the big race – again on Empire Day, May 24th – Newton packed a bag, left his farm and walked the 17 miles into Harding. Here he took the train for the 150-mile trip to Durban, where he was to stay with Bill Payn, an old friend from his days as a schoolmaster. His host was a big muscular fellow, a rugby player and cricketer of some repute, who had also registered to run the Comrades marathon. But in Payn's case, he had signed up late (he was No 111 of 114 entrants) and was not treating the occasion with anything like the seriousness of Newton.

A few days of light running in Durban completed Newton's training programme. He was satisfied he'd done enough, even though his 20-week schedule had been disrupted and adjusted on several occasions. But a structured plan had never been part of his pal Payn's preparations. The bulky Payn was certainly not built for distance work, but he had natural strength and ebullience and had entered purely for the fun of it. He intended to have a good time and the daunting 54 hilly miles to Pietermaritzburg didn't seem to concern him at all.

Payn had no trouble sleeping the night before the race, unlike Newton. The latter woke around 3, nervous and restless. He lay in bed for an hour thinking about the upcoming ordeal, before getting up to prepare a himself a breakfast of three eggs and bacon, plus several large cups of coffee. Payn came downstairs to join him, and they finalised their preparations before strolling slowly the half-mile to the start-line at Durban's Old Toll Gate. Although Newton had socialised with fun-runner Payn and others in the days prior to the race, in the tense moments before the race's scheduled 6 o'clock start he was determined to cut himself off from the laughter and banter in order to be alone with his thoughts: 'When we arrived at the starting point early in the morning I kept away from the great bulk of the competitors so as to be able to sit quietly and rest instead of being called upon to talk loudly amidst the general bustle and noise.'

Only 34 had toed the start-line in the 1921 inaugural race, but this time 114 brave souls signed up. Since putting their names forward, 25 of these apparently fell foul of injury, illness or pure fear, meaning 89 started. It was recognised that this year's race would be much tougher than before, as it was heading up the hills to Pietermaritzburg from Durban, instead of the other way round. This alternation from year to year would become the established pattern in years to come.

By six, in the semi-darkness of a chilly winter morning, the 89 runners were strung across the road near the Old Toll Gate, watched by a crowd of around 2,000. Newton wore his white kit with black trimmings, and was entrant number 77. He was listed as representing Harding Sports, although his shirt bore the prominent black saltire of the Thames Hare and Hounds club. Also in attendance was title-holder and fellow farmer Bill Rowan, who this year had travelled in from the Belgian Congo, and N J Nel, determined to start despite cracking a rib the previous day in a minor road accident.

The Mayor of Durban, councillor Fleming Johnston, after a few words, fired the pistol and sent them on their way at a few minutes after six. Followed by helpers aboard cars, rickshaws, bicycles and motorbikes, many of the field couldn't resist the temptation to 'bolt like startled rabbits' according to one press report. Newton knew better. In his own words, he 'sauntered along quite casually' at the very back of the field, and after a mile was still a couple of hundred yards behind, determined to save energy and make slow but steady progress. He recalled that his sedate speed drew jocular remarks from spectators: one told him he ought to have brought along his motor-bike, while another said he had no chance of making it to Pietermaritzburg unless he got a move on.

As they headed out of Durban, on the dusty, unmade road which climbed to Mayville and Blackhill, back-marker Newton soon found himself passing a few men who were already walking even at this early stage. By keeping to the same steady jog as planned, he found himself overtaking more and more of these under-trained stragglers and headed towards the middle of the field. In the Kloof area, with barely 20 miles completed, he passed three or four groups of men reduced to a walk by the never-ending hills. Before halfway he had passed well over half the field. Up at the front, the lead changed hands a number of times, but this didn't concern Newton, whose progress through the field was going surprisingly well considering he didn't change pace at all. It was the classic 'tortoise and hare' scenario. His hours of training around hilly Harding meant he coped quite comfortably on the severe inclines, while many opponents suffered miserably and looked ready to quit at any moment.

Newton would write later: 'The winner and runner-up of the year before [Bill Rowan and Harry Phillips] were both on the road again, and

I took it for granted that they would be at it hammer and tongs on their own, regardless of the others. It wasn't my business if they killed themselves like this, though I knew it could only turn to my advantage. However, things on the whole were working out so well that when I was approaching the half-way mark at Drummond I was told that there were only four men ahead [of me] – a very surprising and welcome piece of news.'

Before this, Newton had actually thought he might be in the first dozen or so, but hadn't accounted for the numbers who had dropped out altogether after suffering on the crippling hills in the first half of the race. It was stunning news, and must have caused the normally conservative Newton to start dreaming of the debut victory that would achieve his stated need for publicity.

As he passed the 30-mile mark, he had to contemplate the awful prospect of the huge hill at Inchanga Bank: 'I had to take things very quietly indeed as I was already pretty badly tired and knew that I should have to be more than particularly careful if I wanted to reach the other end.' Playing it cautious proved the perfect tactic by Newton in the Inchanga area.

What he didn't know at this point was that the two favourites, Rowan and Phillips, winner and runner-up in 1921, had wasted valuable energy by battling with each other, and the former had left the road earlier in Drummond to deal with cramp in his thigh. Rowan had now fallen well behind Newton and was slipping back further due to having to stop regularly for the problem to be massaged. There were now only three men ahead of Newton and one of these was the ailing Post Office linesman Phillips.

At the top of the Inchanga Bank (around 32 miles completed), Newton shuffled relentlessly on at the same speed, his calm exterior hiding the exhaustion he felt. As he played mind games with himself in order to maintain concentration and focus, he suddenly came upon Phillips, stretched out at the roadside and being massaged. Earlier Phillips had been at least 45 minutes ahead, yet without trying Newton had now caught and overhauled him. This thought encouraged Newton no end. His spirits were lifted even further when someone at the roadside confirmed that Rowan was in trouble well behind him, and Newton was now in fact in second place.

Newton takes up the story: 'Once over the top [of Inchanga Bank] I had enough left to settle down to a steady 6½ miles an hour again. I was getting terribly tired but, on hearing that I was rapidly overhauling the leader [A C Purcell], I felt I had just got to stick at it, though I made a sort of mental note that I ought never again to be called on to put up such an abnormal exertion.'

Meanwhile, back down the field, Newton's pal Bill Payn was having a whale of a time, despite running the race in rugby boots. Such was Newton's conservative pace early on that Payn had actually been ahead of him for around 18 miles, but soon after Newton passed, Payn stopped at the Hill Crest Hotel for rest and refreshment. He ordered up a hearty 'brunch' of eggs, ham, ginger brandy and cigarettes, before attending to his badly chafed and blistered feet. With only hair oil available to him, he rubbed the oily fluid onto his feet, replaced the rugby boots and set off again, leaving a clutch of bewildered and amused onlookers behind him. When he reached the top of Botha's Hill, still a mile or two short of halfway, Payn was invited by fellow runner F K 'Zulu' Wade, to join him at the roadside for a casserole of curried chicken, which an attendant had brought him for lunch.

After consuming the casserole, the pair jogged the short distance to the Drummond Hotel and stopped again for an ice-cold beer or two, to wash down their lunch. By now, Wade seemed unwilling to get back on the road, but Payn was made of sterner stuff and heaved his huge frame out of the hotel. In order to finish the race he would take refreshment wherever and whenever he could, and would later reveal he ate at least 36 oranges en route, not to mention a large glass of home-made peach brandy.

The food and drink Payn took on board made Newton's 'refuelling' seem positively minimal. Spectators throughout the route were offering fruit, confectionery and other delights, but Newton was careful what he accepted. He slugged down a few small doses of Bovril, and later some tea, but towards the end of the race all he risked was a couple of tots of brandy. He did, however, ask for his neck to be doused regularly with cold water, a move that allowed him to get away without having to wear a protective hat.

While Payn was tucking into his casserole, up ahead Newton was making inroads on the race leader, Purcell. At the foot of a gruelling 800 feet climb, Newton suddenly spotted a small white speck just going over the top up ahead. Someone at the roadside confirmed to him this was Purcell, who had unwisely set out that morning without any breakfast as he felt a big meal inside him would do more harm than good. Purcell also failed to stop for refreshment at the halfway point, so when he caved in and ground to a halt just before Camperdown (38 miles) it was hardly suprising. He cut a forlorn, limp and dusty figure at the roadside as Newton went smoothly by. Newton recalled: 'When . . . I caught up [with

Purcell], I was able to appreciate the fact that if I was tired he was even more so. This was tremendously encouraging though I felt so exhausted that even then I wondered whether I should last out to reach the tape.'

With well under one-third of the race left, Newton by now knew the spoils of an unlikely victory were surely his – as long as he could conquer the last of the 'killer hills', the Umlaas Road Bridge area and Polly Short's Cutting. Getting past the former allowed him the relative ease of cruising downhill towards Thornybush, a section in which he could increase his speed a little. By now, with around 40 miles done and 14 to go, he was 30 minutes ahead of the struggling Phillips, who was still plagued by cramp but limping along bravely in second place.

Newton admitted later he 'under-estimated the fearsomeness' of Polly Short's Cutting, which involved a 500 feet climb in little over a mile, with the steepest part at the very top: 'I reduced my stride as I had long since learnt to and gently, ever so gently, crept up the long rise. Great James! It was terrible work! It might have been nothing desperate for a man who was quite fresh, but when you had already run a much longer distance than you had ever tackled before in your life, the thing became a sheer nightmare. Up I went, and still up, but I began to feel that it was impossible to keep going. It got so bad that when it came to the steepest part I stopped dead in a single stride, convinced at that moment that it was worse than absolute idiocy to attempt to carry on. At the same instant I considered that if I permitted this sort of thing I could say goodbye to any self-respect I ever had. The stop lasted no more than two seconds and once more I was slowly, ever so slowly, working my passage up that hill.'

Finally at the top, having now run further than ever before in a single journey, he was mightily relieved to see Pietermaritzburg ahead just four miles away, and downhill all the way. Victory was surely his. A tot of brandy at the Star and Garter Hotel, his second such indulgence in just a few miles, fortified him for the final stretch. What lay ahead was clearly within his physical capabilities, but he could never have imagined the mental ordeal that faced him in the approach to the finish line.

Essentially a shy man who hated excessive attention, Newton was roared home by a massive crowd that exceeded anything he'd seen or experienced before. The acclaim was deserved, but for Newton not a comfortable experience. His exhaustion would be largely forgotten as he suffered acute embarrassment at the jubilant reception. He described the final mile or two thus:

'With a swarm of cars and cycles behind, I guessed there would be a crowd ahead. Crowd wasn't the name for it. As I approached the City

Hall with a mile to go to the finish at the Sports Ground, the people swarmed up so suddenly from every side that I was only just able to get through with the aid of the police. Gently downhill, and then round the corner into the Showground track for the finish. Good Heavens, what a multitude; thousands of people intensely concentrated on watching that final lap. Even then, although more tired than I had ever believed possible, I was still able to feel distinctly embarrassed. But at last I saw the tape ahead and ran to it in a tumultuous roar of cheering from all sides to get a handshake from the City Mayor.'

He had finished in 8 hours 40 minutes, nearly 20 minutes quicker than the previous winning time, and was nearly half an hour ahead of Phillips in second place. It was an astonishing run and press and public were fascinated at the achievement of this 'unknown' from many miles away. Modest Newton confessed to the reporters that he too was surprised, and his awkwardness was compounded when the throng suddenly lifted him off his feet and paraded him shoulder-high off the field.

Reporters followed him and he told them he planned to parcel up his various prizes and rail them back to Harding later, so that he could avoid any home-coming ceremonies, as the last thing he wanted was a fuss. His haul included the Comrades Marathon 'Floating Trophy' valued at 70 guineas, and presented by various sporting clubs of Durban, plus a 25-guinea first prize and a gold medal. Eventually, at his own request, Newton was spirited away from the melee by friends and helpers before being called back again to be photographed, and then being 'kidnapped by ladies who entertained him to tea far from the madding crowd,' according to one report. By the time the runner-up Harry Phillips crossed the finish line, it was noted, Newton had had a bath and was dressed in collared and everyday garb.

Pressed for his reaction to the win, Newton said: 'I rather thought I could run into third or fourth place, but certainly did not expect to win and still less to cover the course in less than 9 hours and 15 minutes. It isn't my fault I won. If Phillips and Rowan hadn't cut out such a terrific pace at the start they would both have finished in front of me, because they are both better runners.'

Like many a distance runner before and after him, he declared he probably wouldn't attempt such a thing again. He told one reporter his parents back home in England would be 'tremendously pleased when they hear about this. After all, I'm 39 and getting on.'

To his relief, Newton was finally able to slip away from the centre of the throng as they began turning their attention to the other bedraggled finishers. Newton's friend Bill Payn lumbered home in just under 11 hours, his exhaustion and various injuries not preventing him playing in a rugby match the very next day. Another finisher was a 16-year-old called Templeton, who had started alongside his father and continued to the end when the older man quit.

The *Natal Witness* newspaper, which sponsored the 25 guineas first prize, was fascinated by Newton and his background. Their editorial deplored the fact that, as a returned soldier, South Africa had treated him so poorly by placing his farm in a native area. This was the sort of publicity Newton welcomed and he was optimistic it would help his cause.

After a short stay with friends in Pietermaritzburg, Newton returned to Harding, but didn't get the quiet homecoming he had hoped for. Townsfolk insisted on presenting him with an address and purse at a concert and dance staged by the local rugby club in the Alfred Theatre. Newton was given a handsome clock with a swinging pendulum and vases, although the main trophy had not been railed up from Durban in time.

The gathering was told that Newton had won because of his 'British pluck allied to colonial acclimatisation'. It was pointed out that he now held the world record for running 54 miles, as well as for the growing the greatest quantity of cotton reaped from a single bush! After a rousing 'three cheers', an embarrassed Newton stood up to give a brief and modest reply.

As intended, the victory made him a star overnight throughout Natal, and the press became interested in his story, thus alerting a sympathetic public and his regional MP. In this regard it was very much mission accomplished. But, once the aches and pains had died away, Newton forgot his post-race comments and confided to friends he had no intention of stopping his training yet. He was now convinced he could become an even better runner in his forties.

Chapter 5

Merely an Artificial Runner

Victory at his first attempt in the Comrades Marathon may have made Arthur Newton well known in Natal, but as the weeks went by in 1922 his new status as a celebrity showed no signs of persuading the Union government to resolve his problems at Lovat Farm.

Newton, claiming financial ruin, continued to write and lobby for the government to do the decent thing and help him move to an area not earmarked for natives, or compensate him. His pleas continued to fall on deaf ears, so he did the only thing he felt he could in the circumstances – he stepped up his training and vowed to make himself an even more famous athlete. By hook or by crook, he would force the mandarins in Pretoria (the country's administrative capital) to change their minds. If winning the Comrades as 'an old man of 39' wasn't enough, he could try for a world record or two, which would get him known around the globe. Eventually, he was convinced, the pressure would force them to act.

Recognising that his days at Lovat Farm were numbered, he had bonded the farm to the Land Bank with the object of releasing funds while the Government made their investigations into his case. This would not prove a good move, for the case would drag on without a successful outcome for far longer than Newton ever anticipated. And so, surviving on limited funds, handouts from his parents, and the goodwill of friends, he ploughed on with his new career as a full-time runner, devoting every day to his training and conditioning. By the middle of the African winter in mid-1922 he was clocking up weeks of around 180 miles of slow, steady running. By the end of that year his log showed a grand total of 4,678 miles covered on foot (1,584 of them walking and 3,094 running). It represented an average of 12 miles per day for his first year as a serious runner. These figures were remarkable enough, but for 1923 the tally would rocket to 9,168 miles (around 25 per day).

Such extreme mileage was unprecedented. Great champions of the past – such as Alf Shrubb and Walter George – had never attempted this sort of intense training, yet both of them had set 10-mile and one-hour records that stood unbroken for many years. Shrubb liked to take long walks as part of his regime, but never contemplated the type of journeys Newton attempted. Newton, of course, had plenty of time on his hands and liked to experiment, but the main difference between him and the legends of earlier eras was that he was totally unconcerned by speed. He felt he could do well at ultra-long distances by conditioning his body to travel for hours at a steady pace. He wouldn't dream of wasting energy by surging or changing pace in the middle of a run.

Newton's success at the 1922 Comrades inevitably sparked thoughts of attempting to set a new 50-mile record, and he fancied that with the right training he could even go beyond this and become the 60-mile record-holder too. Previously acknowledged records were generally set on running tracks, which had the advantage of being flat and accurately measured, but were soul-destroying places to run for long-distance men. Newton decided early in his new career that such tracks were not for him. He enjoyed the open road, however remote or hilly, where he could slip into a state of zen-like calm and appreciate his surroundings. Being scrutinised while circling a tiny track for hours on end would drive him mad, he concluded, and he pushed on with his road-work, trundling up the local hills time and again, his motivation never wavering.

According to Newton: 'I took stock of my position, felt that I had by no means established myself as a well-known public character, and decided that more [training] work, even harder work, had to be the order of the day. Besides, didn't all the other runners know what they were up against now, and consequently they would train until they were able either to beat or approximate it? In that case I should have to do altogether better. In fact it looked as though nothing less than world's records would bring me the publicity I knew was required.'

For 11 months after his glorious Comrades debut he toiled away, getting fitter and stronger, and managing to steer clear of serious injury. One rare setback came when he made the naïve mistake of many a novice runner – he failed to properly 'break in' a new pair of shoes. He recalled the painful episode that resulted:

'At the time I was using chrome-tanned leather shoes. My footgear needed repairing so I set out for a 19-mile run to leave them at the shop I always patronised, proposing to pick up a new pair which I understood were ready for me there. As these were always made to measure I reckoned that breaking them in would spell no more than an odd blister or two. I tried the new ones and they seemed perfectly comfortable. To make doubly sure I had them well oiled all over. Leaving the old ones to be mended, I started off home. After some eight or nine miles the right shoe seemed to be uncomfortable at the toe, and at a gate I had to go through I stopped for a moment to investigate and consider. As it was about as far to return to the shop, as it was to get home, where I had other shoes, I decided to continue. The trouble got worse very rapidly and eventually I tried running without the shoe, only to find it impossible, owing to the very rough country roads. So I put the thing on again and struggled home. "Whew! The three biggest nails on that foot were spatch-cocked!'"

Despite his huge training mileage, the only other known setback from this period involved a muscle strain that kept him off the road for a mere six days. This came after a month when he clocked up weekly totals of 253, 121, 133, and 242 miles. The problem occurred after he ignored soreness by favouring the other leg. This led to what he called 'inflammation attacking a sinew' and brought him to an abrupt halt one day, miles from nowhere: 'I just managed to get to my neighbour's farm. He put me into his trap and drove me home. There for six solid days I sat and nursed that leg, continually soaking it in very hot water, as I found that eased it.'

Throughout this period the Union government's position didn't change, but nor did Newton's resolve weaken and by the time Empire Day 1923 came around, Newton was confident of an even better finish-time at the annual Comrades race, thus proving he was no 'flash in the pan' in sporting terms.

Since his heart scare, he had resolved never to indulge in time-trials, so had no real clue what time he was capable of clocking, but knew an improvement was highly likely given that the race would this time head downhill from Pietermartizburg to Durban. The hills he had conquered (with difficulty) last time would now be mercifully in his favour although, of course, his opponents would also find life similarly easier.

Newton lined up for the 1923 Comrades with 9,000 training miles in 12 months in his legs, thousands more than most of the rest of the field. He was the only man on the start-line who could be described as a full-time runner, a matter which troubled him slightly as he felt it was an almost unfair advantage over the working men lined up against him. Should he win, he vowed, he would pass his prizes to whoever finished second. This was not only the stance of a quintessentially 'fair' Englishman, but also because Newton only really wanted publicity and justice – not material rewards.

Having trained 'properly' this time, Newton performed what can only be described as a Comrades walkover. He arrived at the finish in a remarkable time of 6:56:07, to win by the huge margin of 52 minutes. The previous winning time for the 'down' route had been more than two hours slower. He was so fast he even caught finish-line officials on the hop and not in their proper positions! The race this time featured 67 men, plus the first female to attempt the journey. Miss Frances Hayward of Durban shocked many of the 2,000 crowd by turning up at the start-line in a business-like green gymnasium costume and solid-looking leather shoes. As a mere female, she was classed an 'unofficial' entry, but nobody attempted to stop her and some of the crowd appeared to believe she was a helper, or part of some sort of gimmick. Others had heard she seriously intended to run the 54 miles, and clamour quickly grew to catch sight of her and shout out encouragement. She was accompanied all the way by a chaperone called Rogers, whose main job, it was later explained, was to ensure that her costume was 'suited to the event' throughout. The young typist made steady progress, slowing to a walk on the uphill sections, and eventually came home in 11hrs 35mins, in a respectable (unofficial) 28th place. She told reporters she had been determined to finish 'to shock everybody.' After the race she calmly got changed and went off to the theatre. Having received no finishers' medal, a collection was organised for her and paid for a silver tea service and rose bowl. Later, she wrote letters of thanks to the local press and pleaded for special women's marathons to be laid on in the future (her calls were not heeded; a woman's marathon would not be part of the Olympic programme for another 61 years).

The gallant Mr Newton was quite content to share the limelight with Miss Hayward. Throughout the race he had travelled at a quicker pace than last year but still adopting his steady, economic stride. By the town of Harrison – one-third into the race – the early front-runners were fading and Newton had the lead. Typical of those who Newton overhauled was little John Annan, a telegraphist, who entered with practically no training other than long hikes. Annan made good use of the unofficial refreshment stops provided by locals en route, and the energy he gathered from these saw him put on regular spurts. He revealed later he'd taken up all offers of ginger beer, fruit salts, sherry and coffee. He was never likely to threaten Newton's relentless progress, however, and in the Gillitts area, with around 10 miles left, Newton found himself 35 minutes ahead and increasing his lead with every step.

By now Newton was covered from head to foot by dust, but still moving supremely well. He made several brief stops to sip some tea, but after going through Pinetown began to suffer from cramp over the final ten miles and made one or two stops to have his legs massaged, always resuming quickly and never looking in real trouble. As he entered Durban followed by a huge procession of vehicles, the cheers rang out from the sidewalks, although it was clear nobody had expected the winner in yet.

Harry Hotchin, president of the Natal Amateur Athletic and Cycling Association, was walking to the sports ground to check everything was in place for the afternoon's proceedings when he suddenly spotted the fig-

ure of Newton approaching the Alice Street bridge along Old Dutch
Road, meaning he was just minutes away from an unattended finish line.
The flabbergasted Hotchin scampered through a hole in the sports
ground fence and sprinted across to get the tapes in place and to clock
Newton in. Those out on the road cheered Newton past, but there was
hardly anyone at the finish to greet him. A crowd was in place by the time
second place N J Nel shuffled in an hour later wearing bedraggled socks,
having discarded his shoes en route. This balding figure then entertained
them by suddenly bounding like a child as he reached the line.

All and sundry agreed Newton was a remarkable fellow, one reporter
marvelling at how a 'man of 40 summers had run the distance at eight
miles an hour.' It was all the more merit-worthy, given the tough conditions this year, for the road surface was in a poor state, particularly near
Kloof, where dust was said to be several inches thick. Newton told one
pressman he had tried stimulants to help his progress, but found that
champagne had been harmful so he now stuck to sweet tea and perhaps
a small tot of brandy on days like these. Asked about his unique shuffling
style, often called a 'jog trot', he confirmed that he actually travelled
quicker than it appeared to the naked eye, and reckoned he did 190 strides
to the minute in normal conditions.

When the prize-giving ceremony came around, Newton quietly
shrank back from the limelight, refusing to accept anything. Without
explaining exactly why, he passed a message to the Mayor of Durban that
second man Nel should get the prizes and then he made himself scarce.
After momentary confusion, the officials decided they couldn't possibly
accede to Newton's request, and the whole matter was left unresolved.
Newton explained later:

'I merely intimated that I should wish to climb down and let the second man take the first prize and so on. It appeared that couldn't be done,
and I left Durban with the thing still unsettled. It had been on my mind
for months that no amateur had a reasonable chance against me, provided I was fit, because I was able to, and did, spend the whole of my time
at training. Only those who were comparatively wealthy could afford to
carry on like that, and as the man in-the-street had to spend the bulk of
his time working for his living he could not hope to put in as much training as I did. I was an amateur, of course, but one with an unusual incen-
tive and with the means, temporarily at any rate, to carry on with whole-
time training. It seemed to me distinctly unfair that under these circumstances I should collar the valuable first prize.'

Eventually, following representations from his friends and sponsors in
the village of Harding, arrangements were made for the main prize, a

large ornamental clock, to be sent to Harding where it would 'grace the table of the Town Clerk'. The athletics officials of Natal were amazed by the modesty and dignity of this rather eccentric Englishman, and before long they made it known they were interested in Newton trying out for a place in their Olympic team for 1924, as a marathon runner.

Any thoughts of the Olympics were put on hold by Newton, who had other priorities. Analysing his timings at the Comrades, he was sure he now had an excellent chance of cracking the world 50-mile record. He wrote: 'I refused absolutely to run this on a track, for the monotony would be too sickening: I'd even put up with hills, and bad ones, rather than risk getting bored stiff on a small circular course. This record would make a good starting point. If I could collar it, I might be [then] able to reduce the standing time between London and Brighton [too], and thereby really become better known to the public generally.'

Correspondence with the secretary of the Pietermaritzburg Show and the Natal athletics authorities followed, and it was soon arranged that on the last day of the Annual Show an official record attempt would be made. A 50-mile out-and-back course from Pietermaritzburg was measured, using the same main road as the Comrades. Newton seemed undaunted by the fact that it included the notorious Polly Short's Cutting (named after the gang-leader who built the road), which was 600 feet above the city. The date was set for Friday, 29th June, barely five weeks after the Comrades, and would start and finish at Pietermaritzburg's Royal Agricultural Showgrounds.

Newton's good friends Mr and Mrs Lowe, who lived at the foot of Town Hill, put him up and agreed to escort him in a support vehicle during the attempt. Asked why he was choosing such a viciously hilly route, instead of a flat circular track, Newton replied that he knew every inch of this road and preferred not to have any surprises. He was happy to do it the hard way.

It was an apprehensive Newton who set off at 7 o'clock in a cool mist to run an unfamiliar lonely battle against the clock: 'I was glad to get to work, though more than a trifle nervous, for I knew I should be extended to the limit. Only two years previously I had never dreamt of seriously tackling athletics, let alone such things as records, yet here I was in my 41st year actually being advertised as trying to collar one.'

He set off looking his usual composed and untroubled self, but was covering the ground slightly quicker than his Comrades pace, and on arrival after 41 minutes at the top of Polly Short's Cutting felt some nasty spasms of cramp in the calves. He dropped his pace and the discomfort faded. Most of the course was untarred road and the official cars had to stay well behind or well in front to avoid throwing huge clouds of dust over him. They only came near to call out split timings.

The first 20 miles didn't leave him over-tired, but fatigue did begin to set in at the halfway point, on the heights above Drummond Station. Here he was to turn around and head back, but he astonished the helpers in their cars by going straight past them and carrying on towards Durban! They leaped out and screamed at him, not realising that the naturally cautious Newton was simply adding a few hundred yards to the distance so he could be absolutely sure of running a full 50 miles – just in case the course measurers had fallen slightly short. (It would be revealed later they had in fact measured the road by taking the average figure from several car odometers, and then adding a short distance for safety's sake. Newton's extra yards hadn't been necessary at all).

As he headed back to Pietermaritzburg, Newton felt his body tiring and craving some sort of 'pick-me-up' to enable him to maintain record pace. But his pre-run plan stipulated no stopping until 30 miles and he stuck to this despite the desperation of his thirst. It was the top of the long ridge near Camperdown, roughly 1,000 feet higher than the city, he allowed himself a stop to gulp down a strong mug of tea, with double the usual amount of sugar, and immediately felt a lot better, telling his helpers to get more tea ready in ten miles' time.

The tea did its job and he 'waltzed down the next descent in fine style', to use his own description, but then had to tackle two of the toughest hills of all, including Polly Short's Cutting. Maintaining a decent pace over these twin peaks caused intense fatigue, but Newton dug deep and enjoyed huge relief when he went over the top and saw the city below. However, the mounting exhaustion had rendered his mental arithmetic skills useless, and he was unable to calculate time, distance and pace required for the final section. It was a question of simply keeping his legs moving and hoping for the best.

Crossing the bridge over the Msunduzi River on the outskirts of the Pietermaritzburg, he had little more than a mile to go. At this point his brain instructed his uncooperative legs to increase their speed to ensure the record would be secured. It was the action of a desperate man who was unable to think clearly. Newton had suddenly become scared that if he failed to speed up he might miss the record, and all that mattered was to get the wretched thing and not have to face this sort of pain all over again.

A good crowd had gathered by the time he approached City Hall, and the police kept a lane open, allowing him to pass unhampered through the last half-mile before entering the showground. Here the stands were packed and a mighty roar erupted as he approached. The raucous reception had been anticipated this time and there was none of the crippling embarrassment he had suffered 13 months earlier at his first Comrades. What the crowd knew, but Newton didn't, was that he needed to lap the field in three minutes or less to beat the best time on record. Newton somehow upped his pace to six-minute miling and stumbled over the line, accepting the handshake of the mayor, while doing his best to stay upright. Within a few moments came the good news. Timekeepers Kerby and Farrant announced a time of 5 hours, 53 minutes and five seconds, beating all known previous records, including George Cartwright's long-standing professional mark of 5:55.04 and Edgar Lloyd's amateur best of 6:13.58 set in 1913, both recorded on tracks in London (Westminster and Stamford Bridge, respectively).

Doing his best to steer clear of the back-slappers, a smiling Newton was handed his pipe and rested his weary limbs before then going on a gentle stroll around the showground to relieve his stiffness. And then it was back to the Lowes' home on Town Hill for a much-needed bath and longer rest.

Shortly after returning to the solitude of his farm at Harding, 100 miles away from the cheering crowds of Pietermaritzburg, Newton received a letter from London. It was from the famous distance man Jimmy Fowler-Dixon, now 73, an Amateur Athletics Association official and former 50-mile record holder. Fowler-Dixon congratulated him heartily but explained that as the run had taken place on the road and not a measured track it would not be generally recognised as a world's best. He acknowledged that local officials had measured Newton's route and all the evidence suggested it was the fastest run ever, but the rules wouldn't allow it to stand: 'It's illogical, but there it is old chap', he wrote.

Fowler-Dixon sounded sorry to be bringing bad news, for he clearly admired Newton's feat, having himself chalked up some good times as a veteran athlete (including a mile timed at 6:37 on his 63rd birthday). He finished his letter by suggesting Newton should consider running the 50-miles-plus from London to Brighton, where any 'record' performances would be seen in a better light. This was food for thought for Newton, who was rather miffed that his efforts wouldn't go into the record books. To his dismay, the English sporting press had scoffed at the very idea that an unmade road in the middle of Africa could produce a genuine athletics record.

Newton's resolve was only deepened by all this, and he stepped up his training in the second half of 1923, boldly putting his name forward to take part in the first South African marathon championship, to be held in

September in Johannesburg. There were 28 entries in all, and although Newton suspected 26 miles was too short for him to produce a world class time, he felt confident of matching the best of the opposition. Race-day arrived and after a peremptory examination by physician Dr Brennan at the start, 25 men set off at lunchtime. The road conditions were appalling, with many potholes to be dodged, and lengthy stretches of road thick with dust. At one point a persistent dog snapped at the runners' heels, adding to their problems.

Newton started carefully and was never far from the front. Just before halfway he felt strong enough to open a gap between himself and pre-race favourite Harry Phillips. Spectators along the route helped by calling out the extent of his lead over Phillips, meaning Newton had no need to look over his shoulder, something he hated doing as it indicated weakness and anxiety. The experienced Phillips didn't react to Newton's uncharacteristic move, and would be proved correct in not doing so. By the time they had passed the 20-miles mark he had slowly reeled in the tiring Newton and was able to pass without response. Newton would look back at this episode with horror and castigate himself for 'making a complete hash of the race'. Soon after Phillips left him trailing, another fellow Natalian, Marthinus Steytler, also caught up and overtook. By now most of the field had quit altogether, exhausted by the thin air at this altitude, and only four men were left. Newton and Steytler were shuffling along at a relatively slow seven miles per hour and Newton soon noticed his opponent was in an even worse state than he. He was able to regain second place, but came home looking despondent, more than a mile behind winner Phillips. It had been a slow race and Newton was depressed at finishing 'like a woe-is-me-I-am-undone scarecrow'.

He was frankly embarrassed by his clocking of 3:30:05, and dismissed the day as a complete washout. He blamed his own mistake of trying to speed up – contrary to his normal style – to get rid of Phillips at halfway. But, he added, there were also extenuating circumstances: 'With the exception of the winner, we were all coast-level men or thereabouts, and were quite unused to the 6,000 feet altitude of Johannesburg. Never for a moment did we realise how much difference it would make.'

There was little time to brood, however, for days later he returned to the familiar surroundings of Pietermaritzburg, where he decided to test himself at 10 miles in a road race for the Taylor-Thomas Trophy. He won in 61 minutes, with one report marvelling at how he 'discarded his jog trot and finished strongly'. It restored his confidence and set him up nicely for the 1923 Natal Cross-Country Championship over a four-lap 10-mile course at Clairwood racecourse in Durban. Races were coming thick and fast now, and Newton entered whatever he could, welcoming the opportunity to raise his profile and therefore keep up the pressure on the government. He was by now getting used to the limelight, and learning to overcome his shyness, although he could never shake off his post-race habit of slipping away from the crowds to enjoy a pipe and a few moments of solitude.

The cross-country championships, complete with hurdles and ditches, was a new experience and although the local press reckoned ten miles ought to prove a 'tarradiddle' for a man of Newton's stamina, he didn't share their confidence. It was staged on a relatively new racecourse built on land that was originally a swamp and a big crowd came to see the field of nearly 100 runners, plus the motor-sports events also on the programme. After they set off, Newton found he lost time at the various jumps and had his fluent style was badly disrupted. But he was able to run between them at what he called his top racing speed of 10 miles per hour, and this kept him close to pre-race favourite C B Tod, the 19-year-old reigning champion.

Newton recalled the first hurdle was a permanent fixture about three feet high laced with brushwood, over which most of the others sailed over 'like a covey of partridges'. At this and virtually every other hazard, Newton lost a few yards, but his strength saw him bounce back every time. After nearly an hour of this, and with the final lap underway, he and Tod found themselves the only serious contenders, with the youngster slightly ahead. At this point came an incident which typified Newton's keen sense of fair play: Just ahead of him, Tod approached a hurdle and jumped at a point where it had been partly knocked down. An official immediately leaped out and stopped Tod, ordering him to return and take the hurdle at its standard height. This allowed Newton to gain a considerable lead, but it struck him as 'monstrous bad luck' on Tod, who had jumped the lower section in all innocence. He explained later: 'I felt it would be most unfair to take advantage of his unintentional mistake, and deliberately slowed down to 7 m.p.h. till he had levelled up again. He soon managed that, and once more we were at it hammer and tongs.'

Together they ran on and with about 600 yards left Newton deliberately quickened his stride, as opposed to lengthening it, and built a lead of about 100 yards, the younger man, to Newton's surprise, unable to respond. It gave the 40-year-old a victory in 65:21, well clear of an opponent less than half his age. Newton's win ensured his Comrades Club won the Houghting Shield team prize.

Newton treated the cross-country run as a learning experience, but was relieved a month later to return to the roads where there were no jumps and the longer distance allowed him to control things at a slightly steadier pace. The occasion was the Comrades Club's 13-mile event on the late afternoon of Saturday, November 10th, from Alexandra Park rugby ground in Pietermaritzburg to Edendale and back. Newton and Harry Phillips were the star attractions of the day and ran from scratch, with less talented men given a start of 40 minutes. Newton recorded the fastest run of the day (1:21.30), which was thought to be a course record. His main rival Phillips forfeited any chance of winning by generously stopping to help several runners who were in distress, having under-estimated the difficulty of the conditions.

By now, Newton's Comrades Marathon prize, the impressive ornamental clock, had been put in a prominent place at civic offices in the centre of Harding, according to his wishes. In return for his 'gift' a presentation ceremony was arranged to mark Newton's recent achievements. He was formally handed a sum of money – described as a 'filled purse' – by the proud locals, who were firmly behind his fight with the government, and wanted to help with his living expenses. A grateful Newton had to tell them he was still making little headway with the Department of Native Affairs, who once again in December wrote to reiterate their position of being unable to purchase his farm from him.

Having topped 9,000 miles for the year of 1923 (a remarkable total he would never surpass), Newton was well prepared for what the new year would bring. He planned to continue his busy racing schedule and was made aware that a good showing at the classic 26.2-mile distance might see him asked to represent South Africa at the forthcoming Olympic Games in Paris.

New Year's Day 1924 saw the SOE. Sports staged on the showground in Pietermaritzburg in scorching heat of well over 90 degrees F. Newton suffered in the conditions, but still recorded the fastest time of the day. Marthinus Steytler, who won the handicap prize, happily took his winnings from the Mayoress, but Newton caused a storm by indicating he would not accept his. Having strolled off to recover in the shade with his trusty pipe, Newton had to once again explain that he only ran 'for honour and for sport' and didn't seek prizes. However the clamour was so great from the gathered crowd that he was forced forward, and rather than insult the Mayoress, reluctantly took his trophy.

A few days after this race Newton began to feel unwell but continued with his training, gambling that his condition was merely a bout of flu. He wanted to be fit for the January marathon in Durban that was being staged as a trial prior to the Olympic Games, but the illness hung around for more than a fortnight. Newton stubbornly carried on with his training, only stopping when he virtually collapsed a dozen miles from home and found himself unable to make further progress under his own steam. Fortunately a friend was able to drive him home and he took stock of the situation, desperately unwilling to drop out of the trial scheduled for Saturday, 26th January. He travelled down to Durban and bumped into the editor of one of the leading sporting papers, to whom he confessed he was intending to run despite not being fully recovered. The sensible course would surely have been to drop out, but not for Newton, who said he would 'take my beating rather than funk it'.

Race day dawned bright and the temperature soon soared into the nineties. It was not a day for distance running, and the presence of a phalanx of motorcycles and other hangers-on did not help by kicking up clouds of dust as they accompanied the runners. Progress was slow, with the dust and smoke from the vehicles adding to the blistering heat of the sun. Newton, as ever, shuffled along economically, clutching a handkerchief in one hand, his frame looking stiff and slightly stooped as he maintained a position some way behind the leaders for much of the race. His inscrutable face rarely reflected his misery, for he must have been suffering badly and known he was well behind the schedule for a finish-time of international standard.

Pre-race favourite Harry Phillips was suffering too, but sensed Newton was not at his best and knew he could take the limelight this time. The Olympics were his goal, and by the time he struggled to the 26-mile point, he had forged a lead of around 30 minutes. He came home in a modest-looking time of 3:10.41 and the crowd then had to wait almost 35 minutes before Newton shuffled in for a second place in 3:45.30. The difficulty of the conditions were underlined by the fact that the third man (J Annan) came in a further 38 minutes down in 4:23.30 and nobody else managed to complete the course. Newton commented: 'I was very surprised and pleased to arrive second. Had it not been for the unusual heat many others would have easily beaten me.'

The poor clockings, even given the tough conditions, gave rise to discussion in the sporting press over whether any of the contenders were capable of putting up a decent marathon in the Olympics. It was suggested South Africa should only be represented if they had a runner capable of around 2:45. The consensus was that Phillips was their best bet and Newton should probably stick to the ultra-long distances. These stories didn't meet with Newton's approval and he wrote to several papers, including the *Kokstad Advertiser*, telling them about his illness and suggesting that on a good day he was still capable of a good marathon time. He also took the opportunity to publicise his campaign, confirming he had been 'hopelessly and completely ruined' by a government that was driving him out of South Africa by declaring his locality an area for native settlement.

In order to chalk up better times, Newton and Phillips both wanted a re-run of the Olympic trial race. Eventually, once arrangements were finalised to everybody's satisfaction, it was announced that the two men would each run solo against the clock on different dates in March. Newton went first, at 6 on the morning of Friday, 14th March, using the same Durban-to-Mount Edgecombe route as in January, but this time enjoying far more suitable weather conditions. His progress was smooth and uneventful for the first 20 miles, watched intently by an accompanying car of officials and pressmen, and an official on a motorcycle. He passed 20 in 2:15 and at Queen's Bridge a little further on, he called out for a cup of tea, which was duly provided. Fifteen minutes later, his thirst still not sated, he stopped at a tea-room outside the Lion match factory on the edge of Durban, and drank some more of his favourite beverage. His chances of a sub-three hour clocking began to disappear around now, with time lost at the tea stops, plus added problems with heavy traffic and a head wind that suddenly whipped up, bringing rain with it. He came home to encouraging cheers from a small crowd in a time of 3:05.57, which was better than any of Phillips' recent efforts, but still a long way adrift of the best times in the world (Hannes Kolehmainen's current record was 2:32.35).

Around ten days later, Harry Phillips emerged to stake his claim for the Olympic team, running the same course three minutes quicker, hampered by more severe winds than Newton experienced. It was clear that Phillips deserved the Olympic marathon place and Newton acknowledged this, and to set the record straight he contacted the *Natal Witness* to say as much. He wrote:

'It should be remembered that I am merely an 'artificial' runner, not a natural one . . . if on occasion I happen to beat Mr Phillips it is only because I am able to get the time for training which is denied to him. It seems to me rather absurd for the authorities out here to expect men like Mr Phillips, who can only train after their full day's work is done, to approach world's amateur record time.'

In early April the two men were in opposition again in Durban, as part of the annual Railway Sports. Heavy rain made the going difficult on the North Coast road and officials declared later the distance run had been over 21 miles, even though the race had been advertised as a 17-miler. The previous day had seen Phillips knocked off his bike and rendered unconscious, but he showed no ill-effects winning in 2:25.05, some 80 seconds clear of Newton, with the rest a long way back. Three months later Phillips, who was only three years younger than veteran Newton, represented South Africa at the Paris Olympic marathon, but could only finish 19th in a modest 3:07.13, some way behind gold-medallist Albin Steinroos of Finland (2:41.22).

Newton knew by now his best chances of major success were at distances far longer than the marathon. He made up his mind to return to England later in 1924 to have a crack at the London to Brighton run (52 miles), where he felt an official world record, with the attendant prestige that would bring, was within his capabilities. He wrote to England, to family and to the athletics fraternity, stating his intentions.

In the meantime he continued to spice up his monotonous solo runs on the lonely Natal roads by entering whatever races he could find in Durban and Pietermaritzburg. He even, for the first time, tried track running and in one 10-mile contest in Durban used the experience to experiment with his running style. When the leader lapped him he studied closely the man's footfalls and attempted to keep pace, imitating the man's 'flatfoot' style and abandoning his own low-lift, quick shuffling method. After just 50 yards of this he realised he should stick with his own, sometimes unattractive, gait and not be influenced by others. He finished fourth.

May 1924 brought with it the chance for Newton to create a unique hat-trick of victories at the annual Comrades Marathon before his scheduled sailing to England a week or two later. As part of his build-up for the big 54-mile test, he registered for an 18.5-mile event being staged in Pietermaritzburg, which followed a route from the Town Hall out to the Thornybush district and then to the showgrounds where a 'Sports and English Fair' was being held. In sultry heat, Newton won in 2:06.39, several minutes clear of runner-up Shackleford.

He was in good shape for his third Comrades, and also looking forward to his forthcoming break in England, his first trip back home for a number of years. He was hot favourite to complete a trio of wins, but found his reputation for being 'unbeatable' over 50 miles, not to mention the gruelling experiences of many in the last two races, had helped reduce this year's entry to just 31. On a chilly Empire Day morning, the Post Office clock at Durban struck six and they were set off by a hoarse Mayor of Durban, Walter Gilbert, who struggled to make himself heard, having spoken at length at a political meeting the night before. As the runners departed the wind was strong and the temperature below 60 degrees F, but Newton confident he could set a new record for the 'up' course.

Two masseurs accompanied the race in a smart Studebaker car, and found they were needed frequently as the casualties mounted. This year the road was tarred as far as Mayville, but after that came the usual thick dust and stony surface to contend with. Newton, undaunted, established a lead early on and was never headed. By halfway, at Drummond, he was 18 minutes ahead of the rest and looking relaxed. Many behind were suffering badly, and grateful for oranges handed out by an emergency bus, which would later break down itself. Second-placed Nel quit in the hilly area around Umlaas Road (40 miles), thus increasing the already huge chasm between Newton and the rest of the field.

Newton's first stop was not until the outskirts of Pietermaritzburg when, alarmingly, he gulped down a drink and then suddenly collapsed. Fortunately timekeeper Wise was close at hand to help him to his feet and there appeared no lasting damage. After a few minutes' delay to ensure he was properly recovered, Newton resumed, no doubt wondering if he should have taken refreshment on board a little earlier than this late stage. He negotiated the remainder of the course without problems and was delighted to cross the finish line in under seven hours (6:58.22). He was an astonishing 75 minutes ahead of second-placed Shackleford and this hat-trick of victories would not be emulated for another 44 years.

Chapter 6

An Audience with the General

Newton had an extra weapon in his armoury when he raced during 1924. He was running on anger. His very future as a hard-working resident of his beloved Natal was hanging by a thread, thanks to the situation at his farm – for he was getting nowhere with pleas for help from the government. His case had been handled throughout by its Native Affairs department, whose lack of co-operation left a furious Newton feeling he was being deliberately forced out of the country.

The three options Newton had offered the department since 1920 – to buy his farm from him, to swap it for another in a 'white' area, or to compensate him – had all been flatly rejected. And by now, with his funds fast dwindling to nothing, he could no longer contemplate starting again as a farmer, so even the prospect of a farm-swap had to be ruled out.

Newton regularly told anyone who cared to listen that recent modifications to the Natives Land Act of 1913 meant he was now completely surrounded by a belt of resettled native people, the effect of which had ruined him by making his farm unworkable. If the government didn't help him, his 20 years of hard work would be wasted.

It was a sorry situation, but in the meantime his running exploits were, as intended, certainly getting him noticed across the country. He was no longer simply 'a farmer in trouble', but now 'a white sports hero in trouble'. The publicity he generated in the press led to the local Member of the Legislative Assembly, J S Marwick, and the Farmers' Association, taking up the case on his behalf. Initially they met with the same government indifference, although Newton's hopes rose in April 1924 when 'every available Natal Member of Parliament' joined forces to demand an urgent settlement of the case. Sadly this also floundered, but there was another breakthrough the following month when the Prime Minister himself, General Jan Smuts, agreed to a private audience with Newton and Marwick.

Smuts, in office for around five years by now, was facing a general election in the coming weeks, but his South Africa Party was widely expected to return to power. The abrasive Smuts was a leader who advocated racial segregation and was opposed to the unilateral enfranchisement of the black majority, fearing it would destroy the 'civilisation' of South Africa. Newton had every reason, therefore, to think he would get a sympathetic hearing from Smuts, especially as his beef was with stubborn officials at the Native Affairs department, rather than the Smuts government as a whole.

While he prepared for the June meeting, Newton allowed himself to feel a little more optimistic about his prospects. But he saw no need to cancel his forthcoming trip to England, which was already booked and would come literally a day or two after the meeting with Smuts. Newton had accepted by now he would probably be forced to leave South Africa permanently in the near future, but he did not want to quit without some form of financial compensation. He continued to court publicity for his cause, and among his best supporters was the Natal local press. At the end of May the *Natal Advertiser* ran a lengthy editorial backing him to the hilt. They stated:

'Mr. Newton is packing his boxes and proposes sailing for England, and South Africa loses a good citizen and a good sportsman. It has been an unfortunate chapter, and one which leaves an uneasy feeling that the task of populating the vacant spaces of this country is not being tackled in a spirit which is likely to prove successful. Long before Arthur Newton was a runner he was a farmer, and one who had converted an area of virgin soil into a flourishing farm. A small area of the desert had been made to bloom, miles of roads had been constructed, and tobacco and cotton were being produced where previously there were but weeds. The farm had been purchased from the Government and duly paid for. Then, without warning or legislative sanction, the area was proclaimed a black one, and Mr. Newton found himself surrounded by black men who refused to work for him, and whose presence there was backed by the government's dictum that no white man should hold land within a specified area. Years of work on the farm Lovat went for nought, the pioneer was robbed of the fruits of his labour and was cut off from the society of his kind. But Mr. Newton was willing to try again, and applied for an exchange of farms. This was refused, as was compensation. Negotiations characterised by all the circumlocution which breaks the heart of the man desiring to have something done dragged on.

'Meanwhile Mr. Newton lived on capital, his income was gone, till he had reduced that capital so greatly that even an exchange of farms was of no value to him. He had not the wherewithal to stock and work another area. The people of Harding having pressed his legitimate claims, and Mr. Newton having adopted athletics to bring his name and his case before the public, the authorities relented, and another farm was offered. It was then too late. Indomitable will is good equipment for a farmer, but it is inadequate without capital. Mr. Newton was unable to accept the offer. Then the last move. The farmer offers to the Government, which has taken over the land surrounding his farm and hemmed him without companionship or markets, the property, which it originally sold. It is not prepared to pay for the improvements.

'So ends the chapter. It is a sorry one. The country loses the citizenship of a man of a type, which South Africa badly needs. He leaves these shores with the feeling, and a justifiable one, that he and his kind are not wanted. Sixteen years of his life have been wasted, and the development of the area in question has been set back far more than that. It is probably too late now to repair the trouble entirely, though it is not too late to see that Mr. Newton gets something like fair play. What is of even greater importance, is that the country should realise that these things are possible, and that steps should be taken to avoid a repetition. In Mr. Newton's case the blame rather falls on a Service department rather than on the ill will or indifference of a Government. How easy it is to see what may happen to a great many settlers in this country if and when a native segregation policy and Nationalist antipathy to English-speaking immigrants give General Hertzog and Mr. Roos all the opportunity for British depopulation they desire.'

Newton's elected representative Marwick contacted the Native Affairs department to demand full details of Newton's case history be put before General Smuts prior to their meeting. According to Newton, this request – true to form – was completely ignored. When he and Marwick arrived for their audience with the PM, at the well-appointed Durban Club, they found Smuts had never even heard of their case. Newton was not surprised, for it only confirmed his view that the Native Affairs office were 'doing a winger' on them, to use his phrase. Smuts chatted amiably with Newton and Marwick on the verandah of the clubhouse before retiring to an inner office for more privacy. Here Marwick summarised the facts of Newton's plight while the Prime Minister listened on patiently.

Smuts fired back with half-a-dozen questions and seemed genuinely concerned to find that things had come to such a pass, according to Newton. Smuts told Newton he was delighted to meet an industrious South African citizen and felt the country could not afford to lose men such as him. He insisted that Newton return after his trip to England, and promised in the meantime to look carefully into the issue. Newton was relieved to get a fair hearing and pleased by Smuts' understanding and sympathetic attitude.

As Newton was due to sail within days, the Prime Minister immediately wired a government official called Beaumont, instructing him to go to the farm and value Newton's losses. Newton rushed back to meet Beaumont and give him a tour of the premises. When told that the result of the inspection, and the Prime Minister's subsequent decision, would take a week or two to be announced (by which time he would be in England), Newton arranged for a friend in Durban to receive the news on his behalf. He fired off the following telegram to the Prime Minister's secretary in Pretoria: 'Sailing Wednesday Beaumont telegraphed report my farm Lands Department Friday can Prime Minister possibly notify decision address 139 Essenwood Road Durban.'

Believing the tide was perhaps finally turning in his favour, Newton sailed from Durban on the *SS Arundel Castle* bound for Southampton, looking forward to seeing his family, and ready for a crack at the London-to-Brighton road record. Eager to maintain his fitness, he explored means of training on board ship, but there was little room or privacy and he had to be content with brisk walks up and down the deck in the early morning when most passengers were still asleep. He managed around 20 miles a day of this, but felt frustrated at being unable to run properly. He vowed that on future sailings he would contact the shipping lines in advance to ensure special arrangements would be made to allow him to run on the promenade decks without inconveniencing other passengers. Sailing in mid-June meant his departure coincided with voting in the South African general election of 1924, and Newton was naturally keen for the South African Party to remain in power, now that their leader Smuts was taking steps to help him. Smuts was widely expected to win when polling got underway the same week as Newton's departure. Commentators reckoned anything other than a Smuts victory would harm British interests in South Africa, but his popularity in provinces like Natal (where Newton lived) would surely see him through.

However, as Newton's ship steamed towards Britain, surprising news began to filter through. With record numbers turning out to vote, Smuts lost his own Pretoria West seat and his party encountered shocking and unexpected defeats in the Transvaal area. Newton had set sail on the Wednesday full of optimism, but by the weekend it had been announced that General Herzog and his National Party had swept to power. Newton was horrified, knowing the collapse of the Smuts regime would ruin his prospects of an immediate settlement.

Once in London, Newton sat down with his father and discussed the whole position in depth. The Rev Newton pointed out that no honourable and civilised government would ever knowingly and willingly treat its respectable and diligent subjects in such fashion. He urged his son to be patient and said he had no reason to distrust the integrity of the new Herzog government. He would be best advised to continue with his plan to attack the athletics record, and then quickly return to South

Africa and seek an interview with the new Premier. Funds for his return passage would be provided, he assured him.

In the meantime, Newton received letters from South Africa that confirmed the further bad news he had been expecting. Firstly a letter arrived from the Native Affairs department stating: 'In the absence of provision by Parliament, ministers are not prepared to authorise the purchase of [Lovat Farm].' Then, more pressingly, he received word that the Land Bank was demanding interest payments now overdue from Newton in connection with his re-mortgaging of the farm. Newton had planned to pay these bills with compensation money from the Government, but as the latter hadn't materialised he was now in deep trouble. He had earlier sold his cattle, implements and furniture at the farm simply to survive, and simply had no means of paying the bills.

His only option was to send instructions to the bank to sell the farm right away in order to cover the spiralling bills. The sale was quickly made, but because the farm was nowadays enclosed by a native settlement area and only good for grazing, its value had plummeted. The sum raised was disappointingly low. This had been expected, but it was still a crushing blow to Newton. He was now 41 years old, homeless, jobless and virtually penniless. He reflected: 'After 20 years' good work in the country I was now worse off than when I first landed there.'

Newton shut off from his troubles to focus on his assault on the London to Brighton record. Following correspondence earlier, Joe Binks, esteemed *News of the World* athletics correspondent (and former AAA mile champion) had agreed to organise the 52-mile run to Brighton. It would be a solo affair for Newton, with qualified timekeepers and course measurers involved, and the date was provisionally set for late September. Binks' involvement, plus the support of *News of the World* proprietor Emsley Carr – a big athletics fan – ensured there would be maximum publicity before and after the event. In the build-up Newton stayed with relatives in London and Paignton as well as with his sister Ursula (now Mrs Creighton), at her delightful home in the rural outpost of Frieth in Buckinghamshire.

Daily training on the relatively busy English roads was a new and tricky experience for Newton, who was used to the hot, dusty solitude of Natal's byways. Eagerly he began piling on the miles, and by the end of June was averaging a prodigious 30 miles a day (some of it walking), but soon found his legs giving him problems. Although the lack of dust and relative smoothness of the English roads were a welcome change, he found there was less 'give' in the surfaces underfoot than he was used to. His joints began to rebel. The constant daily pounding soon saw his left shin and ankle swell alarmingly, and he found the only way to relieve the problem was to reduce his weekly mileage to a mere 120 miles or so!

He wrote: 'Ah, me! There is always more to be learnt. Thinking I was now pretty safe, I let out for a couple of weeks in the old style – 251 and 295 miles. The latter was certainly rather more than usual, but the roads were so good in comparison to what I had been used to that the extra mileage was not very noticeable.' It was only a temporary respite, for as the summer went on the problem switched to his right leg, leading to the same sort of pain and swelling on that side. And now he found he was unable to eliminate the problem simply by reducing his mileage. A visit to a specialist in London would be called for.

Despite the sore legs, Newton loved spending the summer of 1924 cruising along the leafy lanes of England and enjoying the 'green and pleasant land' he had not seen for nearly 15 years. His homecoming was all the more poignant for the fact that his record attempt would see him running into Brighton, the very town where he spent most of his childhood. For three idyllic months his typical day involved a long run amid the birdsong at dawn, following by a lazy morning of drinking tea and devouring the much-missed English newspapers. He read intently the news from Paris that Harold Abrahams and Eric Liddell had won gold for Britain at the Olympic Games, Paavo Nurmi had smashed the world 1,500 metres record, and his South African contemporary Harry Phillips had struggled in the marathon. It was a lifestyle Newton enjoyed immensely, and he later described a typical day from the period:

'[I had] to use blinds to keep out the sunlight as I retired at 7p.m., for I wanted to get up at 3 each morning. Why so early? Well, there were two reasons. First of all and quite the more important, it was summer and I wanted the coolest part of the day for my exercise. The other, well, you know, I have always had a desire to pass on my way inconspicuously and find it painfully embarrassing to waltz along a road in running costume with the public agape. It is bad enough when you are with others, but alone! Whew!'

'I was taking pastry (cakes) either once or twice a day, always after my long run. Then perhaps some brown bread (I had a favourite brand), and honey, with a couple of cups of tea to finish up with. After having successfully battled through that little lot I gave the works a chance to get a move on without being hurried, flurried or worried. An hour's attendance to correspondence just fitted in nicely. Then, with a despondent glance at a fat easy chair awaiting an occupant, I'd pluck up courage and set off for a few miles' walk. No hurry over this, merely an average of some 3¾ miles per hour up and down hill. I always tried to get back by 4 p.m. if I could manage it. I lunched at midday and dined at 5.30. Thereafter if I was not obliged to return to correspondence (as I generally was), I slacked it right royally in an armchair near the fire. With a cigar or pipe and a favourite author to help me, I forgot that men ever dreamt of such things as records. Ah me! All too soon it was time for dinner.'

By September, with the troublesome leg injury still reducing his mileage a little, and the date of the event getting ever closer, Newton headed into London to see his Harley Street specialist, check arrangements with Joe Binks, and also called in on his former clubmates at Thames Hare and Hounds in Roehampton. Although he usually wore their club colours in his races in South Africa, he had not run with the Thames pack for 15 years and enjoyed the camaraderie of their opening cross-country run of the new season. The club had taken part recently in a relay on the London to Brighton road, and were fascinated to hear of his forthcoming solo record attempt on the same course. Newton took away with him a club fixture card, so that he could earmark more runs to fit in before he eventually left for South Africa.

As the last few days of September dawned and the day of reckoning drew ever closer, Newton's stress levels began to rise alarmingly. The lack of improvement to his swollen right shin and ankle worried him greatly – not merely because it might scupper the record attempt, but because it might force him to let down all the people who were helping him in his quest. There was Binks and his *News of the World* boss, plus the well-known sporting figures Tony Fattorini and Jimmy Fowler-Dixon, who were officiating on the run, and there was his sister Ursula, who enthusiastically volunteered to travel alongside to dispense cold water at the roadside. If there was one thing Newton hated more than almost anything else, it was letting people down.

Chapter 7

Seaside Shuffle

Newton's plan to shatter the record for running from London to Brighton generated huge public interest, but few knew that behind the scenes he was in turmoil. His preparations were plagued by a catalogue of near-disasters.

For several weeks before the proposed run on Friday, 3rd October 1924, he had to curtail training to take daily train rides into London for treatment by his specialist on an inflamed ankle and shin splints. Then on the eve of the run he chose to stay at a hotel near Trafalgar Square, where the noise of night-time revelry deprived him of a good night's sleep. Next morning the hearty breakfast he'd ordered – essential fuel for the ordeal ahead – completely failed to materialise. To compound matters further, the weather outside was humid and totally unsuited to distance running. Everything seemed to be conspiring against him.

But it was too late to pull out now, and Newton knew he had to be on that start-line beneath Big Ben no matter what. History and the public demanded it. A number of London-Brighton walks had taken place on the same road in recent times, but this was the first organised run for some 21 years. The route had been properly established for foot-racing in 1897, when 50 professionals headed for the seaside, most of them just beating an 8hrs 15mins cut-off time. The first amateur event here was a 'go-as-you-please' contest organised by South London Harriers in 1899, when winner Fred Randall (Finchley Harriers) clocked 6:58.18, gaining himself a place in the GB team for the 1900 Olympic marathon. The *Evening News* promoted a similar race four years later, open to professionals, and a field of 90 was headed by Len Hurst, who chalked up a new course record of 6:32.34.

Since Hurst's superb performance, interest in ultra-distance running had declined in Britain, with the emergence of the 26-mile marathon and of cycling no doubt partly to blame. But tales of exile Arthur Newton and his prowess over 50 miles in South Africa had regenerated interest in 'ultras'. Newton's first major outing in the country of his birth drew big crowds to the start in Westminster, at villages and towns along the 52-mile route, and especially to the finish area on Brighton seafront.

Joe Binks stoked up the fires in his newspaper columns, telling readers Newton was a remarkable man of 5ft 9ins and 10 stones, who was 'hard as nails'. He usually ran in the lightest shoes possible, ordinary plimsolls with the thinnest of soles rather than heavy crepe rubber ones, and employed an economic 'pit-pat' style similar to American indians. Unlike many sportsmen of the time, he didn't go in for heavy massage, just a quick rub-down with a rough towel. He mostly took just cups of tea during his long races, having filled up earlier on a large breakfast of eggs and bacon. For over two years the 41-year-old had averaged between 22 and 23 miles per day. Binks, the doyen of athletics writers, had encountered all the stars of the past 25 years, but had met nobody quite like Newton. He was clearly captivated by him, and passed this sense of awe to the *News of the World*'s three million readers.

Course record-holder Len Hurst turned up at the start line near Westminster Bridge to wish Newton luck, and accompanied timekeepers Fowler-Dixon and Fattorini in their car. It was a touch misty at the 6am start, and with sun expected later, a humid day was in store. Newton had had little sleep in central London and had been unable to get more than a 'sketchy' breakfast, so wasn't in the best frame of mind, although was pleased to note that his right leg felt better than it had for several weeks, just as his specialist had predicted. Nevertheless, the recent enforced reduction of his training mileage worried him.

Newton, with a procession of vehicles behind, some of them official and others not, set off for the coast to a rousing cheer. The first hour or so whizzed by with Newton looking composed and content, and on 60 minutes he was just a few yards short of ten miles. Binks called from his car that he was going too fast, but Newton acknowledged him and indicated he was quite happy. Going through the village of Merstham (18 miles) he was still comfortably ahead of Hurst's record pace, but he began to struggle at the hilly section around Earlswood a little further on. The heavy atmosphere was starting to get to him a little, and he felt much hotter than he'd expected at this time of year.

Action was called for and Newton switched from his usual drink of tea, to a new concoction he'd devised himself, which would be coined in the press as his 'magic drink'. It comprised half-a-pint of ordinary bottled lemonade, half a tumbler of sugar and a teaspoon of salt, stirred together. He had, effectively, created the first sports electrolyte drink. It proved an efficacious means of preventing cramp during runs when the temperature was high. As well as passing on the drinks, Newton's sister Ursula was positioning herself at points along the roadside so she could drench him with jugs of cooling water as he passed. She would receive widespread praise for her efforts in the papers the next day, the reporters impressed this well-spoken wife of a famous author (Basil Creighton) should take such an active part in a sporting event.

The 26-mile halfway point was close to the racecourse that would later become the site of Gatwick Airport, and Newton passed here in 2:45.44, an almost identical time to record holder Hurst, who looked on with interest from the timekeeper's car. By now Newton was beginning to slow, and was feeling distinctly unwell. He began to doubt he would beat the six-hour barrier, which he had privately promised to do, although felt reasonably safe he could still set a course record. At a level crossing in Crawley he was halted by a train coming through, but after 30 seconds of standing waiting, decided his best bet was to take a small diversion via a subway. Through Handcross, Bolney, Hickstead and Pyecombe he pushed on, his pace slightly slowing, but exactly the same had happened to his predecessors and Hurst's record of 6.34 remained in considerable danger.

Coming into the environs of Brighton – the final 5.5 miles – Newton appeared to gain heart and picked up the pace. Ursula was by now dispensing water more frequently from her jug, entirely wrapped up in her important task, but clearly immensely proud of her younger brother. He passed the 50-mile point on the edge of town (the Preston district) after 5:57.48, which was slower than his own best 50-mile time, but still considerably faster than Edgar Lloyd's current amateur record of 11 years' standing, set at the Stamford Bridge track. Newton turned onto the seafront to tumultuous cheers, reaching the finish-line at the Royal Aquarium in 6:11.4. Wearing his favoured white Thames Hare and Hounds kit, he smiled gently and looked a picture of calm.

He had beaten Hurst's professional course record by nearly 24 minutes and Randall's amateur mark by more than 47 minutes, but Newton modestly brushed aside the congratulations, knowing these were records that had rarely been attacked in recent years, and convinced he was capable of much better than today's display. He privately cursed his disrupted training schedule and what he saw as self-inflicted problems with his pre-race preparations 'I had not yet got used to the English atmosphere and was consequently not too good a judge. It always seemed to me to be colder than it really was, probably owing to the moisture in the air. [I decided] the result wasn't good enough [and] I must go through with it again. Knowing that I could considerably improve on 6 hours 11 minutes for 52 miles, I decided to postpone sailing for Natal while I did some more training and took another cut at it.'

Afterwards, there were suggestions that recent road improvements along the route had shortened the course from when previous records were set, so at the request of the *News of the World*, George Hogsflesh, the secretary of the AAA, accompanied by Joe Binks, measured the course by driving with a special odometer fixed to their car. They announced it was a valid 52 miles and 200 yards, a distance they confirmed on their return journey. Within days it was also announced that the highly dissatisfied Newton would attempt another run on the same route exactly three weeks later, bidding to go under six hours. As it turned out, Newton's specialist advised him to postpone this for a while, after examining his leg, and a new date of Thursday, 13th November was arranged, with an 8am start from beneath Big Ben.

Some professional 'challenges' to race Newton were put up following the run, but Newton was quick to indicate he was not interested in relinquishing his amateur status to take these up. He said he was testing his powers of record-breaking merely for the love of sport, and indicated he would be leaving for South Africa by the end of November anyway.

On the day after the run, Newton made a surprise appearance at the Thames Hare and Hounds clubhouse and joined the training pack for their weekend run. Some of the runners there were astonished that he was ready so soon for yet more mileage. Afterwards Newton sat in on their annual general meeting, where he heard secretary Harry Hall sing his praises in the annual report. Now that he knew his schedule for the remainder of his stay in England, Newton told them he would join them for at least four more runs before he left. That same day, the blind soldiers of St Dunstan's completed their annual London-Brighton walk, and when competitor Ingram was close to collapse after hitting a bad patch, it was suggested he try a concoction of the new Arthur Newton 'magic drink' that worked so well the previous day. He did so, and went on to win.

Newton was the talk of the town, and the BBC invited him to give a talk on long-distance running for one of their radio programmes. He submitted a manuscript, to which their editor made only minor amendments, and he travelled down from Frieth to go on air at the Savoy Hill studios on Victoria Embankment on the evening of Monday, 3rd November 1924.

As he'd promised, Newton loyally turned out in late October for Thames Hare and Hounds in their annual cross-country match with Oxford University at the tough Shotover course, coming 11th in 47:12, around 1:45 behind joint-winners Montague, Bell and Bryant, who had sportingly joined hands and crossed the line three abreast. By now TH&H were entering open events regularly, having only recently ended 40 years of 'isolation'. They had originally set themselves up as a club for refined gentleman amateurs, with 'artisans and tradesmen' not welcome, but the recent change of tack pleased Newton, who found some aspects

of the professional/amateur debate distasteful and hypocritical. He
would miss the camaraderie of club life and was full of praise for their
secretary Harry Hall, who, with his wife, 'did me proud' by ensuring he
had exactly what he needed [food, meal timings, sleep etc] in the hours
before his second assault on the Brighton road.

November 13th dawned cold and damp, with conditions appalling for
spectating, but Newton fancied the grey weather might prove a little
more helpful than the humidity of last time. Mr and Mrs Hall had done
their bit and he felt ready for the task. Hall himself accompanied the run,
as did former mile record-holder Walter George. Newton had become
friendly with the latter recently, meeting and running with him at the *News
of the World* sportsground in Mitcham, where George was now caretaker.
George was fascinated by Newton's exploits and volunteered to help run
organiser Joe Binks on the day. As they all gathered beneath Big Ben for
the 8am start, there had been 36 hours of continuous rain, and to add to
the fun there was a strong NE wind and some fog. It didn't dampen the
enthusiasm of the large crowd, however, and Newton got a rousing send-
off, speeding away to complete the first five miles in 29:40.

He reached 10 miles in 59:06 and had only slowed slightly by 15,
clocking 1:30.40. As he splashed through the unavoidable puddles along
the roadside, he noticed his legs were starting to feel extremely cold. At
20 miles (2:02.25) the rain had long since stopped, but the wind was still
strong, and the cold seemed to have spread upwards from his legs to his
hands and arms, which felt numb. These troubles occupied his mind as
he approached the halfway point, but outwardly he appeared to be running easily and effortlessly. The knots of spectators all along the route,
and the bigger crowds in the villages, were highly impressed and gave
lusty vocal support. He hit the halfway point near Horley in 2.41.36, and
then the marathon distance of 26.2 miles in 2:42.52, a time which measured up well against world-class marathon runs of the period. In fact, his
time at 26.2 was nine minutes better than the best Englishman at the 1924
Olympic Games (Sam Ferris), and just five minutes outside the English
record.

At Crawley, the cold became just too much and Newton stopped for
refreshment for the first time, far earlier in the run than he had planned.
He gasped 'I am nearly frozen' to his sister Ursula, who quickly reached
for a thermos flask containing tea and salt. To Newton's horror the flask
had not done its job and the beverage was stone cold. He drank what he
could and urged his helpers to go ahead and organise hot tea further
along. Joe Binks offered him a woolly vest, worried at how his arms
looked blue with the cold, but he turned it down.

Feeling only marginally refreshed, he set off, stopping again outside the Red Lion at Handcross (33.5 miles), where this time the tea was rewardingly hot. As we have already seen, a simple cup of tea galvanised Newton more than almost anything else, and by the time he reached Bolney, four miles further on, he was moving slightly quicker than of late. His limbs also felt much less cold. His helpers had their hearts in their mouths, however, when he suddenly faltered again in Hickstead with an attack of what seemed like cramp, having reached the 40-mile point in 4:23.27. This put a definite frown on his usually inscrutable face, but a third brief stop for more tea and salt outside the Castle Hotel seemed to do the trick. During this episode, Binks called out a warning about an upcoming hill, but Newton's response was a confident smile, for he knew there was nothing in Southern England to compare with the slopes he regularly overcame back in Natal.

With six of the 52 miles still to go, it was calculated he had 48 minutes to beat his own record of the previous month. Only an unexpected disaster would stop him now, for even in his most exhausted state he had managed eight-minute miling in the past. He swept through the 50-mile point in 5:38.42 which beat the unofficial record he set in Natal in 1923 by over 14 minutes. This was a source of great satisfaction to Newton, for it sent a powerful message to the cynical sporting press who'd dismissed the Natal run.

An excited crowd greeted him at the Aquarium on Brighton seafront. It must have been a poignant moment as the accolades rang out for a returning hero, for he was just yards from St Mark's Vicarage and the Lady Matron School where he'd grown up. He crossed the line (52 miles, 200 yards) in 5:53.43, meaning 'every record had been absolutely pulverised', in the words of one report. In typical fashion, the mud-spattered but composed Newton politely acknowledged the back-slappers and walked quietly over to the waiting Joe Binks, who helped him on with his coat, and out from its pocket came the inevitable pipe. A jubilant Binks noted: 'He was no more distressed than if he had just strolled along the sea front!'

At his own request, Newton was hustled away for a bath at the home of local sportsman Harry Preston, which was followed by a lunch attended by the officials and helpers. After they had eaten, a number of speeches were made and more than one speaker admitted they were too astonished by the day's events to express their thoughts fully on the performance. Timekeeper Jimmy Fowler-Dixon said he felt Newton's time would probably never be equalled, while 65-year-old former champion Walter George said Newton was the most wonderful distance runner he'd ever seen. Joe Binks pointed out that Newton's triumph at the age of 41 showed just what a man could do if he was trained properly. The *News of the World* announced it was to create a special gold medal for Newton to commemorate his performance.

The run generated huge publicity for Newton, who could now return to South Africa satisfied he'd done himself justice and, at the second attempt, had clocked the sort of time of which he knew he was capable. He could now book his passage from Tilbury to Cape Town a fortnight hence, with mission well and truly accomplished.

The only sour taste left over from this stint in England came when the AAA announced that the two London-Brighton runs would not be officially recognised for record purposes, as they had been solo affairs and not in open competition. This was highly annoying for Newton, although he knew he had achieved his aim of getting his name widely known for athletics excellence, with or without AAA ratification. Newton argued his case, pointing out there had been nobody sufficiently trained to be capable of getting anywhere near a 50-mile record: 'It would have been a mere farce to invite self-confessed insufficiently-trained athletes to compete.' He said the timekeepers Fattorini and Fowler-Dixon were 'past masters at their game' and both Life Vice-Presidents of the AAA, so there could be no doubting the times recorded were correct and above suspicion:

He sounded bitter as he reflected: 'The English AAA took not the slightest notice of either run. As far as they were concerned, no runs took place. It is amusing to know that a paltry verbal quibble can contradict an admitted fact. However, the records are English, even though its athletic institution cannot admit them. The times were correct and quite above suspicion, although they were so much ahead of any track performances on record.'

By now based at his sister's Gloucester Place residence in central London, Newton did plenty of running in his final few days in the country. Less than 48 hours after the second Brighton run he turned out for Thames Hare and Hounds against Charterhouse, as a 'warm down'. He recalled: 'This was pretty obvious proof surely that the London-Brighton course had not knocked all the stuffing out.' This run was followed by a farewell dinner in his honour, staged by the club at its King's Head headquarters in Roehampton, at which he was presented with commemorative medals. Then, on Thursday 27th November he said farewell to English soil with a fast ten-mile run around the edge of Regent's Park, before catching a train from St Pancras to Tilbury and setting sail for Cape Town on the *SS Bendigo*.

Chapter 8

Down and Out in Pretoria

Newton stepped off the boat at Cape Town and straight on to a train to Pretoria, eager to meet South Africa's new Prime Minister, General James 'JBM' Hertzog at the earliest opportunity. His immediate future depended solely on whether he could winkle compensation out of the government for his farming losses, and Hertzog represented his last chance.

In Pretoria, he approached a previously helpful cabinet minister, who was able to set up the meeting with Hertzog at short notice. He could not, however, grant Newton's request that the Native Affairs department should be barred from the meeting. As they headed to the meeting room, Newton knew his hopes were doomed the moment he saw a Native Affairs official accompanying Hertzog. He recalled:

'As soon as I entered I knew I was wasting my time. General Hertzog chatted away genially and occasionally asked the odd question, apparently with the object of killing time. Beyond an occasional reply I did very little talking. I just waited to see what the upshot was going to be. It came quite suddenly. I doubt if he was aware that he was uttering almost word for word what the [Native Affairs] department had been reiterating for so long – the Government had not acted in any way illegally and could not therefore consider the question of compensation in any form whatever. He was most suave and courteous . . . and when a man has already prejudged a case and determined on his course of action, it is useless to expect him to listen to reason.'

Newton's demeanour at the meeting was, it seems, not welcomed by the government officials and was interpreted as surliness. For soon afterwards he received a letter informing him his 'attitude' had ruined any last chances of compensation, which had still been a possibility even at this late stage.

Newton felt his only remaining route was to approach the Premier by other means. Officials of the British Empire Service League agreed to lobby on his behalf, and then a petition signed by many Natal residents was presented to the Parliament, tabled by his MP, Marwick. While this was going on, there was still an outside chance of success, meaning a near-destitute Newton stayed put at the Warrington House hotel in Pietermaritzburg, where the landlord was a sympathetic and understanding friend. But the weeks of 1925 crept by without a resolution, and it wasn't until June that the matter finally came to a head.

The occasion was a debate in the House of Assembly about Zululand farms, part of the Land Vote issue. Marwick stood up and raised 'the Newton Case' and the Prime Minister was forced to respond. Hertzog said he had been sympathetic to Newton when they met earlier, but it had been pointless to back him before the House then, because they 'would have laughed heartily' at him for doing so. He implied that Newton's position was due to his own mistakes in buying a farm in such a geographical position, and actions during the saga involving native workers and cattle dipping. He said: 'Mr. Newton really put his whole case before me so simply and without any attempt at hiding anything that I openly told him I had got him to come [to Pretoria] in the hope I might do something for him. But I [eventually had to assure him] that if I were to comply with his request, and pay him any of the money he asked for, I would simply be laughed out of Parliament if I had to account for it later on.'

Newton was left cursing the election defeat 12 months earlier of Smuts, who was far more pro-British than the republican Hertzog, and had been ready to make up his own mind about Newton. The new Prime Minister, on the other hand, only seemed interested in rubber-stamping previous actions by the Native Affairs office. The sympathetic pro-Newton letters and editorials continued in the regional press, but were clearly not helping much, and Newton knew this was the end of the road. As June 1925 drew to a close, he regretfully declared it was time to quit: 'Once more my funds were exhausted and consequently there was nothing for it but to clear out [of South Africa] and make for the nearest country where reason and justice were understood and valued.' That country, he decided to himself, would be Rhodesia.

The previous calendar year had seen him complete 7,769 miles on the road (5,161 of running and 2,608 walking) for an average of 21 per day. Although his shin soreness came and went after that, he was generally extremely fit and strong, and capable, he felt, of saying goodbye to South Africa with further record-breaking performances. During the first half of 1925 he maintained high mileages in training and entered a number of events in the Pietermaritzburg area, knowing they were likely to be his last appearances at each.

For a couple of months he laboured on with severe pain in his lower right leg. His London specialist had assured him it was only 'shin soreness' caused by over-use, but he noted that the Americans now had a phrase for the condition: 'shin-splints'. The discomfort didn't prevent him winning a 17-mile race which was the main attraction at the South African Harbours and Railways annual sports in Durban in March. Travelling from the city's railway bridge offices to a point on the North

Coast and back, he looked in great shape, winning in 1:55.30 with Marthinus Steytler second, some six minutes adrift. The pre-race favourite Harry Phillips failed to finish. Big yellow posters had adorned the city to promote the event, proclaiming a 'Monster Sports' of 30 events and the chance to come and marvel at 'Newton, the London to Brighton world record holder.'

Newton decided to defend his Comrades Marathon title in May and go for a fourth consecutive victory, but his shin-splints flared up badly and put the task in jeopardy. Still holed up at the Warrington House hotel, he told a reporter he hoped the sporting public would forgive him, for although the leg would allow him to run, he feared he would be well beaten on the day. He was prepared to beat the pain barrier, he said, for this year's race was to feature for the first time a fascinating battle between man and beast. A 69-year-old farmer from Riet-Vlei in Natal, George Robinson, had successfully applied to do the race on horseback and his chances of beating Newton had excited much public discussion and betting. Robinson publicly proposed that he and Newton formally make a winner-takes-all wager, but Newton was having none of that, and the chestnut horse's involvement ended up little more than a publicity stunt.

In the meantime, Newton and a friend decided to confirm once and for all the accuracy of the Comrades course's distance. They trundled a government measuring wheel the entire length of the supposedly 54-mile route and were pleased to announce at the end of the trip that it measured precisely 54 miles and 1,100 yards.

Newton nursed his injured shin carefully and got himself to the start-line in relatively good shape. He was secretly convinced he could beat the horse to Durban by some distance, even though press and public had come down in favour of the beast. The largest crowd yet for a Comrades start gathered before sunrise in the centre of Pietermaritzburg, and such was the crush that Newton struggled to get through to the start area, and ended up having to give his coat and muffler to a complete stranger as he was unable to locate friends. The good Samaritan promised to pass them to the motorcyclist who would be following the runners to Durban. In the mayhem there was then the comical sight of a 'false start', with half-a-dozen of the 39 men reacting to the chiming of the Town Hall clock instead of waiting for the pistol. After a few moments' hesitation another dozen or so joined them and dashed off. They could not be called back, but Newton and the rest bided their time and were able to enjoy a little extra elbow room when the pistol did sound. The four-legged entrant was asked to start three minutes after the rest of the field, so as not to impede anybody in the early stages.

As they headed out of Pietermaritzburg the route took the runners via a narrow thoroughfare that was badly congested, and when Newton spotted a gap in the crowds he dived to his right, slipped through and found he had a completely free passage behind the lines of spectators. Eventually he rejoined the pack when they had thinned out and for three miles tentatively trotted along at about nine miles per hour. Pleased his right leg was pain-free, he prepared himself for the first of the many hills. By now the sun was getting up and it was clear they were in for a very warm journey, more so than in previous years.

Newton was halfway up a steady 800 feet incline when he first heard the approach of the horse from behind. He exchanged polite greetings with rider Robinson as it passed and disappeared over the top of the hill. Newton was not downhearted, believing that Robinson was pushing his mount a little too hard and would pay later. He was rather more concerned when told Harry Phillips had ground out a good lead, which had been stretched to well over a mile by the 13-mile point.

As pre-arranged, Newton received a refreshing dousing of cold water near Camperdown, and then gulped down some of his 'magic drink' of lemonade, sugar and salt on reaching Cato Ridge. After a long stretch of road where he had to 'prance like a cat on hot bricks' because of the stony surface, Newton collared a native girl who was filling a paraffin can with water under some rocks. At his request, she poured the water over his head, and giggled in amazement as the drenched white man thanked her and ran away. Newton soon hit the halfway point (2:55.0), and was told he'd closed the gap on Phillips to only half-a-mile, but that the horse, which had rested here for fully five minutes, was in good shape and at least two miles ahead.

At the 30-mile mark Newton passed Phillips, who was on his back being massaged at the roadside, and looked ahead hopefully for signs of the horse. Forty miles came and went, his lead over all but the horse growing continuously. Tiredness began to spread throughout his body, but he comforted himself with the thought that the rest of the race was nearly all downhill, dropping from over 2,000 feet to sea level at Durban. As the miles ticked by with no sign of the horse, he began to believe it had quit earlier and had pulled off the road.

Into Pinetown (42 miles) and the heat had intensified, meaning the jugs of cold water being thrown over him no longer felt especially cold. Cramp in his legs was getting more persistent, but he knew he was on course for a new record and was determined to ignore the discomfort and press on. As the race entered its final few miles on the edge of Durban, it struck him that he and his accompanying pushbikes, motorbikes and cars were formed like a 'moving oasis' in the shimmering heat. Into the built-up area and Newton had to contend with a continual stream of traffic which kicked up clouds of dust, meaning he could see no more than 20 feet ahead. Once into the city proper, he came to tram tracks at the top of the Berea and the crowds grew, making him begin to feel a little claustrophobic. He was particularly annoyed when a passing tram deliberately kept pace for several hundred yards, so that its passengers could gawp at him from close quarters. He recalled later: 'I've always been one of those who dislike publicity and anyway, if I was tired I couldn't show it while these thousands were looking on. But, no doubt, the crowd and their encouragement helped to spur me on.'

The final mile to the Town Hall saw him cruising along smoothly, happy in the knowledge he'd run the fastest Comrades yet, and by a considerable margin. He hit the line in a time of 6:24.45, which smashed his own best time by nearly 32 minutes. It would ultimately stand as a course record for 12 years. The euphoria was temporarily dampened a moment or two later when he spotted Robinson and the horse, who had arrived more than an hour earlier (5:11.0). It shattered Newton's theory that the horse would never maintain its early pace. Robinson confessed he had deliberately chosen a mount that was exceptionally good at distance work and had given it three months of hard training. He reckoned it could have managed another eight or ten miles, but he would not have gone much further for the sake of its well-being. Just like Newton, it felt a bit stiff after its long journey, but with a day or two's rest would be as good as ever. If anything, Newton was more impressed by the performance of the rider, who was only a few months short of his 70th birthday. Newton said later: 'I lift my hat mentally to him every time I think of that contest.' Harry Phillips, ever the bridesmaid, came home in second place, 40 minutes down but in a personal best time, thus underlining the true quality of Newton's run.

Desperate for his pipe and a bath, Newton was instead man-handled shoulder high by the cheering crowds. There was no sign of his coat with the pipe in the pocket, so he gratefully accepted a cigar and asked to be transported towards the public baths in nearby Medwood Gardens. The crowd obliged. He would write with amusement about this later on: 'Help! I'm being hoisted – how perfectly helpless a man is in this position, but I must stick it for a shake. Great Scott! Now there's the cinema man grinding his machine at me. Ah, a smoke, many thanks! And here are the baths – won't I just wallow and luxuriate!'

In the wake of this fourth Comrades triumph, Newton was interviewed by the *Natal Advertiser* and confirmed his belief that he had exhausted every means in his power of changing the government's mind over compensation, and that his days as a full-time runner were coming to an end: 'I cannot go on running much longer, I must go to work and one cannot do both.' The paper bemoaned his luck and revealed that a further record attempt by Newton on the Comrades course, to be run solo around nine weeks after the official race, was likely to be his farewell appearance in South Africa.

Newton didn't deny he wanted to say goodbye to the country by setting a recognised world record on South African soil. It seems likely this was partly his way of bidding a warm farewell to his sporting friends, and partly a gesture of defiance at the government. The injustice he felt gnawed deeply at him, and he was desperate not to leave this beautiful country feeling like a defeated man. By carrying out a record-breaking run and immediately disappearing, he felt he would be remembered as a winner. The record attempt also explained his earlier keenness to meticulously measure the exact distance of the Comrades route.

With the help of the athletics officials of Natal, the solo run took place on Saturday, 25th July and saw him repeat the recent 'down' run from Pietrmaritzburg to Durban in his best time yet – 6:14.30. His interim clockings at 30, 40 and 50 miles were also declared the best ever. His finish time lopped ten minutes off his own recent Comrades record and the whole thing was lauded as a truly remarkable display of distance running. It meant he'd covered the hilly route of almost 55 miles at an average pace of under nine minutes per mile and it represented a time that was 51 minutes quicker than any other man had managed in the five years of the Comrades. Newton had certainly marked the end of an era with a flourish.

He decided he would leave the country secretly some 36 hours after the run. His money had run out, and he couldn't face the humiliation of having to rely on his hotel-keeper's charity any longer. He later put his thoughts down on paper: 'I am [becoming] an exile from a British Dominion because I will have nothing to do with a country intentionally misgoverned in spite of the protests of its decent citizens. Still, it is as well to remember that Englishmen are not downhearted; they help themselves. I was merely the first to be despoiled like this. If the Native Affairs secretary [Major Herbst] is permitted to treat a single case with impunity, there is nothing to prevent him carrying it further afield. What is my case today maybe the case of any Natal farmer, provided he is English, tomorrow.'

The run had finished around lunchtime on the Saturday and within 24 hours Newton was back in Pietermaritzburg, alone in his hotel room and gathering his thoughts. It was an emotional time as he quietly packed a small amount of essentials in a suitcase, and wrote a note for the hotel proprietor, detailing his wishes for the storage of his other belongings. He had 'casually let it be known' to a few acquaintances that he was shortly to leave for Rhodesia, but not a single soul realised the full extent, or the immediacy, of his plans.

He had no work or accommodation arranged in Rhodesia, nor did he have any real idea what awaited him there. But because it was the nearest British territory, going there felt like his only option. He had no means of transport and no money for rail fares, but reckoned this need not be a problem. After all, he was the finest ultra-distance man in the world and ought to be able to do the 770-mile trip on foot, especially as there was no particular hurry!

Yes, he would walk the thing, and, what's more, he would set off under cover of darkness and do the walking mainly at night, finding sheltered spots to sleep during the daytime. What could be simpler?

Newton was deeply embarrassed by his poverty stricken state and hated the idea that his famous face might be recognised as he shuffled along the roadside with his suitcase, looking for all the world like a hapless hobo. Therefore, he concluded, the 770-mile trek would largely be done under cover of darkness. Not a single person would know he was going, and not a single person would see him go.

Chapter 9

Walking to Rhodesia

Captain Wearner, the proprietor of the small Pietermaritzburg hotel where Newton stayed throughout the first half of 1925, was charmed by his guest's good manners and highly impressed by his sporting reputation. He also knew Newton was suffering financial problems.

Wearner had a quiet word with Newton and urged him to stay at the hotel for as long as he liked, with no further payment necessary. But Newton was a proud man and would have none of it. His middle-class upbringing meant he felt humiliated and ashamed to be short of money and accepting charity pained him. He assured Wearner he would soon be departing, although carefully avoided giving away details of his plan. Privately, he knew exactly what he must now do: broke or not, he must head for Rhodesia, nearly 800 miles away, and if the journey had to be on foot, so be it!

'Six years of a real sporting fight had changed me from an active and prosperous farmer to an energetic and all-but-penniless tramp,' he reflected sadly.

He was determined not to be seen leaving, and wanted to be well clear of Pietermaritzburg by the time the sun came up. He could not face the humiliation of being seen at such a low ebb by people he knew, and others who might recognise him from the papers. If he set off in the early hours of Monday morning, 27th July, by the time it was daylight he would be well clear of the city and nearby villages. And by the time people deduced that he was 'missing', he would be even further away.

His plan was almost foiled at the eleventh hour. During the late evening on Sunday, a friend who had seemingly smelt a rat came to visit and quizzed him on how and when he proposed to travel. Unable to lie to such a good pal, Newton confessed he was leaving in an hour or two on foot, but insisted it was now far too late to be persuaded otherwise. The friend agreed to a pact of silence, as long as Newton would allow him to wire some funds to a post office en route. They agreed on a small sum for food to be wired to Estcourt, a town 55 miles up the road, with Newton's middle name 'Hamilton' to be used to preserve anonymity.

Newton saw the friend off, changed into a stout tweed suit and finished packing his suitcase. He also decided to take a haversack for various 'odds and ends', including basic provisions to see him through 36 hours. Suddenly the nearby City Hall clock struck midnight, and Newton quietly stood up, ready to go. He gathered his meagre belongings, left a note for the hotelier, and crept stealthily into the night. To his relief the streets were deserted and he was able to make his way unseen through small side-roads, out of the city and to the outskirts. Crossing a rail line near the Show Grounds he knew so well, he strode up Town Hill bound for the small town of Howick.

The handicap of walking with a suitcase soon began to prove bothersome, even with the special carrying straps he was using. After four miles of interminably slow going up the hill, he reached the steep bend at the top, stopped to adjust the straps and took a lingering, wistful last look at the flickering lights of Pietermaritzburg below. It was a poignant moment.

Telling himself he must make this entirely new start in life, and the sooner the better, he sadly set off again. He planned to reach Howick, 15 miles away, before daybreak to avoid being seen, meaning there was no time for rests till he got there. Off he plodded, dismayed at how much slower walking with baggage felt, compared to running unhampered. The case weighed about 25 pounds and he was not a muscular man, quite unused to carrying weight for long periods, so it was quite an ordeal to maintain his planned pace of one mile every 20 minutes. There was a suspicion of frost in the air, and this helped keep him on the move.

The sun came up just as he left Howick on the long hill which winds over the Karkloof mountains. It was a route chosen as being the shortest and most likely to be near-deserted, due to being farthest from the main railway. After around 20 miles of walking, it had passed 8 o'clock and Newton stopped at last for food and an attempt at sleep. To save weight, he hadn't brought a rug or blanket, in the hope his resting could be done in daylight hours when it would be warm enough to sleep uncovered. Afraid vehicles might pass at any moment, he hid himself away in the long grass, had a bite to eat and tried to take a nap. Nothing doing.

'My mind was too disturbed with all the recent excitement and calculations,' he recalled. 'However, I stuck to it for several hours, as it was certain I could not keep going unless I rested while I had the chance. There would be no hope of taking it easy after dark on account of the altitude – it was mid-winter and I was 4,000 feet up.'

Back in Pietermaritzburg, Newton's disappearance caused an immediate sensation. Word got out less than 24 hours after his departure and the next day's papers lapped it up. Headlines in the *Natal Witness* exclaimed: 'Famous Runner vanished – where is Newton?' The *Times of Natal* even broached the possibility that the runner may have committed suicide due to his money worries. Another suggestion was that this was another publicity stunt to draw attention to his grievances. To help readers find him, the *Times of Natal* issued a description: 'He is of medium height, square shouldered, bronzed and has a small toothbrush moustache. He walks with a peculiarly hurried stride, taking short, springy steps and usually wears a khaki-coloured topee [a lightweight protective hat with broad brim] which appears to be a size too big for him.'

One Pietermaritzburg correspondent hit the nail on the head when he pointed out: 'Intensely independent and thoroughly British in his pride, Newton may have feared that if he said goodbye to his friends in the usual fashion, they would not have allowed him to carry out his intention to travel by foot and would have insisted on his accepting the railway fare . . . the last thing he was likely to have anticipated was that his somewhat unorthodox manner of leaving would serve to make him the central figure in a sensation.'

The news soon reached Britain, which must have caused concern among relatives, with the *Daily Express* and then the *News of the World* discussing the 'mysterious circumstances' of Newton's disappearance. When reporters descended on the Warrington House hotel, Captain Wearner told them Newton had vanished without saying goodbye, but had left a note asking for his belongings to be stored away. Wearner said Newton's habit was to stroll in for breakfast after an early morning run, and he knew something was amiss when this failed to happen. He was sure the runner would soon be in touch, he added.

Inevitably the publicity led to people in rural areas looking out for him, and after the story was broadcast on a Durban radio station, reports of sightings began to flood in. Two people claimed to have given Newton a lift, both confirming he seemed perfectly well and happy. And a Miss McAllister of Mooi River said he visited her tea-rooms when passing through the village, and had told her he was heading for Rhodesia.

Over these early days of his trek, Newton was unaware of the fuss he had left behind. After abandoning his abortive attempt to get some sleep in the long grass on the first day, he had decided to push on. His baggage was proving a major handicap, the straps cutting into his shoulders and slowing him badly. In the Mooi River area, a car approached from behind and stopped to offer a lift to a hotel. Newton declined the tempting offer, too proud to admit he had no money for a room. He made up a tale about meeting someone, but asked the man to drop his troublesome suitcase at the post office in Estcourt, further down the road.

Walking was easier without the case, but again attempting to sleep in long grass beside the road proved impossible, particularly now that temperatures after dark were dropping to freezing point. On reaching

Estcourt (55 miles), still without proper food and sleep since departing, a long wait for the parcels office to open proved fruitless, for his case had not been left there. Less than 10 per cent of the trip had been completed, and his problems were mounting. Ascertaining the whereabouts of the case involved walking back to Mooi River, where he swallowed his pride and went into the tea-room. The luxury of his first cup of tea in 48 hours was a treat, but Newton was not pleased to be recognised, even though the locals were able to confirm his case would be waiting further on at Ladysmith.

Heading off temporarily refreshed, and with less to carry, Newton's next target was the village of Colenso. But an hour's roadside dozing before the sun went down only left him glum: 'Night and the cold arrived together and, had there been anyone to ask me, I should have admitted that I was fed up and far from home. After a time I spotted the lights at Willow Grange station and longed to go across and cuddle down by the fire I knew would be burning in the waiting room. These luxuries were not for me, at any rate not for the present, so I kept going until once more sleep seemed a pressing necessity. I even found myself starting to dream as I walked along, with the result that I would suddenly stumble into the side instead of being in the middle of the road.'

Desperately tired, he presented a sorry sight. He occasionally munched on a stash of plain biscuits as he plodded through his second night on the move. By daylight he had reached the bridge that spans the Tugela River at Colenso. Sleep had by now become essential, but no matter how he tried, he was unable to get any at the cold, uncomfortable roadside: 'I could no more sleep in the ordinary way than pigs can shoot snipe. It was merely a succession of dozes, punctuated throughout with endless absurd and annoying dreams.' Even reading his little Shakespeare book by moonlight could not induce the proper rest he needed so badly. After the next start, he was offered and accepted another lift, this driver heading for Ladysmith. The man guessed who he was and further unwanted recognition came at the parcels office when he called in to claim his suitcase: 'The official stared at me as though I had been Buffalo Bill. Being recognised by the public when I was on the tramp wasn't at all soothing!' The effect of being recognised seemed to erode his stubborn resolve to stay anonymous and self-sufficient, for he now found himself unable to decline the car driver's offer of a meal, clean-up and bed for the night. He admitted later he'd been astonished at such kindness being shown 'to a common tramp.'

He was able to organise for his promised funds to be wired on ahead to Newcastle, but couldn't resolve the suitcase problem quite so easily. To save his aching shoulders, he tried strapping it around his neck and on to his back, but nearly throttled himself in the process. After having covered 120 of the proposed 770 miles, he came across a country post office, at which he posted letters updating close friends of his plans. The official behind the counter instantly recognised him and out came the inevitable tea cups and kettle. The man showed Newton the publicity he'd received in the newspapers, and he was shocked for he had naively never expected such a fuss. During their chat it emerged that an old wartime friend of Newton's lived on a farm nearby: 'I made a bee-line for it. Great Scott, wasn't the good man surprised! What a cordial welcome he and his wife gave me. I sat down to dinner with them that night and once more thoroughly enjoyed the many comforts that are the outcome of civilisation and refinement in an English home.'

Eventually Newton tore himself away, nourished and refreshed, but not before a lengthy argument in which Newton persuaded his old pal he didn't need money. Trekking through the night, at midnight he passed a turn-off leading to Dannhauser, meaning he'd completed 140 miles in four days. His main problem remained the unwieldy suitcase, although by now his feet were also rebelling against his stiff walking boots. Arriving in Newcastle he decided to spend some of his very limited cash on sending the wretched case by train to Charlestown, but was dismayed to find the promised funds had not yet been wired to the post office as arranged. Down to his last five shillings, he wired his friend to get them re-routed to Charlestown and bought himself two newspapers which he took to the local sports ground to read. Inevitably they contained stories of his disappearance. By now his plan to move along in secret had been shot to pieces, and he abandoned his idea of trying to walk at night and sleep by day.

Further on, at Ingogo post office, another man recognised him and offered 'another dose of genuine English family life' he was unable to resist in the shape of a bath, dinner and bed for the night. An additional offer of a horse was politely turned down. Newton recalled: 'Scotland Yard! Didn't I sleep! I must have put in eight hours off the reel without a break. I'm sure I wore a very different appearance the next day.'

Heading off with a bag full of home-cooked goodies, he pressed on towards Majuba, close to the Natal border with the Transvaal. Around now he was able to sort out further rail arrangements for his suitcase, and after going straight through Volksrust without stopping his total mileage passed 200.

Newton now found he was down to his last half-crown. To add to his troubles, the nights now seemed to be getting even colder and his feet were perpetually swollen. Spotting the lights of Palmford station up ahead, he found no waiting room with warm fire but instead an open shed where some attempt at sleep was made. Further on at Paardekop, his spirits by now rock bottom due to the various discomforts, he asked a station official if he could warm up by his fire. This led to more hospitality being offered and a gratefully accepted bath and breakfast at the man's home.

On the long walk to reach Standerton, Newton's eighth day on the move, his feet became almost unbearably painful and as a distraction from the torture he concentrated on looking out for station waiting rooms that might have fires inside. At a bridge over the Vaal River he found one, and off came the painful boots. Once he was rested and warmed, the boots were, of course, nearly impossible to get back on. Next morning a half-pound of biscuits was bought to stave off hunger and a few more miles completed before a kindly motorist and his family stopped to offer a welcome lift towards Greylingstad. Newton's final few pence were spent here on a wire to have his promised funds redirected (again) and the lift was extended to take him to Boksburg. He was by now in a bad way, and the help very timely.

At Boksburg his pride caved in and he agreed to stay with the friendly family for a whole six days while his battered feet recovered. He paid his way by helping with a little manual labour. The much-needed funds then finally materialised, as did his suitcase, and all seemed well with the world. Newton was once again 'living as a civilised man should' and felt good. He even went out on the sixth day for a 20-mile jog, feeling fit as a fiddle again. By now he had learned to accept help without embarrassment and even took up the suggestion that he completed his journey on a bicycle provided by his hosts: 'The machine was overhauled and seen to be thoroughly sound and properly adjusted. A big tin was filled with a galaxy of luxuries and strapped on the carrier. A waterproof sheet was added, plus several other real comforts, and on the morning of Tuesday 11th August 1925, I set off in very different style to tackle the remainder of my long journey.'

The trip was now progressing differently to how he'd imagined, but he still urged everyone he encountered not to publicise his whereabouts, and for the most part his wishes were observed: Even though he must have been easy to spot on the well-laden bike, the Johannesburg papers were obliged to report that their efforts to track him down had failed. Cycling speeded up his progress no end, and he soon reached the country's administrative capital Pretoria, passing the very building where the futile interview with General Hertzog had taken place earlier.

A taxi driver, asked by Newton for the direction towards Warmbaths and Nylstroom, recognised him from press photos, but agreed to stay silent. Heading out of Pretoria, the road surface deteriorated badly and the nights were cold. After recent luxuries, it was a struggle again to sleep and stay warm. Some roads were covered in sand and dust to an extent which meant cycling was almost impossible. Eventually things would improve towards Nylstroom, where Newton found an excellent spot for sheltering for the night and building a warming fire. Unfortunately he relaxed a little too much, and allowed his favourite letter-writing Swan fountain pen to accidentally roll into the fire and be incinerated.

Potgietersrust was the next village and then Pietersburg. Regularly arriving ahead of where his suitcase had been sent, he was now getting used to having to issue instructions for redirecting it. Another stop for repairs to a gear cable on the bike and then it was off towards Dwaars River. The nights by now were bitingly cold and a fire essential at every stop. At Bandolier Kop a shopkeeper confirmed the good news that Newton was now 'crossing the line into the tropics' and was barely 100 miles from the British territory of Rhodesia.

With the Zoutpansberg mountains in view, Newton arrived in Louis Trichardt to find his bag was again still on a train somewhere behind him. Undaunted he cycled on into the mountains, enjoying the scenery and glad to be rid of the monotony of flatter areas. Before long he entered what he understood to be 'lion country', a matter of some concern when bedding down for the night out in the open: 'I had been assured that so long as I kept a good fire going I should have nothing whatever to fear. Yet for all that, when you are out alone the mere suggestion is bound to be disquieting. Every time a lizard or some small creature moved in the bush close by would find me stirring up the fire and peering into the blackness to see whether the blaze would show up a couple of yellow eyes.'

As he approached the Limpopo ('crocodile') river, some six days out of Boksburg, the surroundings were proving fascinating and scenic, and Newton's stops to commune with Mother Nature became plentiful. On one such stop, an encounter with a motorist led to an invitation to a prospector's camp at Schelm Water close to the border with Rhodesia. Needing to wait for his baggage to arrive at Messina, Newton accepted an invitation to stay at the camp, under canvas, until it arrived – which would ultimately take more than a week. Inevitably he became interested in the prospector's work and was delighted when a tap of the man's hammer saw him presented with a fine souvenir specimen of mica. For several days he breakfasted with the prospector and then accompanied him with a gun, looking for additions for the man's larder: 'No two ways about it, I was being shown a sample of the genuine thing – a prospector's life in the wilds.'

Newton's next departure, by now precariously balancing the suitcase on the bike, saw him tackle the final few miles to his promised land – Rhodesia. It lay the other side of the Limpopo and for half-a-crown he obtained a ferry ride, complete with bike, in a small and rickety boat. Disembarking, he made for the police post on the Rhodesian side, where he soon found his successful day was about to take a turn for the worse. He recalled later:

'I called on the Police as I had been advised, and explained as shortly as I could what I was there for. It didn't take half-a-minute to see the man thought I was a raving lunatic . . . he was unable to assist in any way or offer any suggestions. There were sundry inconveniences which I might experience if I attempted to enter Rhodesia without £50 cash or a guarantee of employment, so he would have much pleasure in escorting me back to the punt and seeing me safely back into the Union from whence I came.'

Newton produced a newspaper cutting which showed he was a champion long-distance runner, hoping this would carry some weight, but it had the opposite effect, and the officer appeared more than ever assured of Newton's insanity. Counting to ten, Newton showed commendable restraint in agreeing to return across the river to South Africa: 'It amused me afterwards to think how he must have congratulated himself on so easily getting rid of a doubtful character, and how astonished he must ultimately have been to find out that I had told him no more than the actual truth after all. Perhaps I shall enjoy the joke with him some day.'

Newton had misjudged his ability to walk and talk his way into British territory with impunity. Without more funds or a job waiting for him, he was evidently trapped in South Africa. But what he didn't know at this point was that friends had earlier taken the step of obtaining clearance from the Rhodesian authorities for him to enter the country freely at Mafeking, without the normal formalities – but Newton had opted for the less predictable route via Messina, where border police had never heard of him. Newton knew nothing of this, so while he mulled over how to obtain £50, he set up camp next to the Limpopo, having been reassured there were no lions or crocodiles nearby to trouble him.

He came to the conclusion his best option would be to return to the prospector's camp 27 miles back in Schelm Water, where his new English buddy would surely have good advice on what to do next. The prospector was absent on Newton's arrival, so he sat down to wait, whiling away the hours with his little volume of Shakespeare. Finally the man returned and a lengthy discussion over an open fire resulted in a plan for Newton to seek work at the nearby Messina Copper Mines, and then head for Rhodesia once he'd saved the required £50, or had secured a job over there, whichever came first.

Newton had to admit all this was stressful for a loner such as he: 'I must admit after being for 15 years on my own I found this a very trying ordeal. All the more so as I was obliged to explain I knew nothing at all about mining and yet was looking for employment. The position was desperately embarrassing, and I fear the good man I interviewed must have noticed my nervousness.' The manager had no vacancies to offer, but was able to recommend another mining company several miles away and provide an introduction. This was successful and temporary work obtained in the mining company's office.

Before long the fatigue of the long trek had worn off and Newton settled into a new routine here on the edge of the Northern Transvaal. He railed his bike back to its previous owners in Boksburg and resumed his daily habit of a long run before breakfast. The rather sedentary office work at the mine, plus his habit of going to bed early, meant he had plenty of energy for a dawn run of 20 miles per day. He was still phenomenally fit for a man of 42, and remained as keen as ever on distance running.

He also found he had enough spare time for plenty of writing. This mostly involved lengthy handwritten letters, but also the occasional article for publication, including a piece of several thousand words which featured in the *South African Farmer's Weekly* periodical in late 1925. He wrote of his farming days in Natal and the troubles he encountered. He admitted that even after everything he had gone through he would still be willing to return to South Africa, but only if there was a realistic chance of obtaining justice. He still regarded the Union as his true home, but could never go back there unless the government had a complete change of attitude towards him. Ultimately he still hankered after a return to cotton and tobacco farming, and was ready to investigate the possibility of this in Rhodesia.

By now his new acquaintances in the mining industry had come up trumps and work was offered work at a Northern Rhodesian mine, at Bwana M'Kubwa, a post that would involve supervising gangs of native workers. It would certainly do as a temporary job, for it would allow him to enter the country as a *bona fide* working man.

Newton hired two young native boys to carry his baggage, and set off for Northern Rhodesia in late October 1925. Now at least he could afford to travel by train, but the early miles would have to be negotiated largely on foot. Over the Limpopo went the threesome, followed by a visit to the police post for Newton to report his intentions and ensure he was conforming to immigration regulations. A cup of tea with the officer and Newton and his young helpers were free to head into Rhodesia.

'After nearly three months of striving to get there, it made me feel quite chirpy, and I wondered what adventures were to be mine in this new land,' Newton reflected. Lifts on various wagons were obtained to help reduce the mileage and after camping overnight near Mtetengwe they set off early on foot, traversing unchanging bush-covered and flat country. The target was West Nicholson railway station, where two trains a week passed through. A passing motorist unexpectedly stopped and offered the trio a bed for the night and Newton, now feeling less self-conscious than earlier, was quick to accept. Thinking his khaki shorts and stockings were not quite the thing to wear into somebody's home, he vanished into the bushes and emerged changed into his formal 'ordinary everyday garb' to the astonishment of the boys. It was an enjoyable evening (Newton described it as 'top-hole'), during which a civilised and illuminating chat about farming took place. Newton was pleased to pick up tips about farming and life in general in Rhodesia, and it strengthened his resolve to succeed in this country.

Next morning one of the boys was unable to continue due to a foot problem and had to be paid off. Now that he had money in his pocket, Newton's days of carrying his own bags were at an end, so he made arrangements to forward the baggage the injured boy had been responsible for. He set off with just the one helper, a young lad he described as 'a comical youth who was more than inclined to be garrulous with or without provocation'. Tellingly, Newton did not feel at ease with this, explaining: 'The white man has to be becomingly reserved among the natives, and I fear I blighted his hopes. He must have thought me distinctly aloof and unconcerned.'

A tricky day of walking ensued, the pair suffering through lack of water and the difficult terrain they faced, but compensation arrived when another car driver stopped and offered accommodation for the night. The next morning it was a short hop to the rail station where he headed for Bulawayo and the 800 miles beyond to his new job at the mine near the Belgian Congo border. Stopping off in Bulawayo, he established contacts with the British institutions there, a wise move that would prove beneficial later on.

Supervising gangs of natives at the Bwana M'Kubwa copper mine represented a tough daily regime of at least eight hours' work, and

Newton settled into a routine where his training, somewhat reduced, would take place in the afternoons. The roads were poor so he often ran along the rail tracks, taking care to be home by nightfall in the knowledge that lions and occasionally leopards patrolled the area. His plan was to stay at the mine for as long as it took for a more suitable job to come along, with a long-term aim being a possible return to tobacco and cotton farming.

Christmas 1925 was spent at the mine, but the complex closed on Boxing Day, allowing Newton a leisurely 25-mile run along the rail tracks to the source of the Congo river, where he stopped and ate his packed lunch. On the hot return journey he found some deserted storage tanks which he used for bathing. The year ended with his training log recording a further 6,558 miles completed on foot (3,949 running and 2,609 walking) for an average of 17 miles per day. He was nearly 43 years old, but clearly as fit as ever.

Later, when it appeared likely that Newton had left South Africa for good, the *Natal Advertiser*, *Natal Mercury* and a number of other regional newspapers started a 'shilling fund', calling for donations to help put the veteran runner back on his feet. Eventually the fund raised £1,200 for him, and even General Hertzog was said to have donated. Newton was humbled by such a response and felt it had vindicated his stubborn battle with the Union government, and confirmed that most people felt he had been badly treated.

Newton (third left) acclaims a victory by Hardy Ballington (No 41), one of his proteges

Newton (far left) lines up for the 1928 indoor marathon at Madison Square Garden, New York

Newton has his progress monitored in the 1925 Comrades Marathon

Left: A poster advertises a public appearance in Canada by Newton and Pete Gavuzzi.
Right: The cover of Newton's 1947 coaching book

South African star Hardy Ballington (left) comes to stay with Newton at Ruislip

Newton gets encouragement on Polly Shorts Hill,
the toughest part of the Comrades Marathon

Newton leaves St Pancras station in 1924, bound for South Africa, and bids farewell to
Joe Binks and Mr and Mrs Jimmy Fowler-Dixon

Newton in Wiltshire in the early stages of one of his aborted 100-mile runs of 1933

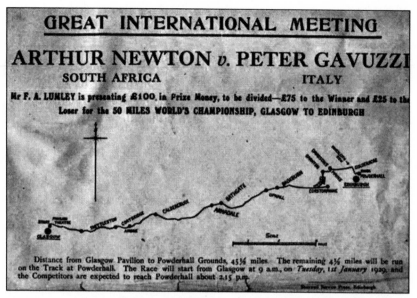

A head-to-head race between Glasgow and Edinburgh is announced

Left: A framed certificate presented to the Comrades Museum by the Thames Hare & Hounds. Right: A cigarette card depicting Newton

An artist's impression of Newton helping other athletes after he quit running in the
Transcontinental 'Bunion Derby' across the USA

Newton is cheered into Durban as he heads for another victory in
the 1927 Comrades Marathon

Newton (left) congratulates Tom Richards (No 21),
who has just won a 42-mile race in Bristol in 1955

Locals shout encouragement as Newton runs the
100 miles from Wiltshire to London in 1928.

Newton close to a triumphant finish at his 1924 London-Brighton run

Left: Tricky conditions in flooded Maidenhead, during Newton's 100-mile run in 1928.
Right: Advice for South African visitor Jackie Mekler

Newton (right) looks on as Hardy Ballington takes refreshment during a record attempt

Newton and Pete Gavuzzi (No 12) take a rest in Montreal after winning a 500-mile two-man relay in the summer of 1930

An enthusiastic send-off for Newton as he prepares to run 100 miles from the village
of Box to London in 1934

'Don't waste time, shovel it down!' was Newton's own caption on this photo of him
breaking for lunch with runners Whelan and Perkin near Berkhamsted in 1952

Newton (right) meets Geoffrey Robinson and his horse, who raced him at
the 1925 Comrades Marathon

Left: A poster proclaims the arrival of the Transcontinental 'Bunion Derby' in the USA.
Right: A bedraggled Newton at the end of his 100-mile run to London in 1928

The farmer wins! Huge crowds greet Newton after his shock win at
the 1922 Comrades Marathon

A Rhodesian news-stand announces Newton's latest plans in 1927

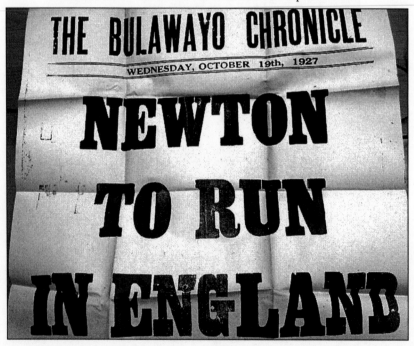

Newton (centre) prepares to set off, with a relay runner, on his first 100-mile run in
England in January 1928

A hand-written note received by Newton in 1927 from
ex-South African Prime Minister Jan Smuts

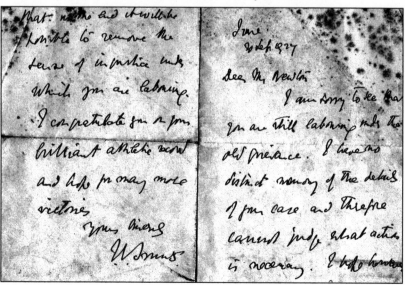

Newton escorts South African ultra-running star Jackie Mekler training at Ruislip

Left: Newton meets former champion Walter George at Mitcham in 1924.
Right: Newton with trophy in Africa

The Bear Inn at Box, Wiltshire, starting point for Newton's
record-breaking 100-mile epics

Newton passes a drink to Wally Hayward as the South African heads for a
24-hour record at Motspur Park in 1953

The start of the Transcontinental 'Bunion Derby' in Los Angeles in 1928.
Newton deliberately started well to the rear

Newton gets a crowded escort into Durban as he heads down Black Hill near the end
of the 1927 Comrades Marathon

A *News of the World* cartoonist depicts Newton as 'the Peter Pan of athletics'

Left: Another cartoonist's impression.
Right: Newton (left) helps young Hardy Ballington with his training

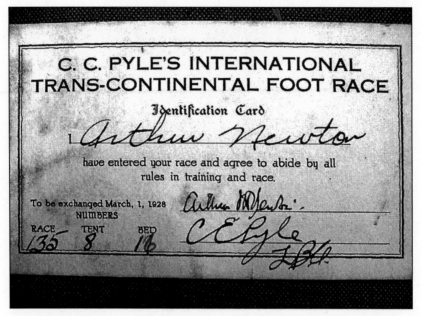

Newton's ID card for the 1928 Transcontinental 'Bunion Derby' in the USA

Australian athlete Trevor Vincent pays homage at Arthur's Seat,
near halfway on the Comrades Marathon course

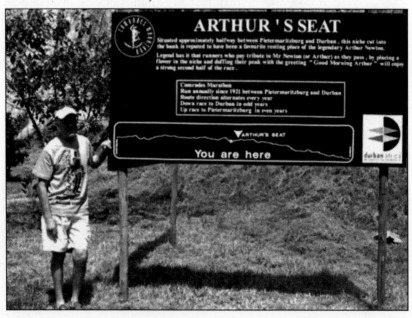

Newton and Pete Gavuzzi (with cigar) congratulate each other on winning
a 500-mile relay in Canada in 1930

Newton (back row, far right) in one of his early coaching roles,
with a group of young Rhodesian women

Refreshment for runners in the Transcontinental 'Bunion Derby' was provided by a
Maxwell House 'mobile coffee pot'

Joe Binks of the *News of
the World* interviews a
weary Newton in Hyde
Park after his 100-mile
record in 1934

Chapter 10

Every Nerve and Fibre Crying for Rest

The break Newton needed to get himself established in Rhodesia came unexpectedly in early 1926 when a letter arrived one morning from Bulawayo, hundreds of miles away in the south of the country.

Contacts he made among fellow Britons on his way through Bulawayo several months earlier had remembered him. The letter asked whether he would be willing to come and try to resuscitate athletics at the prestigious Caledonian Club, if accommodation and employment were found for him. It sounded perfect, and Newton almost snapped their hand off. Within a fortnight he was bidding farewell to his short-lived career in the mining industry and heading south by train.

The Caledonian Club ('The Callies') had been a mainstay of sport in Rhodesia for years, but needed a new and experienced coach-cum-manager to clear the cobwebs and revive former athletic glories. Newton was quickly installed and a special meeting called of all locals interested in athletics. Here Newton gave a short talk on training methods and running in general, and the meeting concluded with the formation of a new club called Bulawayo Harriers, with officials and a committee appointed on the spot.

Thanks largely to Newton's enthusiasm and hard work, the new club soon began to thrive, and before long cycling, swimming and a women's section were added to the roster. Both in running and cycling, the new club had little trouble in setting a whole new raft of Rhodesian national track and road records. Newton enjoyed the coaching and the lifestyle, which allowed him time to maintain his own high mileage routine. He would tot up bumper monthly mileage totals of more than 600 throughout 1926.

The locals took him to their hearts, but he was certainly not forgotten back in South Africa, where in May of that year the Natal Amateur Athletic Association made him a vice-president by unanimous agreement. The pull of Natal remained strong for Newton and he privately yearned to return there for the 1926 Comrades marathon, so that he could defend his title and meet up with his old friends. However, such a trip in late May seemed impossible as he was so busy in Bulawayo, and couldn't spare the many days that would be needed to travel there and back. But, suddenly and without warning, just an hour or two before the last available train for Durban left, the President of the Caledonian Society and the editor of the *Bulawayo Chronicle* called on Newton to urge him to 'drop every-thing and make the attempt'. They explained there had been a spate of last-minute phone calls from people not wanting Newton to miss the 1926 Comrades race.

And so, bowing to popular demand, Newton rushed off to catch the train to Durban via Johannesburg, and for three days and nights sat uncomfortably in his carriage, growing stiffer by the hour and fretting over his lack of preparation for the test ahead. It transpired that barely two dozen men had registered for the Comrades this year, so little won-der the organisers were desperate to boost flagging interest by getting four-times winner Newton to the start-line.

Newton's late entry ensured a good crowd gathered at the start despite the chilly early morning weather outside the Town Hall. Newton, glad to avoid the crowds near the start-line, was spotted sitting in a pressman's car nearby, where his opinion was being sought on one of the chief top-ics of the day in South Africa, the national flag controversy. With just a few minutes to spare, Newton put away his pipe, removed his heavy over-coat and headed for the line, along with old rival Harry Phillips, who stubbed out a cigarette on his way over. Newton, hot favourite to win, was representing Bulawayo Harriers for the first time, while Phillips today wore the gold and black colours of the Comrades club.

Phillips established an early lead up the Berea Road, while Newton discreetly worked his way steadily through the field from the back as usual, and was soon in second place. But by the time Phillips reached halfway at Drummond, he was a full ten minutes ahead and enjoying his best display yet. Over the Inchanga Bank Newton appeared to be closing the gap for a while, but the lead proved simply too big. Not only did Phillips (6:57.46) finally beat his old friend and rival, he also lowered the record for the 'up' run, albeit by a mere 36 seconds. Newton's run was brave (7:02.00) in the circumstances, but the first time he'd been slower than seven hours since his debut four years earlier.

Newton's lack of preparation was widely known and meant he received a sympathetic and rousing welcome when he came home just over four minutes behind the jubilant Phillips. Newton was carried shoul-der-high from the Duck Pond to the pavilion and was generous with his congratulations and tributes to Phillips, but he left for Bulawayo the same night, angry with himself for 'botching things up'. By agreeing to run at such short notice, without his usual meticulous preparation, he had ruined a hitherto perfect record of successive victories.

Later in 1926 Bulawayo Harriers staged an event that would test the 43-year-old Newton's leg speed rather than simply his powers of endurance. A four-way contest was staged over a 26.2-mile marathon course from the King's Grounds to Khami and back. Newton had to run solo against two teams of relay runners, one made up of two men, the other of seven, plus a team of cyclists who were time-handicapped. They all set off in the cool of the morning, but by the time they were returning to the King's Grounds the sun was blasting down fiercely from overhead. One of the cyclists was first back, but the fastest of the foot-racers was Newton in a time of 2:52.07. Given the high altitude, this was probably equivalent to a 2:45 at sea level. Behind him, there was a huge gap before the anchor leg of the seven-man team came in.

If Newton raced against man and clock rarely in 1926, he was to make up for it in 1927. He had a score to settle at the 1927 Comrades, badly wanting to avenge the defeat of 1926. He travelled to Pietermaritzburg with two of his protégés from Bulawayo Harriers, who were also to tackle the race – C M Watkins and H E F Mathews. Last year's winner Phillips had by now stopped racing since achieving his ambition, so Newton was again hot favourite to win. Keen to break his own 'down' record, Newton led from early on against a field of 41, but then hit problems well before halfway. After stopping to have a bucket of cold water thrown over him, he was seen to be struggling badly and Harrison Steytler passed him with worrying ease.

Newton was well outside his planned pace and his record hopes looked in tatters, but fortunately the 'bad patch' only seemed to last for around eight miles (he later put it down to the change of altitude), and he recovered to slowly claw back the advantage. From halfway onwards Newton gave a master-class in how not to panic and haul a leader back with relentless, yet economical running. By the approach of the 40-mile post he was able to regain the lead, having employed an unwavering stride for many miles and never apparently worrying that Steytler had got too far ahead.

He came home looking the freshest of any of the subsequent finishers, and the only minor problem was to find the finish-post, hidden among the teeming crowds. The cheering was long and loud, and after posing for photographs he gratefully accepted a cigar and box of matches, and began to wind down. The time was 6:40.56, a victory margin of 35 minutes, but some 16 minutes shy of his previous 'down' record. Nevertheless he was content with the run, and proud also of Bulawayo colleague Watkins' eighth place in 9:19.00, a sterling effort for a debutant unused to hills. Newton's prize was an HMV gramophone player.

Around 48 hours later Newton was invited to address a meeting in Durban Town Hall to condemn the Flag Bill, still a hot topic across the

Union. Broadly speaking, the controversy boiled down to English speakers demanding the Union Jack be included in a new South African flag, while Afrikaaners wanted this symbol of British imperialism excluded. Newton's arrival on-stage was greeted by a long ovation and the audience clearly expected a lengthy speech, so were a little nonplussed when he simply cleared his throat and said: 'I will come back to South Africa when the government represents law and justice!' and then turned on his heel and left the hall.

He'd always been known as a man of few words, but few here expected such brevity. It left little doubt that Newton was still not prepared to forgive his old enemies in Pretoria. Indeed, letters continued to sail back and forth between himself and the government throughout his time in Rhodesia; he was not willing to let the matter drop, even though clearly getting nowhere with his compensation claim.

Newton and Watkins, before returning to Bulawayo, decided to go for a few days' mountaineering in the Drakensbergs. By train and car they headed up to a hostel below Montaux-Seurces, one of the highest peaks. Many hours of climbing the next day was followed by a night sheltering in a cave, commonly used by climbers in the area. Many had done the hostel-to-cave-and-back route before them, but Newton and his friend reckoned none could do it quicker. Establishing a 'record' for the trek represented a bizarre but irresistible challenge and they returned down the mountain, to fetch camera and stop-watch and give it a go. Watkins went ahead by horseback, to be ready with the watch at the entrance to the cave. Newton changed into running kit and set off later at 11am. He had to follow a mule track, very rough in places, and soon found the steepness playing havoc with his breathing. Certain sections had to be tackled on all fours, but he kept moving regardless and arrived breathing heavily, to be clocked in by Watkins at 2hrs18mins. Before he could head back down, Newton noticed that Watkins' horse had suddenly got loose and the best part of an hour was then spent re-capturing it. Eventually he was able to hurtle back downhill, establishing a final time of 4:18 for future travellers to challenge – albeit a time severely lengthened by the frisky horse.

Back in Bulawayo a few weeks later, the next challenge presented itself. Newton decided he should consider attempting something longer than the 54-mile Comrades. It was suggested at his club that he might have a shot at the 100 miles record, and they offered to put up a relay team to 'compete' alongside and help push him along. Newton had never attempted anything over 55 miles till now, so decided to begin by attempting a low-key 60-miler on his own. He chose a round trip up into the

EVERY NERVE AND FIBRE CRYING FOR REST

Matoppos hills, where he could also visit the burial ground of Cecil Rhodes.

Setting out at 3am after a light meal, he faced the added pressure of needing to be back for work on the same afternoon. He knew there was no danger of getting lost as there was only the one road, and after 28 miles found the hotel near his halfway point, where he'd planned a refuelling stop. Finding few other guests were up and about at this ungodly hour, he ordered a bumper breakfast and within 20 minutes was tucking into porridge and cream, ham and eggs, toast and marmalade and tea. From here he ran to Rhodes' burial tomb, admired the scenery and then set off for home. As the sun got higher, the heat became more oppressive and Newton cursed not having a supply of his 'magic drink' available, for he was sweating profusely and losing salt. He made it back comfortably in time for work, albeit thoroughly exhausted and dehydrated. He concluded that 60 miles was clearly well within his powers – therefore, with the proper precautions, there was no reason why the 100-mile challenge should not be taken up.

So, urged on by Harriers colleagues, Newton 'took the bull by the horns', in his words, and formally requested the athletics authorities make the necessary arrangements for an attack on the 100 miles world record. The amateur best was currently held by Sydney Hatch of the USA, who had recorded 16:07.43 at Riverview Park in Chicago some 19 years earlier. Hatch, a two-time Olympian, had reached halfway in 6:45.28, then slowed to 9:22.15 for the remaining 50 miles; Newton was confident that his even-paced running would wipe this from the record books.

The road chosen for the attempt stretched from near the town of Gwelo (now 'Gweru') to Bulawayo. It included no serious hills of note and by now Newton felt acclimatised to the effects of the high altitude. At Newton's behest, a group of the Harriers rolled a measuring wheel, carefully corrected over a surveyed ten miles, from the proposed finish at King's Grounds along the road to Gwelo till the 100-miles mark was reached. They then went a further 350 yards or so, to make quite sure of the distance, and drove a wooden peg into the verge. Newton wasn't taking any chances.

As no Rhodesian individual was willing or able to run anything like 100 miles at Newton's pace, a Harriers' relay team of six men was given the job of competing against him (Reid, Hendricksen, Zamek, Downing, Watkins and Wilson), and the date of July 11th 1927 settled upon, with accommodation reserved for all beforehand at the Gwelo Hotel.

Early on the Monday morning, Newton demolished a hearty breakfast at the last possible moment and was driven out to his starting point. The journey would be 40 miles longer than anything he'd tackled before and, it seems, the nerves were showing, for he had demanded that the six-man relay team start running some minutes after him, to ensure they didn't distract him by being too close. In the darkness, he removed his coat and muffler and set off at 6.10, the way ahead lit by the headlights of an official car chugging along 50 yards behind him. There was much less dust thrown up than was usual at the Comrades, and Newton was pleasantly surprised by the relative quality of the road surface.

Acutely aware he would soon be entering unknown territory in terms of mileage, he used the first 20 miles to merely settle himself and allow his huge breakfast to digest. At his point he admitted he felt like 'a fellow taking a gentle stroll', but knew it was the right tactic. Going down the long hill to the Shangani River he stopped for tea from a thermos, and between 25 and 45 miles found the temperature rising and the discomfort increasing. An impromptu wash in a roadside pool helped, but he began to feel very hungry and tired on reaching the hotel at Insiza, the halfway point. Here he devoured a pre-ordered meal with relish in 12 minutes flat: soup, chicken and vegetables, and a fruit pie.

Back on the road he tackled the gentle gradient towards Bulawayo. The relay team remained some distance behind. After about 70 miles, the boost from the meal began to diminish and as the sun began to go down, Newton knew the real struggle was beginning: 'The car floodlighted the road while I crept steadily on, feeling that there was still a chance that I might reach the end, though I was in for a real bad time.'

Knowing of Newton's penchant for piping hot tea (and plenty of it), the officials produced gallons of the stuff en route, whipping out a number of flasks whenever required – which was every three miles or so in these latter stages. Grim-faced, Newton maintained a steady six miles per hour, aware he was on course to comfortably beat the record, but unable to summon up the energy to do any detailed calculations: 'Every nerve and fibre seemed to be crying for rest.'

A noisy crowd of around 300 welcomed the weary figure into King's Grounds, and the cheering continued long after the announcement the record had been smashed by more than an hour. Newton felt so shattered he found it difficult to talk as they sat him down and placed his feet in a bath of hot water and passed him his pipe and some drinks. Questions were excitedly fired at him, most of which went unanswered for he remained in something of an exhausted daze. He had completed the 100 miles in 14hrs 43mins, an astonishing 84 minutes better than Sydney Hatch's 1909 mark, even though conditions here had been much tougher than in Chicago. The relay team came in several minutes later, their noble efforts somewhat overshadowed by Newton's superhuman performance. Newton's non-athletic friends and family marvelled at his ability to cover 100 miles on foot, and letters of congratulation poured in. His sister Ursula wrote from Paignton in Devon: 'Very hearty congratulations on your latest record . . . [but] don't let running hinder you in any way in doing all you can to push everyone you can recruit in the interests of your case against the S.A. Government.' There was even a hand-written note from the former Prime Minster Jan Smuts: 'Dear Mr Newton, I am sorry to see that you are still labouring under the old grievance. I have no distinct memory of the details of your case and therefore cannot judge what action is necessary. I hope however that in the end it will be possible to remove the sense of injustice under which you are labouring. I congratulate you on your brilliant athletic record and hope for many more victories. Yours sincerely, J Smuts.'

The 100-mile run was reported in newspapers across the globe, and led to the inevitable calls for Newton to return to England to attempt 100 miles there, where a record time would be taken more seriously and treated as the definitive mark. Said Newton later: 'The improvement on Hatch's mark was so unbelievable to many of these good people [in Bulawayo], they there and then decided to take steps to send me to England to attempt better time under more favourable conditions. Feeling that I now knew something of what was needed for this type of race, I willingly agreed to try.'

Bulawayo, and Rhodesian sporting types generally, rose to the occasion. From all quarters subscriptions came in to pay for their guide and mentor Newton to be sent to England to create a recognised world record for 100 miles on a well-known course such as the Bath to London road. Joe Binks, who organised Newton's Brighton runs, was contacted at the *News of the World* and was happy to put the wheels into motion. Binks publicised the plans in his weekly column, and assured readers there was no danger of Newton contravening amateur athletics rules, for the whole project was being paid for by subscription from his Rhodesian friends, and that his official status on the trip would be as a 'publicity agent' for that country. Binks also made reference to the recent gossip linking Newton with a coast-to-coast run in America being set up by promoter Charles 'CC' Pyle, to take place early in 1928. This would be a chance for hard-up Newton to make some money, but he would definitely lose his precious amateur status as a result.

Newton thought long and hard about the C C Pyle race – which would involve running 3,400 miles in 84 days from Los Angeles to New York. Contact was made between him and the promoter, although it seems his first reaction was to steer clear of such a professional 'circus', instead recommending the semi-retired Harry Phillips as a possible participant. However, as the weeks went by, Newton came to the conclusion that as he was now a man of 44 years old 'with no outlook and no pension', he might be best advised to consider joining the world of the professionals after all. This change of heart must have taken place prior to the forthcoming trip to England. After all, if he had no intention of running in the USA in March of 1928, why was he rushing to attempt a 100-mile record in the middle of an English winter, when he could easily have waited for better weather?

Arrangements were made to head for London in the late autumn of 1927, and in the meantime Newton tailored his training to even longer work than before, committing himself to a number of races and record attempts before leaving Rhodesia. First was a 60-mile solo run in the Bulawayo area: He set off at 5am under a full moon, on rough stony roads, making good progress until the sun came up and the heat intensified. He was distressed to find he'd forgotten to add sugar to his thermos of 'magic drink' and this left him feeling weak after hitting the 30-mile point in 3:25. He tried some salty soup, but regretted this as his stomach reacted badly, forcing him to slow down slightly. He passed 40 miles in 4:46.30, which was just 24 seconds inside Jimmy Fowler-Dixon's recognised record for that distance. His 50-mile time of 6:12 was not a personal best, but still better than Edgar Lloyd's recognised record. This left him with more than two hours in hand to cover the final ten miles and beat the 47-year-old world record set by W C Davies at Islington in 1880 (8:23.30). Newton came in at 7:33.55, meaning he'd averaged around 7.5 minutes per mile, taking the record comfortably, and giving him all the world's best times at distances between 30 and 100 miles.

Over the ensuing weeks, Newton decided to test himself in a couple of races that in his terms were little more than a short stroll – the Rhodesia cross-country championship (10 miles) and its marathon championship (26.2). He was second in the former (1:01.14) and won the latter in high winds in 2:55.32, a highly respectable time, but not a personal best. The marathon result prompted an article in the *Cape Argus* which suggested Newton lacked genuine speed when it came to anything under 30 miles. The paper compared him with South African Ken McArthur, who won the 1912 Olympic marathon in Stockholm with a time of 2:36.54. Newton didn't take kindly to such comparisons, and was quick to point out by letter that the 1912 marathon had been 25 miles long and not 26.2, and therefore comparisons were meaningless. He said McArthur's best time over 26.2 miles was 2:42.58 (Cape Town in 1910) and that his own time was quicker, and had been achieved within a 52-mile run (London-to-Brighton). Furthermore, he added, since the Brighton run he'd gained three more years of experience, so should be even faster now.

Newton wrote to Joe Binks in London to confirm his arrival there in November, and told the athletics writer: 'Thank goodness this heavy racing is now over for a spell . . . I feel none the worse, beyond a stiff sinew.' He added that he was currently coaching top Bulawayo marathon prospects Zamek and Wilson, and all this news was relayed via Binks' weekly column. The subscription fund to pay for Newton's trip closed in mid-October after reaching £235 and was handed over to the Rhodesian athletics authorities as arranged.

In early November 1927 Newton attended a farewell dance held in Bulawayo in his honour. As was usually his way, he remained rather non-committal over when he might return, but promised his friends that, come what may, he would proudly wear Rhodesian colours in his forthcoming runs. He then headed off by train, in good time to board the P&O liner *SS Borda*, which was stopping at Durban, en route to London from Sydney.

Chapter 11

The Greatest Running Feat
the World has Seen

Newton boarded the *SS Borda* at sunny Durban, bound for an England about to be plunged into its worst winter freeze-up for decades. Had he known what awaited him, he would probably have turned tail and headed straight for California and the Trans-America race instead.

And as one great English sportsman left Durban, the port duly welcomed another batch – the MCC touring team, led by their captain Stanyforth, arriving in readiness to uphold the honour of King and country against the South African test side.

The *Borda*'s passenger list had Newton down as a 'farmer and athlete' with his destination address that of his sister Ursula in Upper Gloucester Place, London. The trip took the best part of a month, but Newton was able to train daily, completing 20 miles a day by circling an empty deck at around 3am. Over in London, meanwhile, runners were being urged to come forward to run against him as part of a relay team, in the 100-mile event being fixed for early January on the main road between Bath and the capital.

Disembarking on a bitterly cold day in early December, Newton modestly expressed great surprise that Joe Binks had taken the trouble to come and meet him at the dockside. Binks stated: 'When stepping off the boat Newton looked very fit . . . by nature he is a retiring fellow who thinks anything done for him is undue fuss. I don't think he'll ever know what an extraordinary runner he is.' Newton told Binks he expected to take around 14 hours when attempting the 100-mile record, and that he would welcome a relay team of about six men to give him some competition. By now Binks has whittled the list of relay volunteers down to 'four well-known road runners, plus a junior and an unknown'.

Newton also revealed he had suffered with tendon trouble lately, and he was packed off to see expert Wilfred Smith of Charing Cross for treatment and advice. As they discussed the upcoming record bid, Binks rashly agreed to accompany Newton on a training run – but the 53-year-old reporter, a champion miler long since retired, suffered a bad blister which became infected and kept him off work. Binks reckoned Newton had shortened his stride and adopted a different running style since his previous visit three years earlier, although Newton assured him each stride was 43 inches and hadn't changed. 'He glides along, feet no more than two or three inches off the ground, and noiseless. Not flat footed but more on his heels, and astonishingly silent breathing,' wrote Binks.

Binks noted that Newton still smoked a lot, enjoying a cigar on his way to a training session, and ate anything he fancied. Before one session he amazed Binks by stopping for lunch en route, demonstrating that he had no fear of stitch like most runners. Newton preferred to train early in the day and on the odd occasion when he had to be out and about after 7pm got 'very concerned' at the disruption to his routine. Binks was certain that 'We'll never see another runner who goes to such lengths and methods.'

While based in London, Newton paid a visit to his old clubmates at the Thames Hare and Hounds clubhouse (their secretary Harry Hall was helping organise the 100-miler), and also completed a number of training sessions at the *News of the World* track in Mitcham, under the watchful eye of its caretaker, the former champion Walter George.

In order to be near the Bath Road (the A4) where his run would take place, and to be able to train on quiet lanes, Newton headed out of London to stay at his sister's country residence, a cottage in Frieth. Nestling in the Chiltern Hills, Creighton Cottage sat just 10 miles or so north of the Bath Road, and proved an ideal base for Newton's preparations. The cottage was named after Newton's brother-in-law Basil, from whom his sister was now separated. Basil was a well-known literary figure, a novelist who was a prolific translator of German authors, and who worked for British military intelligence during the 1914-18 War.

Binks had set up Saturday, 7th January 1928 as the date for the run, giving Newton around a month to hone his preparations, but things were badly disrupted by the fact that the wintry weather simply refused to improve. Snow covered Southern England on an almost unprecedented scale during December and Newton – although well used to running in difficult conditions – found his training seriously hampered.

'I remember one day when I gave it up entirely; I had managed to flounder part of the way through a four-to-five foot deep drift that blanketed the path from the house for 50 yards or more, but as it appeared that running would be quite impossible I worked my way back again. Next day, however, I was able to reach the road by getting over a fence, which was invisible in the snow, and crossing a flat field. Once on the highway I found that traffic had hardened the surface sufficiently to allow me to get along. I went over towards Stokenchurch and from there down to West Wycombe, and was surprised to see cars alongside the kerb on the London-Oxford highway deserted and half-lost in the drifts.'

He began to doubt the wisdom of staging the record attempt now, especially after being unable to drive along the Bath Road as planned, to familiarise himself with the course. But, as everything had been carefully arranged, it was decided to press on and hope for a late thaw. Many folk reckoned it was the worst winter in living memory, and when the snow did finally start to melt, several areas were hit by flooding. A less suitable scenario for an ultra-run record is hard to imagine.

Nevertheless, Newton refused to let the snow and ice prevent him entirely from getting out and clocking up the training miles, even though some runs were reduced to farce. Living at or near Creighton Cottage were the children and grandchildren of his sister Ursula, who found the sight of their 'Uncle Tom' (Newton) struggling along the garden path and disappearing into snowdrifts hugely amusing.

Will Steynor, who later became an airline pilot, was one of those grandchildren. He recalls: 'Our nanny Ethel Rodgers had a favourite story about Uncle Tom and his regular training runs in the early morning from Frieth to Reading and back. One morning Tom had risen early to go running and was coming up the lane as Ethel walked to work at Creighton Cottage. It was a frosty morning and very slippery under foot. Tom started sliding about and proceeded to grab at a telegraph pole, hugging it for dear life, his feet flying all over the place. At this point dear Ethel had to pause while she wiped the tears from her face. She found it so funny to see this famous and rather reserved man behaving like somebody in a Charlie Chaplin film.'

The fact that Newton was so keen to see off the 100-mile record quickly, despite the desperate conditions, suggests that by now he had privately committed himself to the coast to coast 'Bunion Derby' in the USA. It has since been suggested that the American promoter C C Pyle offered Newton a cash reward if he could break the 100-mile record before arriving for the USA race, as such an achievement would help him promote the Bunion Derby. If this was true, it raises the interesting point that Newton was using the good offices of the Rhodesian and British amateur athletic authorities for his record-breaking, knowing that he was about to turn his back on the amateur scene.

The big thaw finally began in earnest about three or four days before the run. Some parts of England were deluged by nearly three inches of rain within a 24-hour period, which, added to the slowly melting snow, caused much flooding. Gale force winds added to the mayhem, with shipping along the south coast suffering badly. With less than 24 hours to go, Newton listened with trepidation to reports that the River Thames – which flowed close to most of his proposed route – was rising dangerously, and in West London was at its highest for 33 years. Maidenhead, through which Newton must run, was virtually cut off by flooding, and buses that normally used the Bath Road were being diverted at various points. Floods rather than snowdrifts were now the chief problem, although one road near Marlborough was reportedly still blocked by snow. More rain was forecast for Southern England on the day of the run. Clearly if Newton was to create a new record, he was going to have to do it the hard way.

The state of the roads meant Newton, Binks and other officials were unable to reach the starting point in the village of Box any earlier than the Friday afternoon. It meant Newton only had a few hours to rest before the scheduled 2am start. At least his bed for the night was positioned mere feet away from the start-line, with the accommodation having been booked at the Bear Inn, beside the main road and exactly 100 miles from the Hyde Park finish line. But Newton would write later of his dismay to find that accommodation was severely limited in The Bear, and he found himself expected to share a bed with another man, meaning he went 'mighty short of sleep into the bargain'.

And so, full of anxieties over the hazards lying ahead, Newton pulled on his white Shetland wool jersey and gloves, and went downstairs to join the small crowd gathered in the road.

Also there were his opponents from the relay team, Hubert of Polytechnic Harriers, Norton of Surrey, Wickington of Woodford Green and Terrett of Highgate Harriers, who were each to run 25 miles. Newton regarded their presence as little more than window dressing, for he would be concentrating solely on his own performance. He was aiming to beat his own amateur record (14:43) set the previous July in the heat of Bulawayo, but didn't expect to beat the long-standing professional mark, credited to Charles Rowell at 13:26, which had been set on a track. W C Jewell was referee for the day and the timekeepers were Messrs Fattorini and Findlay. Two more officials, Messrs Pepper and Palmer, were judges.

Emerging from the inn in his familiar all-white running kit, Newton cast his eyes eastwards into the darkness, his teeth chattering slightly, and wondered what lay in store for him in the sleeping towns of Marlborough, Hungerford, Newbury and Slough. Further on awaited Hounslow, Hammersmith and then Hyde Park. By the time he got there, if he got there at all, the day would be gone and darkness would be returning. It was a grim prospect. The snow had largely gone by now, but the fierce SW winds were bringing rain and promised to batter him from the right side all the way.

Olympic sprinter Harold Abrahams was in attendance to officially start the run and at 2am sharp Newton set off to rousing cheers, shadowed by Hubert, the first of the relay men. Disregarding the weather, a surprising number of men on bicycles followed cheerfully to join in the fun. The horrendously early start had largely been forced upon Newton by the demands of the press, who wanted him to finish in Hyde Park no later than 4.30pm, so there was enough light for their photographs. Although he was used to running before dawn, he was not familiar with the conditions at 2am on a freezing English January morning. He would comment later: 'Darkness is a severe handicap to running, for without thinking about it you naturally lift your feet higher off the ground when you can't see the surface, and this tends to waste energy and tire you sooner.'

Nevertheless, he soon forged ahead of Hubert and despite the ungodly hour many people along the route emerged from their homes to wave him on, or called out from first floor windows. In Chippenham cars filled the town square to see him go through. He passed the 10-mile point in a steady 67:40 and then swept through Calne, his friend Walter George's birthplace. He received a particularly loud cheer from people waiting outside Beckhampton stables and chalked up 20 miles in 2:16.47. Progress was good, but Newton didn't feel particularly good, his stomach aching badly by now.

At the 25-mile point he was more than a minute ahead of Hubert, who swapped at this point with Terrett. He was maintaining a solid, steady pace, but not feeling well, and called out urgently to Binks in his car for some hot tea. They had none waiting for him at this point, so a second car was ordered to drive on ahead to get some ready. Unhappy over this, Newton struggled badly on a hill and near the top veered over to the side to be sick. At this point he thought he was 'done for' in terms of records, but vowed to carry on regardless.

By the time he hit 40 miles (5:06) his helpers could tell he was in some discomfort, without having to ask. It was exactly 7.30am as he passed the Newbury clock tower, still a few minutes ahead of schedule. Here he was presented with the long-awaited 'scalding hot tea' as requested. The cup was almost too hot for Binks to hold but, to his amazement, Newton grabbed it and guzzled the brew down. Although his stomach had felt bad for miles now, he knew the importance of refuelling and at a spot just short of Thatcham, stopped for breakfast, a substantial portion of hot minced beef. He wolfed it down in ten minutes and as he grimly resumed running the rain returned. He was soon sick again, and vowed then to take no more solids. On he went, reaching the halfway point of 50 miles in a creditable 6:41.13. By now the relay men had passed him and gained a big lead, but this was the least of his worries and he paid little heed.

Approaching Reading he found the surroundings more familiar, thanks to his training runs, and he managed a thin smile as huge cheers rang out from the gathered townsfolk. Or perhaps it was a grimace, for by now cramp was starting to become a problem. He asked for his 'magic drink', and began taking mouthfuls at regular intervals for the rest of the run. Such repeated requests for fluid were unlike Newton, and gave the game away regarding his condition. His concerned helpers offered various morsels of food, but he refused, indicating that solids would further upset his stomach.

Watching carefully from his car, Binks studied his gait and reckoned Newton was shuffling along at a regular 180 steps per minute, reaching the 60-mile point in 8:07.13. Near to Hare Hatch he again dived into the side to be sick, but didn't let it slow him too much. His lower half was by now filthy from the muddy water splashed up by his own feet, and he became wetter still when going through Maidenhead, parts of which were completely under water. Through the middle of the town temporary wooden walkways had been erected over the floodwaters and Newton gladly made use of them, dutifully smiling for the waiting photographers. Binks calculated that he had now done 74 miles in a time that was just about on course to beat his own record, but 35 minutes behind Newton's personal target.

He passed this rather discouraging news to Newton, who reacted surprisingly positively, grim determination driving him forward. From just beyond Maidenhead and into London there were crowds along the route all the way. A number of enthusiastic spectators reached forward to slap him vigorously on the back as he passed, a well-meaning but highly unhelpful gesture. More than once he was even spun completely around by this, and several times had to waste valuable energy by shouting for the crowd to leave him a way through. After Maidenhead he definitely sped up a little and at the Colnbrook level crossing (85 miles) clocked 11:48, still ahead of record schedule.

He looked to be running well as he approached Hounslow and was seen to smile at some of the well wishers. 'Good luck Arthur' came the constant cry all along. For a short spell in west London, the great marathon runner Sam Ferris appeared and jogged alongside, passing a few words of encouragement. Newton passed 90 miles in 12:35, which was superb in the circumstances as it bettered the equivalent point on his Bulawayo run by 28 minutes. Following another burst of irritating back-slapping in the middle of Hounslow, and accompanied by a flotilla of bikes alongside, Newton reached the Chiswick High Road. He was clearly desperately exhausted and it seemed only regular swigs of his special drink were keeping him going. Huge crowds greeted him in the Hammersmith and Turnham Green areas, and at one point he called out 'How far?' to his helpers, and let slip a big smile when Binks shouted just five miles to go.

He was less happy when mobbed at Hammersmith Broadway, where only the swift action of police allowed him to get through the massive crowd, although even they could do nothing about the scores of noisy youngsters by now running along close behind him. Several times he glanced around with an irritated look, worried that his heels would be clipped, but nothing could be done about the children. He passed Kensington church and then the Albert Hall, and from Sloane Street began the slight climb towards Hyde Park. It was approaching 4.30 in the afternoon, the sky was dark grey and getting darker, but Newton was well inside schedule to beat his own record and surely nothing would prevent it now.

For some three hours or so, a huge crowd had assembled at Hyde Park Corner, and the road just inside the park, parallel to Knightsbridge, was packed both sides with people, cars and horsemen. Movie-men had installed their cameras in all sorts of spots, including the roofs of taxis, but as it slowly grew darker, one by one they reluctantly folded up the stands and stole away. Then, just before 4.30, word spread that Newton was getting near – and furthermore that he would be running along the road outside the park. This caused a furore among those inside the railings who now began pushing dangerously to get into the road opposite the St George's Hospital. It was a chaotic scene, the mob swarming out of control around the mounted police, cars and omnibuses.

For a while, order was just about restored and necks craned in a single direction to watch the white-clad figure, moving at a fair pace and followed by cars, cycles and another shouting mob. Those near to him could see that Newton looked distinctly worried as he gazed at the scene up ahead. Before reaching the official finish line, he appeared to falter. He was then seized by two or three enthusiasts, but shook them off and ran on to cross the line. Then he stopped and for a few seconds seemed bewildered and disorientated. Clearly unsure what to do in all this mayhem, he then turned and for all the world looked as if he was about to head back from whence he came, but was quickly surrounded and swept along helplessly toward the area in front of the hospital. He became lost to view and many people swarmed up onto the Artillery war memorial to try and get a better sight of him. The noise level increased as people cried out their congratulations, while those close at hand worked furiously to give Newton some space. Eventually they bundled him inside the hospital entrance and the police set up a human barrier at the doors. Instantly the crowd began chanting 'we want Newton' and a few individuals at the front made unsuccessful attempts to storm the doors.

Newton had finished in 14:22.10 (beating his own record by nearly 21 minutes), which was a remarkable time given the tough conditions, and the fact that he felt unwell from very early on. Newton had privately hoped to finish in under 14 hours, but Binks, who had witnessed all the great Olympic and championship performances to that point, was in no doubt: 'I consider this the greatest running feat the world has ever seen.' After what seemed like an age to the impatient crowd, but was probably just a 10-minute smoke of Newton's pipe, the hero of the hour appeared at the hospital doors again. The police held the crowds back and Newton emerged, waited for the noise to die down a little and then shouted out as loudly as his weary body would allow: 'Ladies and gentlemen, my greatest thanks to the *News of the World* and the AAA officials for their wonderful work in organising this run for me, and to you for this magnificent reception. Good night all!'

The rather unedifying scenes at Hyde Park corner sparked much discussion over why Newton hadn't simply taken the park road to the finish line, as this would have made life easier for all concerned and prevented the chaos, for the Rotten Row area afforded plenty of space. It emerged that park officials had been to blame, for at the eleventh hour they decided, for reasons unknown, that Newton must finish outside the park in the relatively narrow confines of the road. It had been a bad mistake but luckily for them nobody was seriously hurt.

When a revived Newton sat down later to discuss the day's events, he told Binks he was absolutely certain he could do a much better time for 100 miles. He'd made two major mistakes this time: not acclimatising fully after his switch from a hot region at high altitude, and not getting to the start at Box with more time to prepare. He admitted he'd felt unwell for the final 88 of the 100 miles but was completely mystified by the stomach trouble and had 'never felt so ill in all my life'. A major source of irritation to him had been the woollen clothing he chose to use, which kept him warm early on but made him sweat profusely in the daylight hours. But, despite everything, he had been determined to finish 'because I couldn't let you down after what you had done for me.'

Binks told him he'd succeeded in conditions that would have 'disheartened a lion' and put forward the theory that he'd set off from Box too quickly, but Newton disagreed and said it had been controlled and not nearly so quick as at Bulawayo six months earlier. He agreed he'd made no attempt to race the relay men and had told them to carry on and ignore him. With hindsight he would have preferred proper pacemakers, rather than 'opponents'.

Newton commented modestly: 'I managed to scrape through in 14:22.10 [but] knew it was nowhere near the time that ought to have been put up considering the type of training I had undergone – a type altogether in advance of previous methods. Fortunately the public seemed pleased, but that was only because they didn't realise how poor the time really was.'

Congratulations poured in from all quarters, including Government House in Salisbury. A hand-written letter from Sir John Chancellor, the highly decorated Governor of Southern Rhodesia, arrived: 'I must write you a line to convey to you my very hearty congratulations on your great achievement. All of us in Rhodesia are delighted that you have succeeded in creating a new world's record for 100 miles on road. We shall follow your future arrangements with the greatest interest and with ardent hopes that you will break some more records. All good wishes to you for 1928, Yours sincerely, J R Chancellor.'

A week after the run, Newton was invited to the *News of the World* offices to be presented by editor Sir Emsley Carr with a gold watch, gold platinum chain and gold matchbox as mementoes of his achievement. In his short speech of thanks, Newton said he hadn't set out to win things in athletics but to draw attention to his grievances, so that future settlers in South Africa might not meet the same fate.

A few days later he accepted an invitation from Walter George to speak at one of the regular 'Round the Fire' talks held at the *News of the World* sports ground in Mitcham. George himself missed the event after an attack of jaundice saw him confined to bed at St Thomas' Hospital. Newton told the gathering of athletes and officials how he had studied wild animals in motion in Africa to help him devise his own uniquely economic style of running. He was in big demand as a speaker, and on another evening joined Olympic marathoner Sam Ferris to give a talk on distance running at the Air Ministry Refreshment Club in Kingsway, Central London.

A fortnight after the 100-miler, Newton was back in competitive action, helping the Thames Hare and Hounds beat London University in a seven-mile cross-country match, finishing a modest 13th in 43:03. At a club dinner at the King's Head, Roehampton, later that evening he was made an honorary member in recognition of his record-breaking. He was also awarded the club's silver medal, on a night that would mark his last involvement with them. Within a few days of the club dinner, news broke that Newton was quitting the amateur ranks in order to chase the Yankee dollar.

Joe Binks filed a *News of the World* 'exclusive' that Newton was signing up for the trans-America Bunion Derby to be run in a few weeks' time, in March. Binks wrote that Newton regretted having to take this step as he prized his amateur status very highly, but had little choice because of his parlous financial state having lost a 'small fortune' fighting the South African government. Newton had intended to go back into farming in South Africa or Rhodesia, wrote Binks, but all his friends had urged him to take this great new athletic opportunity in the USA and after agonising over the move, he had now agreed.

It was sensational news to most of the athletics fraternity, and inevitably did not sit comfortably with the traditionalists. Professional running was seen as the abhorrent and seedier end of athletics, a world populated by gamblers, con-men and people not interested in the integrity and purity of athletics. Many men before Newton had quit amateur athletics to make money and there was still a stigma attached to taking this step, even though professional running had been a dying sport throughout the 1920s. Despite his middle-class background, Newton had never particularly regarded himself as the classic 'gentleman amateur' because he had always trained like a full-timer. He sought to defend himself:

'As a nation we decry professionalism in athletics in spite of the fact that every sensible person knows that the pro can spend time and energy on the subject denied to the amateur. To most of those who form the governing authorities in this country, athletics is amateur or it isn't sport at all. A curious illusion without any foundation in fact. These men profess to have kept strictly to amateurism throughout their lives and have spread the impression, another curious illusion, that there was virtue in doing so. Actually of course it has restricted their outlook, and it would seem very doubtful if they were in a position to weigh the advantages of both sides, as can the man who has practised both.'

One morning around this time, Newton arrived back from his daily training run to be handed a telegram from New York. It was from the Bunion Derby organiser C C Pyle: 'Congratulations may we announce your entry our race.' With the cat now out of the bag, Newton could now give them the go-ahead.

Chapter 12

A Magnificently Stubborn Old Goat

USA, February 1928. The so-called Roaring Twenties had reached fever pitch, jazz and art deco was all the rage and a country led by popular President Calvin Coolidge was enjoying an economic boom that fed a frenzy of outrageousness. The Wall Street crash was over a year away and excess was the name of the game. It even spread to the world of athletics, with promoter Charles Cassius Pyle finalising fantastic plans for a three-month extravaganza that would see 200 men race the 3,400 miles from Los Angeles to New York. The United States, let alone the rest of the world, had seen nothing like it before.

This was a country dealing with prohibition, immigration laws based on colour and political persuasion, and the terrorism of the Ku Klux Klan. Yet, despite all this, the United States was a country that knew how to enjoy itself. Mickey Mouse and Babe Ruth were household names, the cinema 'talkies' had arrived and the nation's love affair with the automobile had begun in earnest. The 1920s had been littered with endurance tests and bizarre stunts of all description, including marathon dances, six-day bicycle races, barn storming, and dog-sled relays. Now, the coast to coast run – or the 'Bunion Derby' as it would be coined – was set to top the lot.

Promoter Pyle assembled a cosmopolitan field of runners in Los Angeles that was unique in terms of its sheer size, racial mix and sporting background. The only thing the men had in common was a desire to get to New York first and win a pot of money. A sum of US$25,000 awaited the winner (equivalent to around £220,500 in 2009 terms). Pyle's greatest coup was to secure the participation of Arthur Newton, the man regarded on several continents as the father of modern distance running. Newton's presence added quality and experience to a motley field who were largely ignorant of the horrors and discomforts that awaited them on America's roads. They were being asked to run, over a 12-week period, a level of mileage that exceeded even the prolific Newton's busiest training periods. The number of men in the Bunion Derby who had ever run 50 miles in one day could be counted on one hand. Only Newton himself could possibly have any idea what was required and what it would feel like: He had logged 31,000 miles since taking up the sport seriously six years earlier and nobody else in the field could match that. Newton would soon be installed as hot favourite to win.

On the night of Friday, 3rd February 1928, Newton set sail from London for New York on the *SS American Banker*, one of only 24 passengers, two of whom were Japanese diplomats. On the passenger manifest he was listed as a farmer, but as he no longer had a farm and was gunning for Pyle's prize money, technically he was really a professional runner. He was able to squeeze in some undisturbed running up on deck during the crossing, as long as he rose very early. It left him plenty of free daytime hours to ponder his latest career move.

He summed it up thus: 'It was obvious that, being one of the best-trained men in the world for long distances, I should do well to consider [the Bunion Derby]. The expense would not be great, and although recent sinew trouble might – or very probably would – put me out of the race, the event was expected to be an annual affair and I should be able to learn sufficient about the conditions to ensure making a good job of it on the next occasion. I had my living to think of before anything else, and this race offered a better chance of safeguarding it than any other opening available to me.'

The week at sea allowed Newton to fully recover from the lingering aches and pains from his 100-mile run. He admitted to feeling unusually excited at the prospect of seeing a land he had read so much about. Landing at New York, he was met by Dr Hugo Quist, part of the Bunion Derby organising team, although best known for being trainer/manager to middle distance ace Paavo Nurmi. Quist was under instructions to get Newton safely to the start-line in Los Angeles.

The pair set off by train several days later, following an improvised five-day zig-zag route across the States with Quist agreeing to Newton's requests for sight-seeing diversions. These included Niagara Falls (which he found less impressive than Victoria Falls in Rhodesia), the Mexican border at El Paso, and the Sierra Nevada. On arrival in LA, Newton was whisked to the Ascot Speedway, the stadium serving as the HQ of Charles 'CC' Pyle's International Transcontinental Footrace, to give its full name.

Sixteen large marquees were in place and runners of all shapes and sizes sat or stood around, a few jogging around a track, and some training up in the nearby hills. Newton was issued with race number 135, and told he would be using tent number 8 and bed number 16 when the road-show stopped each night en route to New York.

The extrovert 45-year-old Pyle bowled over to meet Newton, delighted his star attraction had shown up, and keen to immediately get maximum publicity from the fact. He asked Newton to give a speech to the other competitors in the refreshment tent, to pass on advice and tips about running great distances. Pyle was only too well aware that many of his runners were seriously under-prepared and might not make it to New York, and didn't want the event to end in farce. Newton told the men they must treat the run as a 'desperately serious affair', must not set off quickly, and only those who used commonsense and enjoyed good luck could hope to finish prominently.

Newton studied the route they would be following. Much of it would follow the course of the new Route 66, which had opened less than two years earlier, although only 800 of its 2,400 miles were properly paved, the rest being little better than rough track, covered in dirt, gravel or bricks. The road was barely 15 feet wide and would not be properly finished until nine years later, by which time it would have had grown to become the most iconic highway in the world. But for now it was new and raw, dusty and rugged.

Newton came clean with Pyle and warned him he was carrying a damaged Achilles tendon, which required constant nursing, and that this might lead to him having to quit before the end, although he promised to get as far as possible. Pyle accepted the news with equanimity and devised a plan to use Newton in other capacities if his star performer went lame. In the meantime, he grandly presented Newton with a letter just received from London, which relayed the news that the general committee of the AAA in Manchester had accepted Newton's 100-mile run in January into the record books as a 'noteworthy performance'.

Few, if any, of the other runners had ever met Newton, but most knew exactly who he was. Pyle had already publicised his name to the maximum. Newton struck some of his fellow travellers as being a little aloof. He didn't chat easily and exchange banter in the way that most of them did. Peter Gavuzzi, a little Englishman of Italian extraction, called out 'Over here Arthur!' in a friendly greeting, only for Newton to turn and reply disdainfully: 'Do I know you? In future address me as Mr Newton. Only my friends call me Arthur.' The affable Gavuzzi was momentarily crushed, but would soon realise this was just Newton's way, and that beneath the stiff colonial exterior was a man with whom he could, and would, soon develop a close friendship. Gavuzzi knew his place and would obediently refer to his elder and better as 'Mr Newton' for the next 30 years – even though Newton felt it appropriate to use Gavuzzi's Christian name.

Gavuzzi, 21, born in Kent to an Italian father and French mother, was a chef who had recently shown great promise at distance running, having become friendly with London bootmaker Charlie Hart, a veteran and previous holder of the 100-mile record. Hart, now 63, was also here to take part and the oldest entrant in the field. He and Gavuzzi were running as a team, sharing the same sponsor and having agreed to split any prize money they might make. They were a pragmatic pair, Gavuzzi aiming at daily stage prizes rather than overall victory, and Hart hoping his own slow but relentless jogging would outlast all the novices and get him in the placings.

Newton noted that the only name known worldwide, apart from himself, was Willie Kolehmainen. A native of Finland, 'Wee Willie' was now 40, working as a bricklayer and attempting to gain American citizenship. He was just five feet tall, even shorter than the diminutive pair of Gavuzzi and Hart. Part of the famous Finnish running dynasty, Willie was a tough competitor, who had smashed the professional marathon record some years earlier (2:24.32), meaning he was quicker than Newton at this distance, but had no known form over longer runs.

In the days before the scheduled start (Sunday, 4th March), the likes of Newton and Kolehmainen were regularly quizzed by the American press, with Pyle bustling around encouraging such publicity. Pyle told reporters about the 'sensational caravan' that would be heading through dozens of American towns, and how there would be carnivals staged at each of their nightly stops. He said medical attention, food and tented accommodation would be provided to the runners each night, and it would be the greatest sporting event the nation had ever seen. Any publicity was good publicity as far as he was concerned, and he cared little about what they wrote, as long as they wrote something. Newton, however, was a stickler for accuracy and was rather less impressed by the American newspapers. Following one interview with the *Los Angeles Evening Herald*, Newton was furious to read their error-strewn report the next day, and personally called at one of their local offices to complain. Unable to find the relevant reporter, he returned to his tent at the stadium and dashed off a letter to the editor, registering 'amazement and disgust' at the innacuracies in the paper. His list of objections included his being described as a South African and his being in 'fine shape' for the race. He demanded corrections so that the Californian public wouldn't be misled.

Day 1, Sunday March 4, Los Angeles to Puente (17 miles):
The general hoop-la surrounding the build-up to the start hadn't excited Newton at all, and he was pleased when the day arrived so that they could get cracking and head east. But Pyle knew how to entertain a crowd and strung things out as much as possible. Before the 199 men set off he made them process four abreast carrying national flags, to assemble in front of starter Red Grange, the well known American footballer.

Pyle was indefatigable, and rose above all the problems presented him, including the truck with his mobile kitchen getting stuck in the mud, complaints about running shoes being stolen, leaky tents and inadequate bedding. The one man who did seem a little grumpy was Newton (probably due to the tendon injury and head cold which promised to spoil this great adventure for him). But even Newton had to admit that the start of the race, and the public response on day one, was a wonderful and thrilling sight:

'We had no sooner left the Speedway than we were engulfed in an ocean of humanity. Never have I seen the like of it. For the whole [17] miles cars were parked two or more deep on each side of the road, while tens of thousands of people were jammed along the entire route, wildly cheering and waving flags and handkerchiefs. We ran in a narrow lane the whole way, with banks of people on each side.'

Newton was happy to set off with the back markers and came in a modest 24th, knowing that runners in front of him, such as Kolehmainen (first home in 1:38.29), were wasting their energy and would never maintain this sort of pace to New York. The 199 runners were impressed to see their catering and sleeping accommodation erected in a huge city of tents as they arrived in dribs and drabs in Puente. They were not quite so amused by Pyle's adjacent circus, the noise from which kept most awake all night and would be a sore point all the way to Chicago. The circus featured Egyptian belly dancers, Kah-Ko (the smartest dog in the world), a two-headed chicken, a dried-up human corpse and caged reptiles. To add to the runners' discomfort, it started to rain and the tents began to leak badly, but as Newton concluded philosophically: 'Of course, grousing wouldn't help us, so we just had to grin and bear it'.

Day 2, Monday March 5, Puente to Bloomington (34.7 miles):

At daybreak the men were roused, breakfast was ready at 6, and at 7 they were off on stage two. The newspapers were full of stories that up to 76 'bunioneers' had already dropped out of the race after just one day. It only dawned some time later that this figure was incorrect and only arose out of book-keeping errors by Pyle's organisers, for in fact only 199 men started, and not the 275 he had on his official list! As the runners departed Puente, the 15 tents, 250 beds, 500 pillows and 700 blankets were packed on to motor trollies by a 'bull gang' and rushed ahead to the next night's control point. Officials in cars moved up and down the line of runners to provide necessary assistance, while a vehicle shaped like a huge Maxwell House coffee pot took up a position 20 miles along the road to disgorge free hot nourishment to the passing runners. Newton was impressed:

'That famous coffee pot was one of the outstanding comforts of the race, and every competitor who came through has good cause to be grateful to the kindly men who managed it, and who always seemed to be on the spot when most required. I've never enjoyed better coffee.'

It rained incessantly, meaning a procession of bedraggled men, some wearing overcoats, stumbled into Bloomington during the afternoon. Newton again jogged in gently, disregarding the excitable antics of leader Kolehmainen, who again raced home first, seemingly at full tilt. The jingoistic American press seemed delighted by Newton's failure to impose himself thus far, failing to understand the wisdom behind his tactics.

Day 3, Tuesday March 6, Bloomington to Victorville (45.4 miles):

Cool and dry weather greeted this mountainous stage, which suited Newton well, and he moved through the field to take third place and move himself gently up the overall placings. Kolehmainen paid for his earlier pace by sustaining a painful groin muscle injury that would see him quit early the next day. The hills meant a number dropped out and others didn't reach the finish by nightfall. One unofficial runner, dubbed 'Ukulele Jack' and described as 'a musical bum with two dogs' was still going strong and giving great entertainment near the back of the field. His presence didn't please the organisers, who tried to get him kicked off the road, but were told by police he was perfectly entitled to traverse the public highway.

Day 4, Wednesday March 7, Victorville to Barstow (36 miles):

The heat was noticeably increasing now that they were approaching the desert, but it was all meat and drink to Newton, who even with his head cold, came in an untroubled second and moved up to fourth on the overall rankings. Other men were dead on their feet by the end of this stage, some never made it at all, but after a quick bath Newton spent a leisurely couple of hours strolling around downtown Barstow. Many runners went desperately short of fluid in the hot conditions, which was a fault of the organisers, who sent a single car up and down the line of runners to dispense water bottles. But as the gap between leader and back markers was so large, this service took an age to complete, and some men went hours without water.

Day 5, Thursday March 8, Barstow to Mojave Wells (32.5 miles):

Passing lava beds, cactus and other desert features that piqued his interest, Newton strolled to a comfortable stage victory, enjoying the scenery while those behind him groaned and gasped in the searing heat. Not only had he won the stage in relaxed style, he had overcome the hindrance of his cold, his increasingly painful Achilles problem and a nasty touch of sunburn. In Mojave Wells he settled down for his first cigar in

13 days, a quiet celebration of his first day as overall race leader. And he was able to treat his cold symptoms with a welcome 'few drops of the hard stuff', which had been fetched by the generously natured Gavuzzi. The latter explained to author Harry Berry many years later that he had heard Newton complaining about the USA prohibition laws, which he reckoned meant 'a man can't even treat a common cold'. And as it wasn't in Newton's nature to seek out a 'speakeasy' to procure illegal hooch, Gavuzzi volunteered to do the task for him.

Day 6, Friday March 9, Mojave Wells to Bagdad (41.9 miles):

Winning stages was by now a little more important than it had been earlier, for daily prizes were supposed to be on offer, although due to Pyle's procrastinations these would prove elusive. Newton duly won again in the heat, by a huge 42 minutes, extending his overall lead to three hours. But his pleasure was cut short when he realised, for a second successive evening, there was to be no relaxing and cleansing post-run bath. To get a bath, the men would usually have to pay a dollar to a nearby hotel-keeper, but here in tiny Bagdad there were no hotels.

Day 7, Saturday March 10, Bagdad to Danby (31.9 miles):

After a week of running, more than a quarter of the 199 starters had by now already quit. Only 146 men left Bagdad to again face the intense heat. Newton's familiarity with such conditions held him in good stead and he duly won a third successive stage, although even he came home in a state of dehydration, needing to put away three pints of orangeade at the end. He found there was again be no prize money for his efforts, for, as Pyle explained to them, the local community had refused to cough up as anticipated. He assured the men this situation would be addressed on future stages. One runner not concerned about missing money was the German former cyclist George Rehayn, who was fully occupied that night with a sore stomach after grabbing a watering can and guzzling down nearly a pint before realising it was gasolene.

Day 8, Sunday March 11, Danby to Needles (57 miles):

The toughest stage yet meant a 5am start to avoid the worst of the heat. Newton gave another master-class on how steady, even-paced running can beat the elements, as he cruised slowly through the field. Canadian John Cronick ran superbly to beat him by five minutes, Newton complaining about several stops to rid his shoes of grit from the substandard road surface. A soak in a bath (a highly delicate operation due to sunburn), helped restore Newton's good humour. Some men lagging painfully behind were collected at nightfall and allowed to return to that spot the next morning to resume their journey, but this practice would soon stop when Pyle changed the rules meaning everyone had to finish before midnight in the correct place or be disqualified. By now Ukelele Jack had been left behind, arrested for vagrancy when he made an unscheduled stop due to having apparently lost one of his dogs.

Day 9, Monday March 12, Needles to Oatman (20.5 miles):

Today the runners had to trot down to the Colorado River and cross six-by-six on 14 boats, while the race vehicles had to go the long way round, an extra 40 miles. Nearly every boat got stuck on a sandbank in midstream and had to be coaxed and cajoled before the other bank could be reached. The men were given a couple of oranges at this point and warned there would be none of the usual mid-run refreshments as the vehicles would be miles away on a different route. They then had to follow what was described as a 'a villainous, jungle-like track' for miles, during which several got temporarily lost. It seemed little more than a goat track, but was later defended by the organisers as an overgrown stagecoach route. Added to the heat, these difficulties meant stage winner Newton was the only man to cover the 20.5 miles in under five hours. As he trotted into Oatman, gasping for a drink, an enthusiastic town crier bellowed out the news of his arrival to the crowds on the sidewalk. Behind him, the others trickled slowly in, all suffering badly from dehydration.

Day 10, Tuesday March 13, Oatman to Kingman (28.8 miles):

After posting a letter to England, to warn friends and family that they might soon hear news that he was giving up due to his leg injury, Newton trotted admirably to another stage victory – his fifth in the last six days. Coming into Kingman, his overall lead was now nearly seven hours, with American Andy Payne in second. Newton reflected that there were now only about 25 men still running in reasonable fettle, another 20 were weary, worn, sad but otherwise fit; and a further 50 or so were in a really bad way with blisters, sunburn, strained sinews and inflamed tendons. Dozens had by now quit altogether. After the recent heat, the survivors were now about to experience cold air as they climbed to 7,000 feet above sea-level to face sharp frosts at night and snow in patches alongside the road. By now Newton was being referred to by runners and officials as 'the Rhodesian Rambler', a nickname he seemed quite happy with. The question of runner identification saw Pyle come up with the idea of printing off leaflets which listed all the participants, and could be sold to the spectators along the route as 'programmes'. It helped boost income from the various towns, which sometimes fell below what had been anticipated.

Newton's recent dominance of the race was beginning to irritate the American press and public. Initially in awe of his relentless running, they now longed for a more colourful extrovert to grab the lead and the lime-light. As one writer shrewdly put it:

'Beneath the immaculate manners and urbane exterior there was a dogmatic and obdurate streak that had been channeled into [Newton's] running. He was single-minded to a point that reached egotism and the initial enchantment with his superficial English gentleman charm was fading.'

Day 11, Wednesday March 14, Kingman to Peach Springs (51.7 miles):
Today featured a long run to a small desert outpost, but the runners were treated to a cool and windy day. There was still no sign of cash prizes for stage winners, but Newton was rewarded for coming in first again with a hand-made Native American floor-mat, handed over by a local storekeeper. His overall lead over Payne now stretched to nearly eight hours, and he was pleased to see that his new friend from England, Gavuzzi, had moved up to fifth in the rankings. However, the leg injury was not improving and Newton feared a big decision was looming.

Day 12, Thursday March 15, Peach Springs to Seligman (38.3 miles):
Newton came in second at high altitude Seligman, where it felt des-perately cold and nobody was looking forward to camping out of doors. The cheap blankets indeed proved inadequate once nightfall came and the wind got up, and Pyle was forced to lead his runners into a school-room nearby. Squashed tight inside, more than 100 men slept fitfully and the night proved almost as challenging as the previous day's run. Veteran Charlie Hart decided he'd had enough and quit at this point, agreeing to stay with the caravan for the rest of the trip as a judge. Seven-and-a-half hours ahead by now, Newton attended to his bright red right ankle and wondered if he would be the next to go. The ankle was badly sunburned as well as damaged internally, the latter no doubt the result of his favour-ing that leg due the Achilles problem on the other side.

Day 13, Friday March 16, Seligman to Williams (43.9 miles):
Only four miles out of Seligman, the discomfort increased and Newton knew the time was close when he would have to call it a day. It didn't feel like a disaster as he'd foreseen the problem from early on, but it was still a blow to his pride. Nobody seemed in a hurry today, and Newton was able to win the stage despite his sore legs, building his lead over Payne to 8hrs 25mins. Coming up the steep incline into Williams, Newton felt on the verge of collapse and reckoned the only way to fin-ish was by 'driving myself into a sprint stride to keep going'. After a bath and consultation with Dr Hugo Quist, in charge of medical matters, it was decided nothing could be done for the right ankle, for the severe sun-burn made it impossible to massage or manipulate it. Quist thought it

miraculous Newton had got this far and couldn't believe he intended to start again the following morning. One writer noted: 'This was the day that Newton demonstrated just what a magnificently stubborn old goat he had become.' In the evening a number of runners treated themselves to a meal at a restaurant, despairing at Pyle's catering arrangements which had been reduced to a shambles after a dispute with the chef.

Day 14, Saturday March 17, Williams to Flagstaff (36.2 miles):

Waking to find four inches of snow had covered the region, the runners set off on another tough day in the hills. Newton came in a subdued fourth, his right ankle greatly swollen and the left one 'beginning to peter out'. He wrote that 'by now both ankles were so swollen that the ends of my legs were mere shapeless chunks' but pointed out that generally he felt quite fit and well and the daily grind was not proving too much for his overall fitness at all. He gamely decided to make an attempt at the next day's journey.

Day 15, Sunday March 18, Flagstaff to Two Gun Camp (35.8 miles):

Getting out of bed was another ordeal for Newton with his ankles stiff and swollen and needing much cajoling to move into action. Problems were also piling up for the race organisation, with Pyle having sacked his chef, only to find the replacement was incompetent. Eventually Pyle had to start issuing runners with meal tickets for local restaurants, but as they were worth a measly $1.50 a day, they barely covered essentials, let alone the fuel needed for distance running. Once he got moving, Newton found he was able to jog along at a decent pace and came in third, encouraging enough to consider setting off again the next day, but he knew deep down he was merely postponing the inevitable.

Day 16, Monday March 19, Two Gun Camp to Winslow (24.1 miles):

Another agonizing hobble to the start-line and off went Newton again, even finding himself passing some of the others. Then, after about four miles, suddenly and completely out of the blue, his race was over. He recalled: 'Quite suddenly the pain in my right ankle became acute and, knowing what was bound to occur if I attempted to carry on for the rest of the day, I sat down on the running-board of a stationary car and waited until Mr. Pyle's private coach came along. A quarter-of-an-hour later I climbed aboard and notified them that I was through.'

After 500 miles or so, and with a lead approaching ten hours, the star of the show was finished. Putting on his overcoat, he had a long discussion with Pyle and it was decided he would spend the next few stages travelling prone in Pyle's luxury motor caravan to allow his battered legs to recover, and after that could begin duties as the race's 'Technical Advisor'.

And so, for the next six days, Newton stretched out on the top deck of the camper van, well wrapped up in blankets, watching his erstwhile rivals making their way through Winslow, Holbrook, the Painted Desert, Lupton, Gallup and Thoreau.

Newton reflected sadly on his fate, and ruefully on how, despite the huge lead he'd built up over 15 full days of running, all he'd won was the colourful mat handed over by the trader in Peach Springs. Newton had run 479.6 miles during the 15 completed stages, in a time of 74 hours and 21 minutes, and at the point of quitting led the race by more than nine hours.

However, having the unaccustomed comforts of Pyle's personal vehicle at his disposal soon eased his gloom. Having cost more than $25,000 to build, the 12-ton air-conditioned purpose-built camper was more comfortable than most of the runners' homes. Its floor was carpeted to match plush, blue mohair upholstery and interior panelling, which was bordered with hand-finished mahogany. It had a fold-up table, a writing desk, a phonograph and radio, three reclining chairs and a double Pullman-style seat, which could sleep two. There was hot and cold running water, a bathroom with shower, kitchen with an electric refrigerator, a sink, gas stove and water heater. One reporter called it 'the most pretentious land yacht ever built,' and it was certainly the type of rich man's plaything rarely seen by the likes of hard-up Newton.

Once his legs had recovered, Newton threw his energy into his new role. He even started running alongside the men, dispensing advice and help along the way: 'I toddled along some seven miles, after which I sat down by the side of the road until the coach came along and picked me up. As this sort of thing seemed to suit both the competitors and myself I decided to continue with it.'

The huge convoy rumbled on, ploughing through a severe sandstorm at one point and then diverting away from Albuquerque after Pyle had a row with the city mayor. Every kind of weather was thrown at them, but on they travelled, thousands of fascinated Americans emerging from the towns to watch the show go by. Newton kept a fatherly eye on the men struggling at the rear of the field. On more than one occasion he spent days with particular individuals, coaxing them into changing their stride or gait so that they might move along a little more comfortably. When his advice worked and their pain lessened, they were often reduced to tears of gratitude.

By the time the derby reached eastern New Mexico, only 96 of the original 199 starters remained, including three of the five African American starters – Eddie Gardner of Seattle, Sammy Robinson of

Atlantic City, New Jersey, and Toby Joseph Cotton, Junior of Los Angeles – and Afro-Canadian Phillip Granville, of Hamilton, Ontario.

By the time they reached Texas, the handful of black runners participating faced a new problem, for in this region the Ku Klux Klan dominated the state legislature and the city governments of Dallas, Forth Worth and El Paso. Eddie Gardner of Seattle, Toby Cotton of Los Angeles and Phillip Granville from Canada were reportedly forced out of the communal sleeping tents into a special 'colored only tent', and were allegedly bombarded with death threats and racial slurs as they slogged their way across the difficult roads of the Texas Panhandle. In the town of McLean, an angry mob was said to have surrounded Gardner's trainer's car, and threatened to burn it, claiming that blacks had no business racing against whites. In Western Oklahoma, a farmer trained a shotgun on Gardner's back, and rode behind him for an entire day, daring him to pass a white man.

As the days went by Pyle began to fret about the exact time of arrival in New York, and rumours began circulating that from Chicago onwards he would increase the daily mileage of the suffering runners, in order to suit a new finishing schedule. As the official working closest with many of the runners, Newton found himself fending off many a question and complaint, even though he strongly advised the management against increasing the length of the daily runs. He reckoned they were in severe danger of running men into the ground and arriving in New York with only a tiny fraction of the field still standing.

Pyle made his changes anyway, and on one of the excruciatingly long stages (64.7 miles), between Wauseon and Fremont in Ohio, England's Peter Gavuzzi was forced to drop out, plagued by severe pain from a dental problem that had left him unable to eat solid food. Like Newton, he found himself having to quit while in the lead, and there were only about 15 of the 84 days to go. Gavuzzi was found sitting glumly in a roadside ditch, close to tears, and begging for a cigarette. His crisis handed the lead to the tough young Oklahoman Andy Payne, who seized the opportunity with relish.

As the end of May approached, thanks in no small part to the care and attention from Newton, there were 55 men still standing. He was proud of them, and commented later: 'I mentally lift my hat off to them every time I think of them! Those five [high mileage] days had killed the race so far as racing went: there wasn't a decently fit man left; even the best of them had to do a considerable amount of walking in order to retain a trifle for the finish, for they were keen on putting up as decent a show as possible when they got to New York.'

On Saturday 26th May, the final 26 miles of the race were run on the little track at Madison Square Garden in New York and the 3,422-mile spectacular was declared over. Twenty-year-old farmer's son Payne eventually collected the winner's cheque for $25,000, his reward for more than 573 hours of running in the 84 days. In all the mayhem, Ukulele Jake suddenly reappeared, complete with his two dogs. There was a definite atmosphere of anti-climax afterwards, many of the runners admitting they were finding it both mentally and physically difficult to adapt to the idea their daily grind was over. Many were unwilling or unhappy over the prospect of having to return to their former routines back at home. It was as if their purpose in life had been taken away. Some of them were semi-hobo in lifestyle anyway, and were content to simply hang around in New York. Newton was one who was definitely staying put for the near future, although he was fortunate in being able to afford decent accommodation for himself, as most of the others were homeless or in cheap hostels. Newton was greatly touched when some of the surviving runners clubbed together and presented him with a special cup as a token of their thanks for his advice and support.

Various issues over unpaid prize money and scheduling had plagued the race, but when the dust had settled it was declared a success, having attracted major public interest throughout and countless column inches in the press. After returning their deposits to the runners who finished, promoter Pyle was left broke, but vowed to repeat the race in a year's time, when it would head across the States in the reverse direction. He vowed to make changes to the event, to ensure there would be no repeat of the heavy losses next time.

Newton declared he would be in for a second year, convinced if he could avoid serious injury there would be nobody to stop him winning comfortably. Newton even went so far as to publicly defend Pyle, who had a busy time in the wake of the race, settling unpaid bills and dealing with various complainants. Having experienced the event from both sides of the fence, Newton felt a certain sympathy for the much-maligned promoter, whose main problem had been the unwillingness of the various Chambers of Trade en route to pay for the race's visit to their town. Pyle had counted on them being happy to cough up when they saw the business being generated in their locality, but he had misjudged this badly.

Having had a real education in the ways of professional running, and learned much about the game from the likes of Hugo Quist and Pyle, Newton decided to stay in North America indefinitely with the other foreign 'bunioneers' and look for more distance events. The Bunion Derby had created something of a renaissance in ultra-running over here, and it was known that other sporting promoters like Tex Rickard wanted to jump on the bandwagon. Newton had celebrated his 45th birthday during the latter stages of the run, but felt his ageing limbs were generally standing up well to the rigours of long-distance work, and with his achilles problem healing, felt he had plenty more to offer.

Chapter 13

Claustrophobia and Frost-bite

Americans are nothing if not opportunistic, and immediately the Bunion Derby ended, attempts were made to cash in on the wave of interest it had created. Most of the battle-weary and heroic performers were still available in New York, so the promoters had to act fast. Tex Rickard led the way by putting up several thousand dollars of prize money for a two-man 26-hour relay race which would be contested on the indoor track at Madison Square Garden just a few days later.

It sounded intriguing, but like the Bunion Derby itself, would prove a financial disaster. The contest began at 9pm on the evening of Saturday, 2nd June, and saw the men circle the track in relays, with one team member relieving the other whenever he wanted to do so. Those not running rested in two rows of cots nearby. A band played in three-minute spurts throughout, but after a few hours of this, spectators became bored and drifted off. The event, devoid of atmosphere, finally drew to a close at 11pm the next day, finishing in near silence and witnessed by just a sprinkling of yawning spectators. The runners had done their bit, with 16 of the 20 two-man teams bravely lasting the distance, despite the mind-numbing monotony of having to circle the tiny track for hours on end. The Canadian duo of Philip Granville and Frank Van Flue were declared winners of the $1,000 first prize after they completed 183 miles and six laps between them when the signal sounded to stop. Newton and Gavuzzi were second (182 miles, 3 laps), a long way ahead of the rest of the field, and shared a very welcome $750.

Fewer than 150 people paid to witness the finishing stages and no wonder, for the only real excitement on offer had been the sudden collapse into unconsciousness of Italian runner Joe Conto. After he was carried away, a physician declared poor Conto had over-indulged and not rested adequately since the end of the Bunion Derby. He was certainly not the only one. The 26-hour format of the race had tested the runners' resolve to the full, but had proved unattractive as a spectacle, and the meagre gate money, combined with the expensive rental costs of the building, caused another financial flop.

But promoter Rickard was undaunted, and felt there was still an opportunity to revive the glory years of 1910 and 1911 when the MSG and other venues in the area cashed in on 'marathon mania' and pulled in huge crowds to watch the world's top runners – Alf Shrubb, Dorando

Pietri, Tom Longboat, Henri St Yves et al — competing for big bucks. Newton had already indicated his willingness to stick around, despite a hatred of running indoors, and all Rickard needed to do was recruit a handful of other big names. Before long he had persuaded El Ouafi, the Algerian winner of the recent 1928 Olympic marathon in Amsterdam, to turn professional and come and race in New York. All-American hero Joie Ray and another Olympian, Hannes Kolehmainen, soon signed up too, and a date was set for a 26.2 mile marathon showdown — Sunday 21st October 1928.

Newton, now 45-years-old and clearly best suited to 50 or 100-milers, didn't have the basic speed of an El Ouafi or a Ray, but knew that strange things can happen in distance events, and felt sure his experience would see him get among the prizes. Twenty-eight-year-old El Ouafi, born in Bisra, Algeria, would be a tough opponent, a strict vegetarian weighing around 114lbs, who was said to have learned to run by racing camels in the desert. He was a former dispatch rider with the French Army, and drank only mineral water and the odd root beer.

Meanwhile, the stocky 36-year-old Joie Ray, known as 'the Kankakee Flier' from just south of Chicago, was a former miler who came a surprise third in the most recent Boston Marathon, having only turned to distance running in the twilight of his career. Ray welcomed turning professional as it meant he could quit his taxi driving. Ray's presence in the race was crucial, for he would carry partisan local support, and his gutsy style usually won over neutrals, too. He was well known for cheekily running close behind the great Paavo Nurmi and mocking his running style, which involved the frequent checking of a watch. In typically cavalier style, Ray prepared for the MSG marathon by taking part in a dance marathon which lasted 1,730 hours!

Newton spent many pleasant summer days in 1928 training for the race up in the Catskill Mountains, away from the bustle and grime of New York City. During this period he accepted a further invitation, this from Hugo Quist, to compete in another marathon later in the year. This would again feature El Ouafi and Ray, this time in Boston. It would be another wretched and claustrophobic indoor affair, but it represented a rare chance to significantly boost his income and Newton felt obliged to sign up. Finding himself running for money in the USA was a situation he'd never envisaged until recently, although globe-trotting and free enterprise had become a trademark of the five Newton brothers. By 1928 Arthur, Cyril, Harry, Ambrose and Bernard were spread far and wide around the globe, all working in different fields. Their sisters were keeping their end up in England, with Ursula, an accomplished pianist, having just had a book published in London and New York. Called simply *Music*, it offered an acclaimed historical perspective on the evolution of music. Ursula was well known in her field, having earlier studied in Berlin with the celebrated Italian composer, pianist and conductor Ferruccio Busoni.

Newton's first professional marathon would be run on a specially laid tan-bark track in Madison Square Garden and, just as Tex Rickard had hoped, it pulled in a bumper crowd of 13,000. They cheered wildly to the smoky rafters as El Ouafi ('a bushy-haired and spindly-legged running machine') set a new world indoor best of 2:44.55, leaving eight opponents in his wake. He beat the game Joie Ray by more than two of the tiny 176-yard laps, with the home favourite fading in the last three miles despite huge crowd support. Newton trundled along quietly into third place (and a prize of $750) and was rather rudely described in the press as 'shambling gaited' for his trouble. Of the rest, only Olympic silver-medallist Juri Lossman of Estonia and Sam Richman of New York crossed the finish line. Newton maintained a steady pace throughout and was never higher than third. His finish time was not published, but is thought to have been around 2:54, for he was a mile behind Ray (2:47) by the end.

Afterwards a big clear-up operation went into swing in the MSG, in preparation for the arrival of Herbert Hoover, the Republican candidate, who was booked in for the following day to give his last speech in the run-up to the forthcoming US Presidential elections.

Barely a month later, feeling a shade unhappy at having to leave the invigorating Catskills for the train journey to urban Boston, Newton mulled over his chances and cursed the fact that he was having to run again on a small indoor track. He recalled:

'This was quite the worst [aspect] of the whole business, for having done all my work on open roads, the continual circling of a small indoor track made me giddy and actually physically sick. Still, you never know. I could at any rate try to put up a decent show and, if my luck were very much in, for I was every bit as well trained as either of my two rivals, might even win.'

The race was talked up in typical American style, thousands buying up tickets to attend at the newly-created New Boston Garden complex, recently built as Boston's answer to the MSG in New York. Promoted as the 'Boston Professional Marathon' (to distinguish it from the popular Boston AA road event, established since 1897) it was, said venue manager Sheldon Fairbanks, to be run on a specially constructed cinder track and a crowd of 17,000 was anticipated. The Boston papers revealed Newton's participation just four days before the race, and those who wanted to check his form were told to go see him training beforehand in the Hub Parkway area. The favourite, El Ouafi, arrived in the city three days beforehand and based himself at a local gym, still nursing battered pride after defeats by Joie Ray in a couple of races below the marathon distance.

Wearing race number 3 and his familiar 'Rhodesia & Natal' shirt, Newton looked the tallest of the seven starters as they lined up for the photographers. He was slightly taken aback to find all were happy to set off at a modest pace and for two or three miles the pace was so slow, even Newton had to brake a little to avoid becoming exposed at the front. He began to worry that the crowd would start jeering at the funereal pace, for it appeared the runners were not even trying. Eventually, for probably the only time in his career, he decided this waiting game and tactical nonsense should be dispensed with, and he speeded up and pulled away at the front of the pack. Before long, El Ouafi and Ray had caught and passed him and he settled into third place, worrying more about the giddiness he experienced in such surroundings than his opponents. He wrote later:

'I felt the usual symptoms of giddiness and nausea, which always spoilt my running on a small track, slowly coming on. To fend it off as far as possible I reduced the pace. Not so the other two; having disposed of me they held on to their ten miles an hour and after a mile or two both of them lapped me. The further I went the worse I got, and I lost a couple more laps to both of them during the next half-hour. I still had plenty in hand, but was so groggy that I daren't attempt to go any faster.'

While Newton suffered back in third place, the ebullient Ray went on to smash the recognised indoor record to win in a time announced as 2:34.54, beating the favourite El Ouafi by two laps. It was a popular victory. Newton came home around ten laps down on the Algerian, his time not widely published, but based on his position behind the leaders would have been around the 2:45 mark. However, all the clockings at this race would become shrouded in doubt, with the validity of Ray's sensational record questioned. When quizzed by the press, official starter Arthur Duffey promised that the timekeepers and checkers had all been experienced men and he denied there had been errors, but many were unconvinced.

With little else on the horizon to boost his earnings, Newton decided to head back to England for the Christmas holidays of 1928, but planned to return to New York as long as the second 'Bunion Derby' was confirmed as going ahead. He arrived in London during December on the ship *SS American Banker*, again giving his sister Ursula's Paignton address as his destination, although he would spend much of this trip based in Southampton, a guest of Peter Gavuzzi. The latter had returned to England some weeks earlier, and had spent most of September and October running the 1,087 miles from John O'Groats to Land's End, via his home town of Southampton, a task that took him 30 days and which he claimed as a new record. Gavuzzi was by now fully captivated by the idea of giving up his work as a peripatetic chef so that he could attempt to earn a living from running. He was desperately looking around for challenges in Britain, and had a return to New York later on at the back of his mind.

Newton's arrival in December was publicised by journalist Joe Binks, and he was soon invited to make his British debut as a pro by racing Gavuzzi from Glasgow to Edinburgh on New Year's day, as part of the annual Powderhall carnival celebrations. The pair would race on the road between the two cities and finish with several laps of the famous Powderhall track to make a total of 50 miles covered. Promoter Fred Lumley offered a £100 first prize and boldly advertised his race as the '50-mile World Championship', stretching the truth by claiming that the English-born pair were representing 'South Africa and Italy' in his posters and flyers. Newton, who liked to tell people he represented 'Rhodesia and Natal', would not have been impressed. He felt more comfortable preparing for a 50-miler, following his recent struggles in claustrophobic shorter races. He even welcomed the bitterly cold weather in Scotland – anything rather than smoky indoor tracks!

Newton and Gavuzzi – a rather oddly matched couple, both physically and in their backgrounds – travelled from London to Edinburgh by train with Binks, and were installed free of charge at the city's Imperial Hotel. For Gavuzzi, this was a particular treat, for his working life usually involved hard labour in the sweltering kitchens of such establishments. He wasn't used to being an honoured guest upstairs, and it felt good. Newton and Gavuzzi agreed between them that whoever won the race would pocket £60 with the runner-up taking the remaining £40. They were bussed across to Glasgow and spent New Year's Eve in another hotel, two sassenachs preparing to entertain the Scottish public and going easy on toasting in the new year.

They awoke to find severe snowy conditions awaited them, the roads frozen and dangerous. An hour before the race Newton downed a bowl of porridge and a plate of cold mutton, while Gavuzzi chose porridge followed by scrambled eggs, and both rounded this off with tea and toast. There was no point in risking a shortage of proper nourishment in such conditions! They chose warm running kit and set off at 9am from the Glasgow Pavilion, finding conditions underfoot appallingly slippery and with a bitterly cold east wind making things even worse. Most of the roads were like sheets of glass and there was deeper snow awaiting them once they left the Glasgow hinterland.

After four hours of difficult but steady progress, Gavuzzi stopped and had a nip of port and whisky, complaining of severe stitch. Perhaps it was the copious amounts of porridge he'd downed at the hotel. Newton's first stop was at the town of Broxburn (33.5 miles), troubled by a minor leg injury, and at this point the recently fortified Gavuzzi coasted past him. But then, out of sight of Newton, and without warning, Gavuzzi suddenly jerked to a halt with cramp. A salt drink was sought and this kept him going with difficulty, but soon afterwards cramp seized his right calf, and he called out for tea, coming to another standstill. Before long he took the decision to quit, even though he was less than five miles from Powderhall. Newton passed him and his time on reaching the grounds was said to be the best on record, despite the dreadful conditions. There was still a distance to be covered on the track, but Newton was under no pressure and two laps from the finish he called out to Binks to fetch his pipe. This was lit and jammed into his mouth and he began to feel better instantly, finishing the race puffing away keenly, the crowd vastly amused by this eccentric Englishman. His last 4.5 miles were all on the frost-bound track while another 10-mile race was in progress, Newton courteously allowing them to pass on the inside as he puffed away and finished his own business.

He was declared winner in 6:39:50, which constituted a course record that would stand for years. In the wake of his huge hotel breakfast he had taken no solids en route (mindful of the horrors of the 100-mile run a year earlier) and the crowd seemed amazed at his strength and pluck. The weather was so bad that the White City Carnival, due to follow the races, had to be called off. Newton revealed that it hadn't been as easy as he'd made it look:

'We hadn't allowed sufficiently for the intense cold and, worse still, the abominable surface. Every atom of the road was a criss-crossed maze of ruts in hardened snow and ice, and the trouble of trying to maintain balance added greatly to the exertion required. [But] a thaw had been at work on the Edinburgh side for some hours, for the further we went the dirtier it became underfoot, and at 30 miles we were running in pools and slush.'

In the days after their Caledonian venture, Newton and Gavuzzi pondered their prospects for 1929 and discussed the likelihood of a second Bunion Derby taking place. Meanwhile, a challenge arrived from Welsh runner R E Cole, who proposed the three of them do battle at 26.2 miles on the Moor Park track in Hereford, with the winner claiming the title of British Professional Marathon Champion. Cole reckoned he was the fastest British pro at the distance, but to claim the title he needed to beat Newton, who on paper had a better time to his name. There was no wager or prize money, it would simply be a case of dividing up the gate money proceeds. In the absence of other more lucrative challenges, Newton and Gavuzzi agreed to take part.

The date was set for Saturday, 16th February 1929 and the pair travelled to Hereford from Gavuzzi's Southampton base by coach, stopping off at Bath and Bristol en route, where they got off to stretch their legs and have a run, despite the nasty wintry weather. The further they travelled the worse the weather became (they noticed the River Wye had frozen solid) and Newton spotted a thermometer than indicated it was only 10 degrees Fahrenheit. They arrived at Hereford to find a sloping 440-yard track at Moor Park awaiting them, with the conditions underfoot in a bad way. Not surprisingly, given the weather, barely 50 people had turned up to see the contest. It all looked like a big mistake, but the arrangements had been made and they had to go through with it.

Newton pulled on two woolly sweaters and gloves, cursing the weather and the fact that no fewer than 105 laps of this appalling track had to be covered. He thought back longingly to those long, sun-drenched days of running free through Natal. Cole seemed far more motivated than his opponents and he set off enthusiastically, although allowing the lead to be shared in the early stages. Said Newton:

'The surface was absolutely rotten, simply great blobs of frozen and slippery snow, and we were running of course in gym shoes; there wasn't an atom of decent going anywhere, and a lot of our energy was wasted in overcoming slips and slides.'

Gavuzzi quit at around 15 miles of this rather farcical contest, while Cole, wearing spiked shoes as opposed to Newton's canvas tennis shoes, opened up a lead that he wouldn't relinquish. He came home relatively untroubled in 2:48.45, three minutes and five seconds ahead of Newton, who immediately grabbed a cigar and set off indoors to warm up.

Newton and Gavuzzi needed cheering up after the events at Hereford, and some good news duly arrived in the shape of a cable from C C Pyle in New York, confirming that a second trans-American Bunion Derby would definitely be going ahead, and that they should make their way across the Atlantic Ocean right away. The race would start at the end of March, meaning the pair 'were sent scurrying for London to get passports put in order and fix up a passage,' according to Newton.

In an attempt to avoid the financial losses of the previous year, Pyle made different arrangements for his 1929 race, recruiting a more streamlined and manageable field of runners, imposing a hefty increase in the entry fee and stipulating that competitors must this time organise their own food, board and medical care throughout the event. He would also by-pass much of Route 66 and the towns that had spurned him in 1928, and take the procession through places 'more susceptible to the spirit of uplift.' Another change would be dispensing with the seedy sideshows and adding a quality vaudeville act comprising '21 young ladies of gentle breeding and excellent social standing'. The $300 entry fee and the need to pay for one's own food and lodgings stunned the potential entrants, but they knew it would certainly weed out the no-hopers from the men who were serious about winning. This would be a very different Bunion Derby, and Newton and Gavuzzi immediately put their heads together to discuss how to tackle the situation.

Both remained desperately keen to take part, despite the level of personal investment that would now be needed, and Newton proposed a brand new approach. He suggested Gavuzzi discontinue his search for personal sponsorship, and said they should pool their resources right away and then find a 'Man Friday' to drive a personal support vehicle across the States with them. This vehicle would be fixed up to carry cooking equipment and food, and would also be big enough to allow the three of them to sleep inside in reasonable comfort. The man they chose to drive them from New York to Los Angeles was retired athlete George Barren from Southampton, an old hand who understood running, had a degree of expertise in mechanical matters and was also a competent cook. Barren was delighted to join them for he had relatives in Los Angeles he could visit once the race was over. With this 'road manager' appointed and their tickets purchased, the problem of finding a suitable vehicle could be left until they arrived in New York in March.

Newton and Gavuzzi had both failed to complete the race in 1928, so there was an element of unfinished business influencing their determined outlook, in addition to the pecuniary angle. Newton's Achilles problem had cleared up and Gavuzzi's teeth were in better shape now, and they felt stronger and wiser after the 1928 race. Both could consider themselves among the finest ultra-distance men in the world, so they felt obliged to go for the big prize again. For all its faults and hazards, this was the biggest, brashest, greatest running competition ever devised – and as men with a spirit of adventure and no pressing obligations to tie them down, they had no good reason to resist the pull of the Bunion Derby.

Chapter 14

Run Over by a Cleric

The 54 passengers on the SS *American Trader*, sailing from London to New York in early March of 1929, were a rare and lively bunch. Many of them were in show business in one way or another, and one large group comprised members of a dance troupe. Their extrovert antics, added to Newton and Gavuzzi's daily habit of running around the deck as the sun came up, must have baffled the less gregarious travellers. On the passenger manifest, Gavuzzi had taken great delight in registering as a 'professional runner', whereas Newton steadfastly preferred to describe himself simply 'farmer'.

The ship docked around ten days before the scheduled start of the second Trans-Continental 'Bunion Derby' and immediately Newton and Gavuzzi began searching for a support vehicle they could sleep and eat in. A number of fellow runners did the same thing, anxious to be self-sufficient and not suffer the discomforts of 1928.

After visiting several sales lots, Newton and Gavuzzi found exactly what they were looking for – a one-ton Chevrolet for manager George Barren to drive – and set about equipping it for the long trek ahead. Two Simmons beds were installed in the back for the two runners, plus a refrigerator, portable stove and shelving and a collapsible bed for Barrett. And, at Newton's insistence, a wind-up gramophone and a couple of dozen classical 78s were thrown in for good measure. After a night successfully testing the vehicle's facilities, Barren dropped the two runners in New York City and drove on to Elizabeth, the race's first overnight stop place.

Following the financial troubles of 1928, it was quite a surprise that Pyle was able to stage another Bunion Derby at all, but news that it would definitely go ahead brought out many of the previous year's heroes again. Andy Payne chose not to defend his title, but came along to enjoy the ride. Part of his duties as assistant director of the race would be to entertain the crowds with rope tricks, taught him by movie star Will Rogers, who was the celebrity starter of the race.

Day 1, Sunday 31st March, New York to Elizabeth (25.1 miles)

Rogers and footballer Steve Owen fired starting pistols and the noisy procession of 69 runners got underway under a warm sun from Columbus Circle. An estimated 50,000 watched the scene and, in the excitement, inevitably a number of runners streaked off like sprinters, but the old hands stayed well back. Newton was one of them, and would finished the stage in an untroubled 17th hardly breaking sweat.

Day 2, Monday 1st April, Elizabeth to Trenton (46.4 miles)

Newton was delighted at the work of Barren ('He was quite an admirable Crichton'), who dutifully rose early to provide scrambled eggs for breakfast and sent his charges on their way, refreshed and nourished. Newton was far happier being looked after like this compared to the communal inconveniences of last year. There were frequent light showers today, followed by a rousing thunderstorm and a lot more rain in the evening, but by then Newton had safely arrived in Trenton in 6:47.30. Overall he was now handily placed just outside the top ten, Gavuzzi about an hour or so down.

Day 3, Tuesday 2nd April, Trenton to Frankford (29.3 miles)

A headwind and heavy traffic added to the runners' problems today as they headed into Philadelphia, but at least the road surface was good and true. Newton and Gavuzzi both ignored the hot pace being set at the head of the field, knowing their time would come later when the headstrong speed merchants began to fade. Newton came in a solid tenth in 4:14.05.

Day 4, Wednesday 3rd April, Frankford to Wilmington (37.5 miles)

Leaving Philadelphia's urban sprawl seemed to take hours and irritated Newton, but he was nowhere near as frustrated as Gavuzzi, who led for quite a distance before taking a wrong turning due to a badly placed direction post. The official responsible was later sacked. Gavuzzi made up the ground eventually and came home joint-first, which pushed him up in the overall rankings to within a few places of Newton, who was by now sixth.

Day 5, Thursday 4th April, Wilmington to Havre de Grace (37 miles)

It was out of the suburbs and into the countryside today, to Newton's great relief, and even having to run through a heavy storm failed to curtail his enjoyment of the sights. He gazed around like a tourist as he passed farms, bridges and other landmarks of interest. Gavuzzi eased passed him in the overall placings, as the experienced runners began making their mark.

Day 6, Friday 5th April, Havre de Grace to Baltimore (44 miles)

A massive thunderstorm saw many of runners don raincoats, others wearing wool, while some unwisely piled on several layers of cotton shirts, which simply absorbed the rain and weighed them down. But the road surfaces felt better than the early days of the 1928 race, and they all knew that a warm bath awaited them in a Baltimore hotel that evening. Newton and Gavuzzi coped easily with the inclement weather, and also eschewed the post-race socialising, continuing their habit of parking their vehicle well outside the downtown area to guarantee a quiet night.

Day 7, Saturday 6th April, Baltimore to Frederick (45.6 miles)

A big city-centre crowd cheered the field away after the referee sounded his whistle, although Newton and Gavuzzi caused confusion by arriving at the start several minutes late and had to give chase alone. It gave them the chance to see the struggling 'also-rans' who brought up the rear. This area was mostly populated by the men carrying injuries or stiffened joints, who were doggedly refusing to give in so early. Newton recalled: 'When we caught up the rearguard we were nearly convulsed with the antics of a couple of the worst cases, and had a passing joke with them as we went on. One or two of them were extremely stiff from over-speeding during the first few days, and these unfortunates were no less than astonishingly comic in their amazing contortions to start running, so much so that they were highly amused at each other. It was a pretty tough business for them, and it says something for their stamina and determination that so many of them held out until they had recovered.' Gavuzzi strode through the field to win the stage by 13 minutes, moving up to third overall. Newton continued to hang back, but was still in contention. Many runners finished feeling light-headed and giddy due to the heat, and sunburn was rife.

Day 8, Sunday 7th April, Frederick to Hancock (54 miles)

Another hot, high-mileage day that suited Newton's talents, and he came in third, his time of nearly nine hours illustrating the toughness of the conditions. Manager George Barren had a bucket of water slung on to the outside of their van with a large sponge floating in it and Newton and Gavuzzi were able to douse themselves regularly. At Hagerstown, halfway through the day's journey, they even dived out of the scorching sun into a restaurant to enjoy a lunch of fruit salad and ice cream. Such a stop was rare, for Newton's normal policy was to have a major breakfast and stick mainly to fluids during the day: 'Except for the big meal each night it was sugar that sustained practically every one of us; sugar and a liquid to dissolve it in lemonade or tea or, in a few cases, wine,' he said.

Day 9, Monday 8th April, Hancock to Cumberland (39 miles)

Newton is again in his element as they hit a hilly district, and he comes home an excellent second, nearly half-an-hour ahead of Gavuzzi, a man half his age. It takes him to fourth on the overall list, and by now it is clear the big hitters are starting to dominate. Several of the novices have already quit, and others are finding the going tougher than expected. Dr. Arnie Souminen of Detroit was one of those brought to a grinding halt by the hills, and he dropped out altogether, cursing insufficient training.

Day 10, Tuesday 9th April, Cumberland to Uniontown (52.8 miles)

A long, hilly journey over the Allegheny Mountains, one of the ascents climbing to 4,000 feet and dropping severely the other side. Newton was one of several complaining of stomach trouble, and he found himself forced to walk for long stretches. He said: 'One of the symptoms was that food of any sort was distasteful, and you get remarkably weak if you try to average over 40 miles a day with half or no nourishment. If others could stick it, so could I. When I found that considerable walking had to be indulged in I knew that things were bad indeed. It had its compensations, for I met many of the men on the road whom I had hardly ever seen. I had [previously] always been fairly well up towards the front and they at the other end. Walking! This was new to me in a racing event and I didn't like it.'

Barren and the support vehicle stayed ahead to be near Gavuzzi, and Newton was helped by others, including Dwight Houfstater's manager, who passed him soup. To add to Newton's woes, he developed bad blisters and had to cut away part of his shoes to prevent further chafing. The result of all this was a clocking of over 15 hours for the 52 miles, a time that dropped him to sixth overall, well behind Gavuzzi, who was now imposing himself on the race leaders.

Day 11, Wednesday 10th April, Uniontown to Waynesburg (34 miles)

An easier day with fewer hills, but continuous light rain, and Newton found he was still troubled by his stomach. In earlier years, when running the Comrades marathons, he would never have dared slowing to a walk for a mere trifle like a stomach upset, but had quickly learned that in an epic like the Bunion Derby it was wiser to be more circumspect, and allow problems to subside before they became chronic.

Day 12, Thursday 11th April, Waynesburg to Wheeling (52 miles)

A tough day involving unexpected long stretches of muddy terrain, made worse by recent rains. The vehicles had to detour, which meant runners went without their usual comforts during this long day's work. Gavuzzi brushed this off to win in just over eight hours (now second overall), but Newton struggled badly again and came home outside the top ten, in 12 hours.

As per usual, they didn't bother to view the nightly vaudeville show at the control points, which, sadly for Pyle, was often ignored by the public too. The great 'Follies' show was proving a regular washout. On one occasion the show was halted when the roof of the tent blew off, meaning another night's meagre takings went west.

Day 13, Friday 12th April, Wheeling to Cambridge (53 miles)

The more Newton struggled, the better Gavuzzi seemed to get during these tough sections. Today saw the latter chalk up one of five successive stage victories, on hilly, bricked roads in downpours of rain and sleet. Very few men managed the 53 miles in less than ten hours and many reached the check point only minutes before the midnight cut-off. The temptation to cheat on such difficult stages was strong for some of them, and after the Dane Niels P Nielsen succumbed and grabbed a lift on a truck, he was spotted and thrown out of the race.

Day 14, Saturday 13th April, Cambridge to Zanesville (25 miles)

More rain but fewer miles today, and the entire field seemed to obey an unspoken agreement to take things fairly easy while they had the chance. Gavuzzi won comfortably to take the overall race lead for the first time. The road surface had by now changed from smooth tarmac to rough brick, a far harder surface to run on, and many feet were suffering. The Italian Guisto Umek, however, was simply glad to be still among the contenders, having been struck a glancing blow by a drunken driver and lucky not be in hospital.

Day 15, Sunday 14th April, Zanesville to Columbus (54.8 miles)

As it was a Sunday, the citizens of Columbus came out in force to welcome the bedraggled procession and the roads became badly congested. Newton allowed manger Barren to devote himself exclusively to race leader Gavuzzi's needs, assuring him he need only worry about Newton when the little man had finished each day. This ploy helped Gavuzzi to come in joint-first with his closest challenger, Eddie Gardner from Seattle. Once Gavuzzi was safely in, Barren would then motor back down the field to find Newton and tend to him.

Day 16, Monday 15th April, Columbus to Springfield (43.4 miles)

The rains vanished today, but a cold northerly wind proved troublesome and the road surfaces were wet and difficult. It was not easy remaining cheerful but Newton, who was in tenth place overall, took consolation in the excellent progress of his partner, who won a fifth successive stage. One man who didn't get away from Columbus was promoter Pyle, who was having a little local difficulty after being served writs in connection with unpaid vehicle hire fees.

Day 17, Tuesday 16th April, Springfield to Richmond (63 miles)

Two great man-made dams had to be crossed by concrete highway, which temporarily took the men's minds off the difficulties of another long day's running. Newton remarked: 'I had recently been getting so weak that I was frightened as to the outcome of this prolonged stomach trouble, but today I began to regain my appetite and, in spite of the distance, certainly felt distinctly better. This dose of indisposition had cost me dear: I had dropped from fourth place in elapsed time to 11th.'

Day 18, Wednesday 17th April, Richmond to Kingstown (34.7 miles)

A relatively easy day saw Gavuzzi beaten to the finish by the popular Finnish-American Johnny Salo, who was looking ominously strong again. Salo had recovered from stomach trouble now that his wife had returned with some home cooking, meaning Salo no longer had to resort to the doubtful delights of the Pyle mess-tent.

Day 19, Thursday 18th April, Kingstown to Indianapolis (35.3 miles)

The sun came out at last on another shorter leg, and Salo came home first, ahead of Gavuzzi, in front of a big crowd in downtown Indianapolis. A pale Newton arrived later and expressed no desire to see the bright lights of the city, hopping straight into the Chevrolet so they could head out of town for some food and sleep.

Day 20, Friday 19th April, Indianapolis to Brazil (57 miles)

The weather has become distinctly warmer for this long stretch, and Newton spoke for many of the men when critical of the management for allowing so many 50-mile-plus sections, especially close together. At least he was more suited to longer distances than many others, and as a result came in an improved seventh, despite continuing to feel unwell. A great run by Gavuzzi in second (7:56.15) extended his overall lead to nearly four hours. By now the field had been reduced by withdrawals to barely half the 69 who started in New York.

Day 21, Saturday 20th April, Brazil to Marshall (36 miles)

Disaster. Just when he was starting to feel a little better, and ready to claw back some of his lost time, Newton came a cropper at the hands of a careless driver. The traffic had been busier than usual on leaving the Indiana town of Brazil and Newton had done around seven miles when a car driven by the Reverend A F Schmitz of Anderson apparently failed to notice him and clattered straight into him from behind, sending him flying to the ground. Newton was left badly dazed in the road with a broken bone in his shoulder, and it was immediately clear his race was over. With manager Barren unavailable to help as he was tending to Gavuzzi up ahead, the small crowd which gathered summoned an ambulance and Newton was sped to hospital in the nearby town of Terre Haute. His fracture was set and his arm strapped so it wouldn't move. Advised to rest in bed for around three weeks, Newton immediately telephoned instructions for Barren to collect him as soon as possible. He reasoned: 'I felt that recovery would be far quicker in the open air than surrounded by ailments. So I transferred to the caravan and Barren drove mighty carefully to avoid shaking me about. Occasionally we would strike a real jolt that made me quite sorry for myself, but Barren was an expert driver and most considerate.'

As in the 1928 race, Newton had to resign himself to seeing out the rest of the race, firstly as a lame passenger watching from a prone position, and then more actively as Pyle's 'technical advisor'. The normally cheerful Gavuzzi was devastated when he heard what had happened to his partner. His diary entry for that day read: 'There is not much I can say about today's race concerning the actual running. I am much too upset.'

Newton had been ousted at a time when he was still feeling unwell, and although the race was still not even 30 per cent complete, it seems unlikely he would have recovered sufficiently to challenge for the top prizes. For now there would be plenty to keep him occupied, particularly as he could concentrate on advising Gavuzzi in the tremendous duel that was developing with Johnny Salo. Coming a cropper on day 21 of 78 meant there was plenty of time for Newton to recover his health before the exciting final stages. As it transpired, the race had barely reached halfway when Newton began emerging from the Chevrolet each morning to walk and trot gently alongside some of the slower runners. And by the time his sling and bandaging could come off, there was no stopping him. By early June the race had snaked into Arizona, and Newton was able to run almost as normal. He kept busy all day long, helping those still in the race. After they stopped in the copper mining centre of Miami on day 65, the local townsfolk were quick to tell the entourage about a local running record, which they reckoned was beyond the talents of this motley crew of Bunion Derby runners. Such fighting talk was bound to strike a chord and before long Newton decided he was fit enough to get out there and beat this so-called record. These loose-tongued locals needed to be put in their pace.

The record of which they spoke involved the same road the 'bunioneers' would be tackling the next day – a stretch of around 22 miles between Miami and the small town of Superior, which went over a very steep hill en route. The locals claimed their man's record of 3hrs 22mins for this stretch was unbeatable, but after a quick glance at the hill and a few mental calculations, Newton knew it should be well within his grasp. The challenge was on: 'All of us wanted to see that record put in its proper place. I was the only man running with them who was no longer competing in the race and was just getting reasonably fit and was now almost entirely recovered . . . we had a short meeting that night to discuss the matter and it was decided that the best way to pulverise that record without giving the actual competitors any extra work would be for me personally to attend to the business.'

About 30 minutes after the runners set off the next morning, Newton went off alone, enjoying the smooth tarmac surface and undaunted by the steep climb awaiting him. Over he went, past a garage and café called The Top of the World and down the other side. By now he began catching and passing the slowest of the 'bunioneers'. He cruised into Superior in 2hrs 11mins, more than an hour inside the locals' proud record. He quickly deduced that not only had the local record been far from impregnable, but the distance was well below the 22 miles advertised too . . .

The run gave Newton plenty of satisfaction after his bad luck of earlier, but he soon returned to the more serious business of his job as technical adviser. They were by now closing in on Los Angeles with Gavuzzi and Salo still locked in glorious battle. The latter produced a tremendous performance over a gruelling 79-mile stage when he roared into Dallas to take a large chunk off Gavuzzi's lead. He then managed to overhaul the Englishman at Big Springs, once a resting place for gold prospectors heading west to California. Gavuzzi hit back as they crossed New Mexico, recapturing his lead as the tension mounted. By Deming on Day 61, with only 20 of the 69 starters still going, the battle at the front was enthralling – for, after 390 hours of running, Gavuzzi's lead over the stocky Salo was just 21 minutes. The pair even tied for second place at the end of the 62 miles into Lordsburg, a stage won by a superb display from the veteran Australian Herbert Hedemann.

By the time they hit the California border, the lead had gone to Salo and then back again, and promoter Pyle pulled his familiar trick of rescheduling the final few stages meaning five of the remaining seven legs would average a crippling 64 miles each, far further than anticipated. Pyle did this, not because he was a sadist, but because he wanted the race to finish on the same weekend as the *LA Times*' inaugural marathon, thereby achieving maximum publicity and attention. The runners had to accept their fate and get on with the business of racing, and when the final day arrived in mid-June, thrillingly, Gavuzzi and Salo were separated after 522 hours of racing by a mere 10-minute gap.

The final section – on day 78 – involved a four-mile run from the previous night's finish (Huntington), to the Wrigley sports field in Los Angeles, followed by a 26-mile run on the grass oval there. Sadly, proceedings would end under a cloud of controversy and ill-feeling. Confusion over whether the four-mile section would actually count towards their finish time led to Gavuzzi merely jogging down to the sport field, while unbeknown to him Salo was up ahead sprinting for all his worth. Gavuzzi's passage to the field became even slower when he had to wait at a congested railway crossing. He arrived well in arrears, dismayed to see battle well underway on the oval. He was able to put up a brilliant fight as they circuited the field and at one point looked set to catch Salo, who occasionally looked near to collapse. But somehow the New Jersey man clung on and they finished with Gavuzzi narrowly falling short. The gap was just 167 seconds, after nearly three months of daily racing!

Gavuzzi was furious and felt he'd been badly misled and unjustly treated over the last day's arrangements. There were even dark rumblings about the situation having been manufactured to ensure an American would win. To make matters worse, Pyle had again made heavy losses on the whole venture and was unable to hand over the winner and runner-up cheques, providing promissory notes instead. Not only did Gavuzzi feel robbed of victory, he was robbed of money too. He was determined to lodge a protest, to the pressmen if nobody else, but was quickly talked out of it by Newton, who told him he would appear 'a poor loser' and do himself no good. Newton knew it would be pointless to complain, and also believed it was best to maintain a low profile as they didn't want to spoil their chances of future engagements by upsetting the apple-cart too much.

Discussions in the aftermath confirmed that originally the four miles to the sports field had not been intended as part of the day's racing. If there had been an official change to that rule, it was certainly not properly communicated to all. Furthermore, the chaos caused en route by heavy traffic and trains crossing had made it even more damaging to anyone not running that section hard. Newton was sympathetic and told Gavuzzi quietly: 'You were robbed Peter – that stretch to the stadium should not have been included.' Gavuzzi had no argument with winner Salo, who had battled magnificently, but his sense of injustice would never fade and was deepened by the fact that he never got paid. He kept Pyle's credit note until his dying day, but as the promoter went bust it was worthless.

The dreadful way the 1929 race ended left Newton upset and Gavuzzi bitter. It was clear there would be no more transcontinental races in the near future, but the pair of them were in no position to simply turn tail and head home as they were committed to seeking a living from running in North America. Newton was philosophical and pragmatic about it all, and immediately settled down to spend some months working with Hugo Quist in order to 'learn the ropes' of professional running and keep himself available for any forthcoming events. A number of the other 'bunioneers' also kept in touch and an information network grew up, which kept them abreast of potential races in which they might make some money. Most, however, slowly drifted back to their old occupations.

For a while the Bunion Derby spawned all manner of hare-brained plans for endurance events in the USA – some happened and some never took off. These included dance marathons, tree-sitting, flagpole-sitting, an ultra-distance swim and even a 'gabfest' (continuous talking). None would have quite the impact of the Bunion Derby, and nor did any lose quite the same amount of money or cause quite so much grief.

A few weeks after it finished, in July 1929, a six-day footrace for two-man teams was arranged at the American Legion Speedway Stadium in Los Angeles. Newton chose not to enter and must have been pleased with his decision, for again the winners pocketed far less than they'd been led to believe was on offer. Newton did run, however, when a 15-mile race was arranged in Passaic, Johnny Salo's home town in New Jersey. Sadly, the star local man looked out of condition, as did 1928 Bunion Derby winner Andy Payne, and 46-year-old Newton showed them a thing or two as he raced to victory in 1:32.22.

Curiously, although they were much younger, the two Bunion Derby winners Salo and Payne would run far fewer miles than Newton in the wake of their victories and before long would see their sporting careers fizzle out completely. Salo eventually settled down as a police officer in his home town but within a couple of years was dead, killed in a freak accident while working at a baseball game. Entering the field of play to deal with over-enthusiastic fans, he was hit on the head by the ball and died later in hospital, aged just 38.

Meanwhile, in New York the new 'network' of pro runners continued to work hard to set up races and keep the sport alive. The next promotion was another six-day challenge, this time against teams of horses in Philadelphia. It took place in the October of 1929, within a few days of the great Wall Street Crash, an event that was to trigger a worldwide economic depression.

Newton and Gavuzzi paired up in Philadelphia to tackle opponents of both the two and four-legged variety. Five two-man teams were pitted against five pairs of horse-and-riders. The two members of each team ran alternately, changing when they wished, and it was a simple case of seeing who got the furthest after six days of this. Tents for sleeping were positioned inside the indoor track. The horses soon began to show they didn't enjoy the enclosed surroundings of the hall and eventually refused even to trot, and just walked listlessly. Unknown to the spectators, new horses were then substituted, but soon they too ended up in exactly the same state, and once again had to be replaced, this time by the original horses. By this time the runners were firmly in the lead and there was a definite lack of excitement in the air. The eventual winners were Salo with partner Joie Ray, who chalked up 523.3 miles, ahead of Newton and Gavuzzi whose tally was 521.25 miles. The horses Redwing and Fleetwood came third with 510.5 miles.

Again, there were the inevitable money problems at the end. The first two teams of runners should have received $500 per man, but the failure of the horses had meant a greatly reduced attendance on the last two nights, and thus a reduction in the runners' prizes had to be negotiated. It wasn't the first time that insufficient gate money caused a problem, nor would it be the last; every time runners were sent home with reduced prize money or credit notes it seemed like another nail was hammered into the coffin of professional running.

Chapter 15

Teardrops in the Snow

The aftermath of the Wall Street crash in 1929 meant professional running was on its last legs in the United States, but Newton kept faith, hung around and began looking towards Canada in a bid to make a living from the sport.

He fancied a dabble at race promotion, as well as continuing to run himself, and as part of the Empire, Canada appealed as a place to live and work. Between spells in Montreal, Newton would choose Hamilton as a base, finding it a convenient and welcoming city where people loved their sport. To underline this, the first British Empire Games were held there in 1930 and were hailed a big success.

Newton was greatly encouraged to discover that the Distillers Corporation of Montreal was injecting sponsorship cash into long-distance events. Their first major venture would be a revival of snowshoe racing, a minority sport that had begun in earnest a few years earlier when the first major race went 300 miles from Montreal to Swindon, Ontario. Distillers announced a 200-mile snowshoe marathon for the winter of 1929-30, and before long arrangements were being made for a summer equivalent – a 500-mile road relay from Montreal to Quebec and back, for teams of two men.

Distillers was a thriving company which enjoyed substantial growth in the 1920s, in part due to prohibition in the USA, and had recently acquired the well known Seagram company. They named their two races – the Usher's Green Stripe snowshoe marathon and Peter Dawson International Relay – after two of their brands of Scotch whisky. Newton noted that the entry fees were moderate, the organisation looked impressive and the prizes substantial. He relayed the good news to racing partner Gavuzzi, by now back in England, and they made plans to link up again.

Newton was a little reluctant to run in snowshoes, fearing it wouldn't suit his economic low stride, so didn't enter the first Distillers race, but a number of fellow 'bunioneers' weren't so fussy. One of them, Philip Granville, a big Jamaican exile now living in Ontario, got himself among the prizes, securing second place behind winner Edouard Fabre, the former Olympic marathoner. Newton and Gavuzzi looked on with interest, but concentrated their own efforts on preparing for the inaugural Peter Dawson International Relay, where the small matter of 500 miles had to be covered in eight days, by teams of two. The first six months of 1930 saw Newton pile on the mileage, averaging around 700 per month, nearly half of which was brisk walking, often in the snow.

The Peter Dawson relay began at noon on Sunday, 20th July 1930 from the Fletcher's Field baseball stadium in Montreal and a huge crowd gathered to see the runners head for Granby, about 50 miles away. Joie Ray and Johnny Salo of the USA came home first in 5:22, chased by Newton and Gavuzzi, who came in less than two minutes adrift. The following day featured another 50 miles leg to Sherbrooke, with a tortuous hilly section that suited the two Britons well and they built a big lead as the Americans struggled. A new rule was suddenly introduced to prevent runners changing over more than once every five miles, which caused initial confusion, but Newton and Gavuzzi had no problems and won the stage in 5:15, 17 minutes clear of Ray and Salo.

Roughly 60 miles to Victoriaville was the following day's task and Newton admitted his surprise at the lead they were able to extend over their nearest rivals by coming in first in 7:30. Day four was a run of 82 miles to Quebec which was a major test for all, Newton and Gavuzzi exchanging their baton every ten miles to keep themselves fresh. They clocked just over nine hours to extend their lead over Ray and Salo to almost an hour. This was beyond their realistic expectations but brought with it extra pressure to maintain the momentum. The Canadian crowds were disappointed at the showing of their own men, but were generous in their applause of the dogged Newton, who was by now in his 48th year.

Ray and Salo set off quickly but both encountered trouble with their feet on the fifth stage from Quebec to Ste.Anne de la Perade (59 miles), and the overall leaders passed them and extended their advantage to almost two hours, coming home in 7:23. Newton and Gavuzzi were now looking untouchable and on the sixth stage to Three Rivers they lowered their pace to ensure no calamities occurred. Newton would admit later that by now they looked certainties to win and for the sake of 'making a race of it' for the crowds they had to keep themselves in check. There was nothing the sporting public liked less than a complete walkover. The final day meant a 26.2 mile run from Joliette to the stadium in Parc Jeanne-Mance, Montreal, and for this stage all were permitted to run in one-mile relays. Newton and Gavuzzi finished with a flourish extending the lead to more than 2hrs 20mins. They completed the 500 miles in 48:04 with Ray and Salo runners-up in 50:24.

After coasting in and acknowledging the cheers of the crowd, Newton and Gavuzzi settled down in the sun to recover, Newton with his pipe and his partner with a cigar, to quietly watch the novelty two-mile sand-bag race which followed. But it was not to be the relaxing hour or so they had envisaged: A large part of the 18,000 crowd in the stadium was plunged into panic when some wooden seating collapsed. Many were injured, several sustaining broken legs. In the section along the Ontario Street side of the ground, people were seen tumbling down onto the rows in front. Others leaned over to see what had happened and made matters worse. Items of clothing and belongings were lost and abandoned in the chaos. Many were taken to the Notre Dame hospital, although nobody was fatally injured.

Despite the chaos, the sandbag race was allowed to finish and was won by burly David Courtois, a strapping fellow of 63, who carried his 200-pound bag for two miles around the track and beat 18 opponents. Courtois won huge sympathy from the crowd, most of whom knew about his tragic background. As a grizzled woodsman from the remotely populated Mistassini area near Lake St John, he had recently been declared the hero of an episode in which his two sons went missing in the wild forests of NW Quebec. Courtois reportedly trekked for hours before finding the boys, but while attempting to carry their frozen bodies to safety, one died in his arms.

The success of the first Peter Dawson relay was encouraging to both participants and sponsors and the prospects looked good for more events to be set up over the next 18 months or so. Newton was keen to make hay while the sun shone, and a number of ideas were on the table in addition to the big Distillers races. Now that Gavuzzi was staying this side of the Atlantic for the time being, Newton began making racing plans for the next 12 months or so. He put aside his worries about running in snowshoes and decided to have a crack at the second Usher's Green Stripe Snowshoe marathon in Quebec in early 1931. This would require several weeks of specialist training, but as there was likely to be plenty of snow around, it seemed a good way to maintain fitness and perhaps win prize money into the bargain. Afterwards, he and Gavuzzi would return to conventional running to prepare for the second Peter Dawson relay in the summer of 1931, and in the interim Newton would seek to promote and run in his own 24-hour race in Hamilton during the spring.

To help him set up the 24-hour race he began working closely with Tom Crompton, a former race walker from the North of England who was now an estate agent in Hamilton. Crompton had been a helper during the Bunion Derby and he shared Newton's optimism that professional distance running had a future in Canada. In an August 1930 letter to Newton, Crompton urged: 'This city [Hamilton] is alive at the present time with athletes and athletics and both you and Peter will be well advised to get to Hamilton as quickly as you can and make your head-quarters with us, while we are arranging other races . . .'

But the first task of Newton and Gavuzzi was to familiarise them-selves with the difficult skill of running in snowshoes. They knew they had the stamina, but would they be able to tolerate the change to unfa-miliar footwear? It would prove a struggle. Snowshoes designed for recre-ational purposes were, typically, teardrop-shaped and around 40 inches (110 cm) long, resembling a tennis racquet, with a tail that kept the shoe straight while walking. They were made of a single strip of tough wood, often white ash, which curved and fastened at the ends to be supported by a light cross-bar, the space within the frame filled with a webbing of hide strips, leaving a small opening for the toe of the wearer's moccasined foot. It was fastened to the moccasin by leather thong or buckle. Newton and Gavuzzi's early attempts to run in such items were, by their own admission, frankly laughable. Newton wrote later of this episode:

'We bought showshoes and went outside the city to a flat, grassy field where we could practise on them unobserved. We didn't want spectators. Continuous and exasperating troubles were what we were in for, and we should be quite content to face the daily battle without appreciative remarks. Snowshoes, when you are unused to them, are fiendish affairs. Imagine strapping a thing like a tennis racquet, but double the size, on to your everyday shoes and then making an attempt to run! To begin with you must keep your feet somewhat wider apart than usual or the shoes will foul each other. This led to a sort of-glorified duck's waddle for the first few days, but after that we settled down to it and discovered the cor-rect technique, allowing one shoe to slide over the other at each step. Used to more than 20 miles of running per diem, I found that a mere three was ample for my first attempt at this new game, and those three probably took the best part of two hours. Every few steps ended in a calamity, and most calamities exhibited an astonishing entanglement of the abominable contraptions tied to my feet.'

When proper snow arrived during the winter of 1930-31, matters improved and Newton and Gavuzzi began to look more competent and became less self-conscious about training in public. Over a few weeks they chalked up around 800 miles in the snowshoes, and became quite adept at the new skill. The February morning of the race itself dawned crisp and cold and excitement levels were high as nearly 3,000 people crunched across the snow to Quebec's Jacques Cartier Square to witness a spectacle the newspapers had been talking about for weeks. The racers' 200-mile journey to Montreal would be broken into eight daily stages, and there was big money to be made, with the winner guaranteed $1,250 (equivalent to about £175,000 today).

The highly experienced Edouard Fabre, a lithe six-footer dressed all in black, was the favourite, having won comfortably last winter. But the limelight would soon be grabbed by a man less than half his age, Frank Hoey, a northwoodsman of Irish origin who had used snowshoes for years. The mayor of Quebec, Monsieur Lavigueur, was assisted by the Green Stripe Queen Miss Germaine D'Arcy in sending the 46 racers on their way. Hoey took an early lead in the intense cold and was never headed. After 20 miles Newton crept up to the leader but couldn't hang on. Further back, the Australian Mike McNamara, another Bunion Derby veteran, suffered from snowblindness and a fellow runner had to take his hand and guide him in safely. It was a hazard that struck a number of the less experienced men. The *Montreal Gazette* reported that some of the hot drinks being handed out en route were spiked, and this led to Omer Quellette being picked up 'drugged out of his mind' and needing medical help. Another man suffered a hernia and quit.

Newton came in second on the first stage, some eight minutes down on Hoey, and on the second day repeated this position, shaking off Canadian Fred Desroches after the 29 miles into Ste Anne de la Perade. Five more men were victims of the cold including the crowd favourite Fabre, who quit after a reported attack of gripe. A huge crowd estimated at 50,000 came out to see the climax of the third day's racing in Three Rivers, (26 miles). Newton maintained the pressure on Hoey, but admitted later he was astounded by the talents of the 27-year-old ahead of him. Hoey was going so strongly the horse following with his equipment became exhausted and had to be replaced.

Snow was forecast for the following day which delighted the local runners, who felt it would hamper the 'foreigners' and inexperienced men more than them. Overall Newton was 53 minutes down on the leader as the halfway point approached. They had to cope with snowdrifts once leaving Three Rivers for Louiseville and Hoey, wearing the colours of sponsor Quebec Box Company, stretched his lead to 59:50 over Newton, who nevertheless coped well with fierce 35 mph winds and heavy snow. The fifth day saw them heading for Berthierville (25 miles) for their severest test yet. Gavuzzi dogged Hoey all the way and even grabbed the lead briefly, but the local man prevailed. Joie Ray, as inexperienced with snowshoes as Newton, suffered badly with frozen cheeks and had to keep stopping to adjust the bandages on his face. Newton, meanwhile, got his head down and performed solidly and without fuss to hang on to second place.

On the sixth leg to L'Assomption, there was high drama as Hoey suffered his first defeat, McNamara coming home first after the leader was
slowed by stomach trouble. The ex-Olympian and 'bunioneer' Phillip
Granville then disappointed his local following by having to quit with a
leg muscle problem. By now around 10 men were in with a chance of
prize money and Desroches was beginning to put heavy pressure on
Newton in second place. The last day was a short eight-mile sprint from
Longue Point into Montreal's Lafontaine Park and the crowd awaiting
them was one of the largest ever seen for a sporting gathering in
Montreal, the police estimation being around 100,000. Hoey won in 55
minutes to the jubilation of the fans, completing his 200 mile journey in
26:43.40. It left him 74 minutes clear of Newton who won a fierce battle
with Desroches to narrowly maintain second. Newton's aggregate time of
27:58 left him a mere 170 seconds ahead. Gavuzzi came in fourth, meaning the British pair were both among the top prize pay-outs. Only 17 men
completed the entire journey, and the Canadian press were full of praise
for Newton in particular, astounded that a man of 47 could do so well in
his first snowshoe contest, particularly as he did the whole thing bare-
headed, which they had called highly unwise.

Newton was delighted with his showing, but glad to unstrap the snowshoes for the last time: 'Neither Gavuzzi nor I liked snowshoeing at all.
We considered "racquettes" hideous nightmares to men who were used
to running with unhampered limbs. Besides, it seemed so abominably
slow: six miles an hour on snowshoes took every bit as much energy as
eight an hour in the ordinary way.'

The success of the event and the massive interest shown convinced
Newton he was on the right lines by planning the 24-hour race in
Hamilton for the spring. Several well-known runners were preparing hard
for the Peter Dawson relay in the summer and welcomed the chance to
make the most of their training by joining the Newton event. Newton
wanted to recruit well-known names from the Bunion Derbies, although
signing these men up and satisfying their demands certainly kept him and
Tom Crompton busy. Correspondence from the period illustrates how
tricky it was to: (a) get a definite commitment from runners, and (b) reas-
sure them about the financial arrangements.

To promote interest generally in running and to keep their income
ticking over, Newton and Crompton's enterprising activities around this
time included public speaking engagements in which Newton would
show audiences a film of the Distillers races and demonstrate running
techniques on an early version of a running 'treadmill'. People were fascinated to see the new-fangled machine in action, and found it amusing

to see the well-spoken, middle-aged Newton trundling along on it, but rapidly going nowhere. Often the show would include an invitation for members of the audience to try out the machine, which would raise even bigger belly-laughs, and a 'winner' would be picked who would take home a wristwatch or similar prize.

Having descended into the shark-infested waters of race promotion, Newton was grateful to the canny Crompton for working so hard with him. He said: '[Gavuzzi and I] were fortunate enough to find Tom Crompton enthusiastic over the idea [of the 24-hour race]. We both knew him well, for he had convoyed one of the transcontinental racers across America with us the year before. He was a resident of Hamilton, which place would suit us perhaps even better than Montreal, as winter conditions there were not so severe or so prolonged. Whereupon we went there by train and took up our quarters at the Stafford House Hotel. . . we couldn't have made a happier choice, for Hamilton is one of the keenest of athletics men and everyone knew him and volunteered to help.'

Ultra-running historian Andy Milroy says Newton's decision to go all out for the 24-hour record was probably motivated by professional pride, for when he and the other 'bunioneers' had competed over 26 hours at Madison Square Garden in June 1928, they were unflatteringly compared to the six-day racers of 40 years earlier. Charles Rowell had in fact set the 24-hour professional record in 1882 (150 miles, 395 yards/241.763 km) on the first day of a six-day event. Newton felt his own 100-mile experience gave him a great chance of cracking Rowell's figure – and it would complete a full set of records at distances exceeding 30 miles. Newton felt his biggest problem might be the dizziness and discomfort he felt when circling a small track, so he came up with the idea of a square-shaped course which might eliminate the problem.

While Newton wanted the 24-hour mark, Gavuzzi was more interested in going for a 40-miles record and decided to attempt it within the 24-hour event. Newton signed up men like Lin Dilks and 21-year-old Paul 'Hardrock' Simpson from the USA, Phillip Granville and Thomas Ellis who were on home soil, and the Aussie giant Mike McNamara – meaning he had four of the top seven from the 1929 bunion derby in his race. He wrote: 'I knew that the figures then in the books for the 24 hours were unreliable, as there had not been enough officials to check the laps, but after talking things over with one of the actual competitors in those far-off races I got a fair idea of what was required . . . For a start we cast around to find someone who could attend to the actual details of organisation. Jacques Girling, another [Hamilton] resident, mustered a posse of young men from the local university and took charge of the lap-scoring

. . . Then the City Surveyor came along and measured the track . . . Never have I known a more perfectly arranged competition. In the mean time Crompton was insisting on publicity to ensure success from a business point of view, and suggested that we [first] tackled the existing Toronto-Hamilton road record of approximately 45 miles which then stood at 6:56.50.'

And so, with arrangements made by the local journal the *Hamilton Herald*, on Tuesday, 24th March Newton and Gavuzzi set about obliterating the Toronto-Hamilton record set by George Begley in October 1909 of just under seven hours. They rose early in Hamilton and were taken by car to City Hall in Toronto for the start. They visited a tea-shop to supplement their breakfast of earlier, and then set off about 50 yards apart at a strictly controlled speed. About halfway, one of their leading cars took a wrong turn and led them a mile out of their way before the error was spotted. But this failed to put them behind record pace and they came home in 5:52.15, comfortably beating the old time. It had been embarrassingly easy and Newton hustled his partner away to a local hotel to shower and change before disappearing. This inadvertently foiled the City Mayor, who had to call off a civic welcome when the runners were nowhere to be found.

Hamilton's ice-hockey and skating arena was chosen for the 24-hour race of April 1931, and arrangements were made to lay the desired square-shaped track immediately after a hockey match finished. Newton reckoned wood was too tough and noisy for such a long run and asked for something with moisture and 'give' to be laid. Crompton duly came up with a surface that Newton described as 'a builder's composition, a sort of mixture of felt and paper, which provided exactly the conditions we required.' The corners of the square track were well banked, and it was measured at 12 laps to the mile. The problem of the faster men being slowed by the need to constantly overtake led to an agreement that all competitors step aside if a faster man approached from behind. Newton reflected later: 'This [etiquette] was carried out both in the letter and in the spirit throughout the entire race, even when fellows were desperately tired . . . That such methods should be willingly and intentionally observed by professionals makes one wonder when amateurs, who are definitely taught by amateurs to make way for no one, will learn what unadulterated sport ought to be.'

When the big day arrived, Newton experienced all the nerves and pressure that came with managing an event as opposed to merely running in it. Crompton took most of the weight off his shoulders, laying on entertainment for the crowd by way of a cycling exhibition by internationals William 'Torchy' Peden and Reggie 'Sonny Boy' Fielding, plus several boxing and wrestling bouts in a ring inside the track, and a live orchestra. At around 9pm the runners were photographed and led on a lap of introduction around the track, followed by the signal to start. The new surface was ideal for running and all coped well in their crepe and rubber-soled canvas shoes. Gavuzzi set off in convincing style, going specifically for the 40-mile record, followed by McNamara and Newton, and began lapping the others. All went according to plan for 20 miles but then it became clear Gavuzzi was in trouble, as he stopped lapping the others and slowly ground to a complete halt, before leaving the track for good.

At the time McNamara was just over two miles behind Gavuzzi and called out that he felt quite capable of taking over the bid for the 40 record. This suited Newton, who adjusted his own pace to his 24-hour requirements, and the plucky McNamara suddenly sped up. He surprised everyone by flying through the 30-mile mark in a new world best time and had no problem in cracking the 40-mile record too (4:31.31), and wasn't ready to stop there either. With nearly 20 hours of running still ahead of him, Newton was obviously far more circumspect, but pleased his event had already made the record books. Every six miles or so, each runner would stop briefly for tea or coffee and, very occasionally, for something to eat. Newton opted for a fruit salad which he gulped down while standing still, but several others had cheese sandwiches which they slowly consumed on the move.

With Gavuzzi and two others out of contention, Dilks and Granville settled into a battle royal for third place, behind McNamara and Newton. It was approaching noon when the officials broke the monotony by announcing excitedly that McNamara was nearing the 100-mile point and that a new record was being set up. He passed it in 14:09.45 – an achievement which astonished Newton, who called it 'the most brilliant long-distance running I had ever seen'.

The preconceived plan at this point was for McNamara to depart briefly for a proper wash, to be followed by Newton, with the Aussie waiting so they could resume running again at the same time. It meant both men would benefit from a bath or shower, without losing ground to the other. Newton postulated:

'A short and really hot shower at this stage is more refreshing and reinvigorating than any food or drink, probably due to the fact that it cleans out all the refuse with which prolonged exertion has clogged the pores of the skin. Whatever the cause the effect is almost magical, as we knew from previous experience.'

Just before the wash break could be taken, they were intercepted by the photographers who urged them to pose for pictures having completed 100 miles, before they left the track to freshen up. One photographer then experienced problems with his camera which caused a long delay, and by the time McNamara had disappeared to the changing rooms his weary legs had stiffened up and a bad attack of cramp struck him. After a lengthy massage, it was fully 19 minutes before he reappeared, which meant Newton had to spend 19 minutes off the track himself, in accordance with their pre-race agreement. The upshot was that Newton returned fully refreshed but having lost momentum and rhythm. McNamara quickly decided he would stop altogether, happy with his new records, but disappointed not to be helping Newton go for the 24-hour mark. Newton wrote later:

'Quite unexpectedly, I was left alone to try for the 24-four hour title, for I had confidently reckoned on a fierce battle with McNamara over the last 20 or 30 miles. I daren't look at the big clock too often – I chanced it about once an hour – because I was getting very tired myself. But I knew that if I just kept up a gentle seven-an-hour or thereabouts I'd collar the coveted record all right . . . at long last there came a time when [official] Jacques Girling informed me that I was within a mile of 150 miles and at that I knew for a certainty that I was safe. The news gingered me up considerably and I increased the pace to eight, then nine, and finally ten-an-hour in an effort to crowd a few more yards into the final total. For the last lap or two Girling was running round with me, telling me just how long we had to go, and then I heard *"Time"* and knew that at last it was all over. I had covered 152 miles and 540 yards in the 24 hours.'

It was a two-hour improvement on the record and Newton left the track smiling, but behind him poor Dilks had run himself senseless and was still plugging along, the call to stop not having penetrated his addled brain. Officials chased after him and eventually persuaded him off the track. A long bath and the news that he'd finished third (117 miles) finally revived him.

With four recognised records set, the day was a great success in sporting terms, but the attendance was lower than anticipated and once the final figures were calculated, Newton reckoned he'd lost about £200 on the venture. He pointed out: 'The various runners, instead of the percentage of gate profits they were entitled to, had to be content with all expenses paid and a trifle of $10 (£2) apiece as a douceur, and within a few days they were on their way back to their respective homes.'

Newton's new mark for 24 hours completed his personal 'set' and would remain unbeaten anywhere in the world until November 1953 (22 years later) when South African Wally Hayward claimed it in London. As a North American all-comers' record, Newton's mark would last even longer (47 years) with Park Barner finally surpassing it at Glassboro, New Jersey, in 1978. Soon afterwards, Newton was able to resume 'normal' training before the planned assault on the Peter Dawson relay in August. But before then, he and Gavuzzi decided on a second crack at the Toronto-Hamilton road, and beat their previous record by 30 minutes, chalking up a time of 5:21:48. They were clearly in fine shape.

The pair sailed for Montreal from Toronto across the Great Lakes to prepare for the big relay on Sunday, 2nd August, their eyes fixed firmly on the $3,000 dollar first prize, which would wipe out the loss made at Hamilton. Most people had them down as favourites for this two-man event, but Newton had been amazed by Mike McNamara's display at Hamilton and feared that he and Joie Ray would give them a good run for their money.

Even though a run of 500 miles lay ahead over the eight days, most of the 15 teams seemed to set off at break-neck pace from Montreal for Ste Hyacinthe on the opening day of the relay. Not so Newton and Gavuzzi, who held back, knowing the fast starters were likely to become 'spatchcocked' within a day or two, to quote Newton. In fact Newton took the lead in the race earlier than expected, on only the second day to Sherbrooke, benefitting from a muscle injury to McNamara and from the fact that Joie Ray and others looked less than fully fit.

To Thetford Mines on the third day and another 15 minutes were added to their lead and by the end of the 82 miles to Quebec on the fourth day they were 40 minutes to the good, delighted but not wanting to be guilty of over-confidence. It had become evident that a number of the big names were not in tip-top condition, and the Brits could 'amble along casually' as Newton put it, only putting on a spurt when entertaining the big crowds at the finish lines. The $3,000 first prize was emphatically theirs and any ideas of impending poverty could be cast aside for the time being.

Regular exhibitions by Newton and Gavuzzi of their films and 'running machine' were organised in the wake of the Montreal relay success. The response was generally good and Newton and the enterprising Crompton pondered over whether this show could be toured across Europe too. At one point, they tried to take it across the border into the USA, but immigration officials were having none of it and turned them back. Treadmills were not a brand new concept, but to see one adapted for a runner was quite a novelty; the very first one had been introduced in 1817 as a method of reforming offenders in prison. Nevertheless, despite the best efforts of Newton, the machines would not catch on as keep-fit devices for the home until many years later.

The third annual Green Stripe snowshoe marathon in early 1932 again offered big cash prizes, but it held no attraction for Newton, even though the great economic depression spreading around the world was slowly killing off sponsored events such as this. It was obvious there would soon be little to keep Newton in North America as far as professional running was concerned, and for a spell he immersed himself in learning about American coaching methods, which he felt were far advanced compared to those in Britain. Newton knew his own days as a competitive runner were nearly over, and the idea of coaching appealed. One of his first proteges would be a middle-aged French Canadian called Felix Forget, who would benefit from Newton's tutelage by going on to create a Canadian 100-mile road record of 17:56.24 in Montreal.

Newton was said by one reporter to be keen to stick around and see the 1932 Los Angeles Olympics, but as work and income began to dry up, he began to make plans to head back to Europe.

Chapter 16

Neck or Nothing

One hundred miles. For the ultra-distance runner it was, and remains, a magical distance. Hellishly difficult, but if conquered, the most satisfying of them all.

With his 50th birthday looming fast, Arthur Newton craved one last crack at the 100 miles world's best time. Old Father Time was by now tugging at his elbow and gently suggesting that retirement from competition might be a sensible option. He could not be ignored much longer. But Newton wanted to go out with a flourish, and felt he owed it to himself to hang up his canvas shoes as the undisputed king of the centurions.

He always felt he was better at the 100 than any other distance, even though his worldwide reputation was largely built on his performances at or around 50 miles. He was certain he could achieve a better clocking than his 1928 excursion along the wintry Bath to London road. In good weather and without the irksome stomach problems of that day, he felt confident of setting a new 100 record that would do him justice and stand unbeaten for years. His 1928 run may have thrilled thousands of onlookers in London, but privately Newton had always been dissatisfied by the performance.

In addition to this, he was also desperately keen to claim back the record from Mike McNamara, who had cheekily snatched it from right under his nose on the track in Hamilton.

During December of 1932 Newton bade Canada farewell after his two-year stay, and sailed for Europe. His opportunities to make a living from running had just about fizzled out in depression-hit North America, and he had new plans to tour France with his film-and-treadmill show. Newton told Joe Binks of the *News of the World* it was a relief to leave behind the intense cold of the Canadian winter, and the pair also chatted about the possibility of setting up one more 100-mile record attempt in England. Binks was happy to organise it, but frankly astonished that his old friend should want to take on such a task at his age.

Newton was a globe-trotter by any standards, but even he never quite got used to the physical demands of switching continents. He admitted: 'I found it took me anything up to three months to get used to an entirely new climate. England after South Africa, America after England, or the other way round. Each time I shifted, the symptoms occurred all over again, though on [later] occasions they were not perhaps so marked.

Youth is more adaptable and a young man might possibly acclimatise in few more weeks than it took me months.'

In February 1933, Newton was still kicking his heels, awaiting finalisation of a contract to take his show on a short tour in France, after which he planned to focus entirely on his swansong 100-miler. By Easter it was being announced that the run would take place on Saturday, 20th May, which just happened to be Newton's 50th birthday. The press thought it an admirable, if eccentric way for the old warhorse to celebrate his half-century, and an awe-struck Binks wrote:

'He fully believes he can improve on his sensational run in the floods and snow when 50,000 people greeted him at Hyde Park corner last time. He will run for nothing but the glory of the sport and will make this his final race. He is already busy training on the Bath Road and is confident of putting up good figures. In training during March, Newton ran 1,084 miles – he is truly an amazing fellow. Last week he did 270 miles – think of it, marathon experts!'

Training in the early spring mornings meant traffic on the A4 was light and Newton didn't have the distraction of having to make small talk with passers-by. But one morning he was unnerved to suddenly notice a policeman on a bicycle following him close behind. After three miles of this, during which only basic pleasantries were exchanged, the officer politely enquired if he might be the Mr Newton he had read about in the *News of the World?* Newton was never comfortable at being recognised by strangers, but at least it meant he didn't have to explain his presence on the road.

Staying again at his sister Ursula's home in Frieth, Newton spent around six weeks running up and down the main road from Newbury and then moved further west to Marlborough to get familiar with that end of the route. Then, out of the blue, a cable arrived to confirm details of the lucrative French stage engagements in Nice, which, to Newton's horror, clashed directly with his proposed run in May: 'I was quite fed up at having to alter all my arrangements when I was on the point of achieving my purpose, but after travelling to London and seeing Binks, who had all the arrangements in hand, I decided to go straight on to France and postpone the 100 till my return. Six weeks later I was back once more and Binks had picked on Saturday 1st July for the attempt.'

In France, Newton used his spare time to pile on the training mileage and even issued a challenge to the best French distance runners to tackle him in a match, but there was little response. While in Nice, he was able to link up with former champion wrestler and fitness guru George Hackenschmidt, whose writing he had long admired. While Newton sampled the coffee and croissants of the chic Mediterranean resort, he will have heard the news from South Africa that unknown 20-year-old Hardy Ballington had won the Comrades Marathon in Durban in 6:50.37, the best time ever posted by anyone other than Newton. The emergence of new talent like Ballington must have stiffened Newton's resolve to make sure he captured one more 100-mile record before retirement.

On his return from France, Newton put in a guest appearance at his former club, Thames Hare and Hounds on the occasion of their summer run in SW London, having kept in touch with them in recent years by way of regular letters and the occasional donation to club funds. It was purely a social call, for having spent five years or so as a professional, Newton was not permitted to rejoin the AAA-affiliated club or represent them in any way. But naturally he was by now taking a keen interest in the London running scene again, and applauded the news that Finchley Harriers was launching a brand new annual 20-mile race, to be staged in the Ruislip area. Newton backed promoter Vic Sellars' opinion that British marathon men were currently 'hopelessly undertrained' and that new events like this would aid their progression. The 'Finchley 20' would grow to become an annual classic on the road-race calendar, and for the remainder of his life Newton would become a regular supporter, attending the event as either a judge, steward or spectator. He would be an inspirational figure to its participants.

A blocking anti-cyclone plonked itself to the south-west of the British Isles on the last day of June 1933, meaning the next day was guaranteed to be warm for Newton's much-publicised return to action in England after five years abroad. Recalling the snow and floods of his last race here, Newton was pleased by the prospect of running in the sunshine, thinking it would be reminiscent of his halcyon days in South Africa. Sadly, his delight would turn to despair; race-day became far more humid than expected, and it was the type of muggy, stifling summer day that endurance athletes hate.

The day's proceedings started in darkness, as before, outside the Bear Inn in Box village. Giving the signal to depart was 19th century champion Walter George, who had risen from his sick bed in London to be there. Loud cries of 'Good luck Arthur!' rang out as Newton set off in the gloom, some 45 minutes before sunrise. By the time he had passed Chippenham, the birds were singing and rabbits scuttling in front of him, in direct contrast to the previous frozen trek on this road in 1928. Timekeeper George once again enjoyed the entourage's passage through his birthplace Calne, where the locals showered him with as much attention as they did Newton.

Newton maintained a remarkably disciplined pace in the early stages, completing 15 miles with five-mile blocks of 34:35, 34:40 and 34:35. Apart from the regular knots of well-wishers who rose early to help him on his way, some country folk were already hard at work by now and as he passed Fred Darling's racing stables at Beckhampton, the staff there cheered raucously. He passed the 20-mile point in 2:18, which was eight minutes quicker than last time, but by now the sun was shining bright and conditions seemed just about perfect. Newton felt good, passing the marathon distance in 3:01.15, and seemingly unconcerned that he still had the equivalent of nearly three more marathons to go.

By the 40-mile point near Hungerford (4:40.10) there had been a gentle acceleration and shortly after Newbury he hit the halfway point, with 50 miles covered in 5:56.30, some 45 minutes ahead of schedule. It was splendid running, particularly as the existing 50-mile record for a track was 17 minutes slower than this. However, a mile or two later, the first cracks were starting to appear. For a spell Newton appeared to be limping slightly, although he made light of the problem when Binks' car drew up to ask about it.

There were still nearly two hours before noon, but the sun felt hot and his support team were kept busy throwing iced water over him from the side of the road, and supplying intermittent gulps of his 'magic drink'. Newton wasn't happy with the soreness developing around his heel and ankle, but his pace never slackened and the concern didn't show on his face. At 60 miles he was clocked at 7:15.30, which Binks quickly confirmed was a remarkable new record for that distance, obliterating his own 1928 mark and that of W C Davies, set on the Islington Agricultural Hall track in 1880. Great going, considering he was on an undulating road and under an unforgiving sun. Binks' report the next day would express his astonishment at the 60-mile record, and he insisted athletics fans should be aware the likes of Newton and Paavo Nurmi may never be seen again, and 'we should appreciate what we are seeing'.

What Binks didn't fully appreciate, as Newton hit the 65-mile point in 7:57.30, was that beneath his relatively calm exterior, the runner was beginning to suffer badly. His Achilles hurt, his stomach felt bad and the heat was getting to him. More iced water was poured over his head as he headed towards Maidenhead, grim determination on his reddened face. He reached the centre of the Berkshire town (74 miles) in 9:41.50, an estimated 52 minutes ahead of record pace, silently cursing the fact that the day they'd chosen was proving to be the hottest of the year so far.

After Maidenhead, Newton's condition continued on a downward spiral. Knowing he was ahead of schedule and getting close to London, he was desperate not to give up, for he might have enough time in hand to break the record even if he slowed badly. But Binks and George were thinking differently and could see from their escorting car that he was in a bad way. The 11 miles between Maidenhead Town Hall and the level crossing at Colnbrook saw Newton slow to a shuffle, his pace slumping to a pedestrian 9mins 30secs per mile. He was in serious trouble and Binks and George agonised over whether they should stop him now before he deteriorated further. Newton was having none of it, convinced he should press on in the hope the worst would pass. The idea of giving up after having covered more than 80 of the 100 miles filled him with dread and was almost impossible to contemplate.

Binks could see it was useless to continue, for only his extraordinary will-power was keeping him going. His posture was poor, he was limping, his stride was uneven and his face contorted with misery. He'd never seen Newton look this bad. When he stumbled past the Colnbrook level crossing (85miles) in 11:24.30, it was mid-afternoon and the hottest part of the day, the mercury rising into the 80s. Despite his condition he was still 23 minutes inside record pace and this fact alone made stopping very difficult indeed. When a man is so close to his goal, the decision to say 'no more' could not be taken lightly and Binks mopped his brow anxiously, wondering what was for the best.

A mile or so beyond Colnbrook they noticed Newton was beginning to sway badly and at this point they raced across to him and insisted he quit now. It was several minutes before they could persuade him it was the best course of action. It was the first time in his 12 years of running that he'd been forced to abandon a record attempt in this manner. It was little consolation that his time for the 86 miles completed was phenomenal (11:33.0, some 15 minutes quicker than in 1928). After he was examined later on, it was declared that a nasty case of sunstroke had been the main cause of his gradual collapse.

Newton seemed fully recovered after 24 hours and praised Binks and George for their common sense and for persuading him to quit, and agreed with their verdict that he had been slowing so badly he would have lost his 'time in hand' during the remaining 14 miles into London, and more importantly would have put his health at serious risk. He reflected that the day hadn't been a complete waste of time, for he was delighted with the new 60-mile record.

Having to almost physically pull Newton off the road had been particularly upsetting for Walter George. Shortly afterwards he wrote to Newton: 'What I particularly want to tell you is that it almost broke my heart to get out of that motor on Saturday to advise you to stop, although

I was absolutely convinced some distance before we reached Maidenhead that it would be the wisest thing to do . . . what happened to you was that nature cried "Enough!", but you wanted and would have more cold drink, and this excess, and the hot weather, then brought about fermentation in the stomach and bowels – and so complete collapse.' George urged Newton in future attempts to only use his 'magic drink' for emergencies and not to guzzle it down randomly; to be very careful what he ate, and to save energy by limiting his conversation with helpers, and his acknowledgements to the well-wishers at the roadside. Having seen Newton's torment at close hand, George seemed desperate for him to succeed, and he ended his letter: 'Let me know what you think about all I have said, and if you will try once more, and please, please, please, please do so.'

Newton couldn't be blamed for having chosen the hottest day of the year for the run, but he was surely making a huge mistake when he arranged a re-run for only three weeks later, on Saturday, 22nd July. Surely his battered body needed more time to recover? Binks certainly had reservations, but agreed to make the arrangements again, knowing that Newton was no ordinary athlete and could usually judge his own capabilities accurately without advice from men who had never tackled such mileage.

On Saturday, 15th July, the same day that Jack Lovelock of New Zealand broke the world amateur mile record (4:07.35) in the USA, Newton formally confirmed he would be having another attempt at the 100-mile record on the same course the following Saturday. He was desperate, he confessed later, 'to make amends' for the events of 1st July and even ignored continuing worries about his Achilles problem when setting the new date. The ankle area was painful with a week to go, but he knew Binks had made all the arrangements and he couldn't bear the thought of pulling out at this stage. He revealed later:

'The week before I went [back to Box] I was alarmed to discover signs of serious inflammation at my right Achilles tendon. I cut down the daily mileage at once and the trouble eased considerably; in fact the foot got so much better that, with the trial still a week away, I went out for a 30-miler to see how it would stand up to it and, as it appeared to be no worse, decided to go ahead with the race. Ah! If only I had known!'

On the day before the run, the leg felt painful again but he reckoned it was probably a case of 'muscular rheumatism', the sort of thing he'd suffered before and had often been able to run through with no ill-effects. Even so, he knew most people in his position would have called off the next day's run, and admitted it put him 'in a deuce of a fix'. He convinced himself there was no point in wiring Binks to postpone the run as it was probably too late to prevent him and the other officials travelling down from London. He also convinced himself he could conquer this injury as he had many before – by simply continuing running, albeit with more care than usual. Binks and George arrived later on the Friday and agreed that at this late hour Newton should start the run but insisted he make a sensible early decision whether it was worthwhile continuing. They didn't want to see the prolonged agony he suffered last time.

And so, for a third time in five-and-a-half years, the road outside the Bear Inn in Box was a hive of activity at 3 in the morning. Newton came gingerly down the wooden stairs and into the street, pleased to find his ankle didn't feel too sore at all. With dawn more than an hour off, he received a tremendous send-off, with more than 100 people following him on cycles, both children and adults, with their lights bobbing strangely into the distance. For the first 12 miles or so all seemed to be going well, apart from the worries in the back of his mind, he seemed to be progressing in his usual smooth, metronomic style. But before long Binks believed he could detect a slight limp, Newton admitted later the pain was slowly growing by now at the site of the previous inflammation. By Marlborough (25 miles) his limping was plain for all to see.

He was not prepared to give up easily, however, and pushed on grimly until the 30-mile point when it was clear that further progress was a waste of time. He had by now slowed to a walk and was dragging one leg badly behind him. He had given himself more than a fair chance to 'run off' the injury, but it was only getting worse. Binks and George passed him his coat and were full of sympathy, but for Newton the mental turmoil was far worse than the physical. He was visibly distressed and close to tears, his normal reserve giving way to frustration and embarrassment, despite the reassuring words of his escorts. Newton confessed later: 'I was quite shocked at the disaster and at having given the officials so much work and travel for nothing. Good sportsmen as they were, they seemed to be far more concerned over my ailment than their own loss of time.'

Newton's final record attempt would have to wait, for it was clear this was a nasty injury and would have to be allowed to heal properly. It would be some time before he could even put full weight on the injured leg. Even walking briskly became a problem, particularly when carrying anything heavy. His mileage for the following month, August, was by far the lowest since he'd taken up the sport. His body was so used to its daily average 'fix' of 20 miles that he felt desperately miserable to be inactive. The trouble would last for the remainder of 1933 and when trying to analyse why this injury was proving worse than others, Newton recalled ankle trouble in his childhood:

'As a boy my ankles were somewhat weak, and the approved medical remedy for this was to wear boots to support them. They provided the support all right, but in doing so further weakened the ankles, which, having no particular work to keep them lively, didn't get any stronger. I should have been saved from a load of trouble later on had I been made to wear shoes and take suitable exercise.'

Newton seemed resigned by now to settling and making a new life for himself in England, believing his future might lie in coaching and writing, but in the meantime he was keen not to quit 'serious' running until that 100-mile record had been secured. By the end of 1933 his training mileage was more or less back to normal Newtonian levels and the ankle trouble had diminished if not entirely disappeared. He would go for the record one more time in 1934, he decided, and then probably call it a day for good.

He was happy to mix with the running fraternity and other sportsmen of the London area, sharing his experience and wisdom and giving talks to groups when asked. One such visit was to Headstone High School in Pinner, where the youngsters listened to Newton's tales of running and training around the world. It seems unlikely too many will have been inspired to take up the sport, for these were days when the only people you might see going out for a run would be the occasional grizzled eccentric from an athletics club, always male. The jogging and fitness booms were still decades away, and Newton's audience was far more likely to spend its leisure time on stamps, cigarette cards and birds eggs, or maybe whipping tops, hoops, and bagatelle. Newton was keen to spread the word, however, and asked local papers to publish his current address (Cambridge Terrace in central London), so that schools could write and request his services free of charge.

By the spring of 1934 Newton's Achilles trouble appeared to have cleared up and a June mileage total of 724 confirmed that all was well and he was ready for the swansong 100. It had been a real ordeal reaching this point but Newton was determined to go out with a bang, not a whimper. He recalled 1933-34 as one of the most difficult training periods he'd ever experienced: 'I went out for a short distance every day [after the aborted July 1933 runs] though it could hardly be called a run. I limped dreadfully and went on limping for the next ten months [up to mid 1934], improving so slowly that progress was only noticeable at intervals of many weeks. Of all my physical troubles this Achilles tendon was the most exasperating. I knew I was in for months of annoyance yet underestimated its duration – it was almost exactly a year before I had completely recovered and knew it was really safe to make a last attempt [at 100 miles]. Once more I approached Binks and found him as ready as ever to undertake all the arrangements and see the thing through. July 20th was the day decided on and, with a week to spare, I was down at Bath once more. It was neck or nothing this time and I knew it. Already 51-years-old, I couldn't expect to keep up 700-800 miles a month on my feet indefinitely.'

Binks publicised the details of the run and confirmed the speculation that this would be Newton's last hurrah, after 95,000 miles in nearly 13 years as a runner. Interest was huge, big crowds guaranteed and journalists and friends even sailed from Africa to witness the event.

When a great performer leaves the stage for the last time it is often a bitter-sweet occasion, and the final competitive miles of Arthur Newton would be no exception. As we have already seen (in the Prologue to this book), Newton duly completed the 100 miles on Friday, 20th July in 14:06.00, which beat his own best time by 16 minutes, and was also ahead of the mark set by Mike McNamara at the track race promoted in Canada by Newton himself.

It was a sensational performance by any standards, let alone by a 51-year-old, and a wonderful way for the curtain to come down on a unique career. In the press it was even dubbed 'the running feat of the century.' But the perfectionist Newton was left feeling a little empty, a little frustrated. He was disappointed he hadn't taken the record under 14 hours, something he'd been sure he could do. Once again his legs and lungs had been up to the job, but his stomach let him down in the later stages. And even though he had still managed to annexe a world's best time, it was not done in the controlled, even-paced way he would have liked. He would look back on his four 100-mile runs in England as a 'sea of troubles'. Bad luck and, arguably, an over-optimistic early pace, had prevented him from reaching his full potential at this distance.

But, as he sucked on his post-run pipe, he was ready to accept that time had caught up with him. He'd nothing more to prove. He'd devoted most of 1933 and early 1934 almost exclusively to his love-hate relationship with the Bath-London road, and now it was time to sit back and let others take over. As he put it himself: 'There remained only one useful alternative, and that was to put my experience at the disposal of other athletes so that they could carry on where I had left off.'

Chapter 17

Open House at Ruislip

Newton may have announced his retirement from competitive running in 1934, but he was certainly not ready for a life of carpet slippers, sherry and P G Wodehouse by the fireside. As a fancy-free bachelor of 51 he could still indulge his interests without restraint, and within a few months was back up to previous training levels of 20 miles per day, not to mention a new love – cycle touring.

By 1935 he had moved into a smart new house in Ruislip, on the western fringes of London, tucked away on the newly built Manor Estate. The developers, Manor Homes, seduced buyers like Newton with brochures painting the new homes as 'palaces in miniature'. Newton paid at least £500 for one of the bigger houses on the estate, a bay-windowed three-bedroom semi. Ruislip Gardens underground (ironically running above ground) station was a short walk away and a mile or so in the other direction was beautiful open countryside. It was a slice of classic metroland and suited Newton well, for he knew he would need to find office work in London to tide him over, but wanted quick access to the rural lanes and by-ways for his running and cycling. He recalled:

'I took to a push-bike in order to see something of the English countryside from which I had been absent for about a quarter of a century. I hadn't ridden one of these machines for a very long time, yet soon discovered that a hundred miles in a day was a reasonably moderate jaunt, provided it was tackled, like my running, at a strictly moderate pace. Such a mileage would have been out of the question had not running developed my stamina to an unusual degree.'

Newton was given his bike by the Hercules Bicycle Company, and he made full use of it right away, but without cutting down on his running. He had no more races or time trials to aim at any more, but would not, or perhaps could not, give up his daily ritual of an early morning run, and often exceeded 600 miles a month. There could not have been a fitter over-40 in the land. He explained: 'I probably had more continuous hard physical training of its sort during 13 years [1922-35] than any modern pedestrian . . . Yet at the end of it I was still good for seven or eight hundred a month just as casual and ordinary training, and was almost absurdly healthy not having once gone stale after the first few months.'

The Newton house at 9 Cottingham Chase, Ruislip, would emerge as a sort of Mecca for distance runners. Before, during and after the 1939-

45 War, runners from throughout Britain and its Empire used the house for bed-and-breakfast stopovers, or simply called round for tea and a chat. Newton provided endless slices of yellow Madeira cake, the kettle was constantly on the boil, and everyone was welcome. He would advise his visitors on training, racing and lifestyle, draw up personalised schedules for them, or simply sit and listen to their latest adventures.

Newton began work on a coaching book, submitted articles to newspapers and periodicals, and slowly his reputation as a dispenser of commonsense advice and refreshment spread throughout the athletics fraternity. He was like a friendly schoolmaster, carrying the aura of someone who had achieved great things and gained great wisdom. Sunday was the most popular day for visitors, but Newton welcomed his disciples at any time, glad of the company, and glad to be of help.

After his farewell performance on the road, Joe Binks revealed that Newton 'had hit hard times and was looking for a position'. This appeal, one way or another, led to the offer of work in an office in the city, but it never became a major part of Newton's life and was probably a short-term or part-time arrangement. Newton preferred to fill his days with only running, cycling and writing if he could possibly get away with it.

His first book came out in 1935, called simply *Running*. Published by Witherby's of London, it was a coaching manual for runners based on the tried and tested methods of Newton's own experiences. Having by now taught himself the rudiments of writing (he is thought to have done a correspondence course in basic journalism), he dotted the book with little gems of commonsense advice and pithy observations. His writing had a light touch and was entertaining. Unlike some other coaching books, his was rarely stuffy and condescending in approach and did well, selling at six shillings a copy. The foreword was contributed by the former mile champion and old friend Walter George, who wrote:

'In 1924 I stated that Arthur Newton was the most wonderful long distance runner I had ever seen. I have no cause to modify that opinion, for he was then and still is unquestionably the most phenomenal distance runner the world has ever known. No man in the past has succeeded in doing what he has done and it may be centuries before his records, are surpassed, or even equalled. That is my opinion. Newton, like the modest fellow he is, says that any man can beat his records if he sets about it in the right way. I will grant that a large measure of his success is due to the great pains and trouble he has taken to discover the best way of attaining perfect results, to his meticulous care over every detail and to his capacity for work. Future runners of all ages will realise how much they are indebted to him on reading [this book]; sprinters, middle and distance performers will be benefited by the able and splendid advice he gives throughout. If I could have my way this book would be placed in every school and public library in the Empire.' Another big fan of the book was Olympic medallist Lieutenant Godfrey Rampling (father of film star Charlotte), who said: 'Although this book has been written by a long distance runner, it should be read by every runner, irrespective of what distance he may run: the sound advice and commonsense principles can help everybody.'

After his daily morning run, Newton would deal with his correspondence from around the world, which arrived in vast quantities. On his living room table, next to a battered old typewriter, was a small black ring folder which served as his address book. It was a home-made affair, with the holes hand-made and the whole thing held together with sticky tape, but its contents were meticulously typed. Over the years it would build into a veritable 'who's who' of athletics, listing addresses and phone numbers of the sport's great and good.

Newton also kept little pieces of notepaper with favourite training routes typed carefully on them, with the locations and mileage en route clearly signified. In many cases the mileage was so precise it must have been properly measured and not merely estimated. Cycle routes included the 94.75 miles from Ruislip to Peterborough, travelling via Watford, Hemel, Dunstable, Bedford and Thrapston, and a 65-miler to a canal-side pub called the Spotted Dog, which had to be reached via Leighton Buzzard, Aylesbury and Tring. His favourite running routes were similarly scribbled down, including a circular run of 21.9 miles via the Rickmansworth area, and two of 13 miles featuring Harefield and Amersham.

Meanwhile, Newton's old sparring partner Gavuzzi had stayed on in Canada. He'd heard all about Newton's 100-mile swansong, and was inspired to have a crack at setting a new professional road best himself. In August 1935 he made what would prove his final competitive appearance aged 30, running the 105 miles from Buffalo to Toronto. In tricky weather, he hit 100 miles in 15:25.34, a time which comfortably beat Newton's best, although the route was considerably less hilly. It was a time that would not be surpassed in North America for 36 years. Gavuzzi and Newton kept in touch and discussed Canadian runners who might come to England for events that Newton was helping organise in 1937.

Newton helped arrange the arrival of a number of ultra-runners from around the Empire, for an assault on his own records at 50 and 100 miles. He was the driving force behind the *News of the World*'s staging of an international London to Brighton race, at which Hardy Ballington, 24, of

South Africa, and Norman Dack from Canada would compete. There would then be a 100-mile run on the Box to London road. The various participants were invited to stay at Ruislip for the duration. Newton paid special attention to the rising star Ballington, escorting him by bike on training runs during which Ballington logged a reported 1,100 in one month alone, a phenomenal total only ever exceeded once by Newton himself. All the help paid off, for Ballington beat Newton's record from London to Brighton by a single second, despite heavy winds and generally unfavourable conditions. Dack came second, and the success of the event would ultimately lead to the race being staged annually from 1951. Early in July of 1937, Ballington then attacked the 100-mile record and achieved the sort of time Newton had dreamed about for himself a year or two earlier, clocking 13:21.19.

Newton and Australian Mike McNamara accompanied the trek and supplied food, drink and advice from the roadside. Having four times attempted the run himself, Newton now experienced things from a different viewpoint, and had to deal with an unfortunate episode in a tea shop, where the haughty proprietor would only serve tea in cups for drinking on the premises, and wouldn't allow Newton to fill a flask to take outside to thirsty Ballington. In the week after Ballington's new record, he and Newton held court at daily public appearances in the *News of the World*'s sports department.

By now Newton was establishing his reputation as something of a coaching guru, although not all his theories were easily digested by the world at large. In order to ensure maximum attention for his magazine articles, Newton often adopted a controversial tack in which accepted thinking went out of the window. It verged on the downright provocative sometimes, but most editors approved of this approach for the interest and reaction it generated. In *World Sports* Newton revealed that an athlete from Iran had been in touch to pass on 'some friendly criticism' about Newton's training advice, and quoted German and Scandinavian techniques to counter it. As always, Newton was quick to defend himself with long and reasoned arguments.

After the outbreak of the 1939-45 War, Newton, by now 57, served his country by working in the supplies department of London County Council. During the early days of the conflict he had his second book published, called *Running In Three Continents* (published by Witherby), which adopted a more autobiographical approach than his previous effort, and gave a full account of his conflict with the South African government. It was widely reviewed in the press and Newton eagerly collected all the cuttings via Durrant's press cuttings service in London.

Athletics coach Wilf Richards, from the Manchester area, recalled meeting Newton for the first time during the war, having been billeted in London while in the forces. Richards was keen to tap into Newton's experience and visited the Ruislip house for several chats. They kept in touch after the war and Newton began contributing a regular column when Richards helped launch the magazine *Athletics Review*.

Another disciple of Newton from the Manchester area was Harold Wood, a leading marathon runner of the era. Wood recalled: 'I was advised by Arthur Newton who said when I was in Cairo on war service that I should get out every day [to run] if it's only for 10 minutes. And the same went for when I was stationed in the Far East. He wrote to say keep up the running every day, even if it's only five miles into the desert. One letter apologised for not writing sooner as he had just been on a 3,000 mile cycle tour around Britain.'

As Britain picked up the pieces during the austere post-war years, Newton redoubled his efforts to boost his income from freelance journalism. December 1945 saw the launch of *Athletics* magazine, edited by P W 'Jimmy' Green, which would within five years morph into *Athletics Weekly*. Newton was quick to contact Green and offer his services. Green produced the first few issues in the back bedroom of his bungalow in Kent, and was told the project would never catch on in post-war ration-ticket Britain. 'I thanked them for their advice and completely ignored it. I was pig headed,' said Green, whose magazine soon became established as the sport's 'bible' and has appeared weekly ever since.

Newton's first contribution caused a stir by attacking the system of training intensely for three or four days a week and resting on the other days, which is exactly what most serious runners of the time did. Newton said it was folly, and advocated training every day of the week, albeit at a lower intensity, and said fast running should be done in competition only, not on the training track. What's more, he suggested, athletics and its training methods in Britain fell way short of other nations in terms of knowledge and practices. Editor Green was shocked by such views and at the end of the article added a long footnote disagreeing with Newton. He said Newton was advocating that runners concentrate on good base work but shouldn't bother trying to sharpen up. Whether by design or not, Newton's radical approach brought a flood of letters. Many thought it was ridiculous to suggest training every day, as most working men simply didn't have the opportunity to do this.

A while later Newton declared that massage could have a detrimental, soporific effect on a runner. This would also draw criticism from some of the magazine's readers, with a Liverpool masseur called Cooke saying massage did exactly the opposite of what Newton suggested, and stimulated rather than relaxed an athlete. Before long Newton was accused of being controversial for the sake of it, but his unconventional views were certainly outlined in a lively, colourful style of writing (with many exclamation marks!).

Before long Newton had publicly agreed with his editor's contention that 'I seem to be out to give athletes highly controversial stuff to make them hot under the collar'. That is correct, he wrote, for you learn more and quicker if you get your ideas so stirred up that you welcome the chance to debate points instead of accepting everything cut and dried from the books. He added: 'Don't accept anything I now tell you, but experiment and decide for yourselves.'

Green would continue to publish occasional Newton articles, despite finding it necessary to castigate him by private letter for views that Green believed were sometimes just plain wrong. He got particularly animated when rejecting Newton's ideas on tactical running and on the great divide between amateurism and professionalism. Newton's articles were soon being reduced to just occasional appearances as the magazine began to establish itself as the leader in its field, no doubt aware of its need not to upset the athletics establishment too much. *Athletics* began giving more space to material submitted by official AAA coaches such as Geoff Dyson.

Newton, evidently, had to turn elsewhere to get his thought provoking material published – *The Scots Athlete* and *Athletics Review* being two examples. Newton apparently never asked a penny for his work for *AR*. In return for writing for free, the editor gave him plenty of leeway and even printed his bizarre proposition that black athletes possessed thicker skulls and therefore had smaller brains than their white opposite numbers.

Newton hit back at those who called his ideas 'poppycock' and said he did his own thinking whether the authorities liked it or not. His critics were not slow to respond, and one particularly hot debate saw his '20-miles-a-day' regime condemned as being simply unsustainable for it could not be done by ordinary mortals without 'draining the tank'.

Athletics editor Green confessed in a private letter to Newton: 'I get considerable amusement from the fact that you consider our coaches 50 years behind the times, while Stan Cox and others think *you* are 50 years behind. It's a funny world.' The relationship between Green and Newton seemed spiky, although generally respectful; they addressed each other as 'Green' and 'Newton' in the old school way, and were certainly not afraid of a frank exchange of views.

Newton's critics became so vociferous on one occasion that Newton suggested to Green that he write anonymously under a pen name, so as to 'sugar the Arthur Newton pill'. He also offered to amend and camouflage some of the earlier articles that were sitting unpublished (unpublishable?) on Green's desk: 'Either that or it would be better to return any stuff you have to hand, and leave me to fade out unhonoured and unsung,' he wrote. Green refued to use Newton's articles under a penname, as he said this reeked of dishonesty and would be a waste of time as readers would recognise his style anyway. Newton's habit of responding to readers' criticisms at great length caused problems. Like all good editors, Green always gave Newton the right of reply, but often had insufficient space for what came back from Ruislip, some of it in hefty instalments.

By the late 1940s Newton was still running for pleasure and fitness, although his days of excessive mileage were plainly over. By the time of his 65th birthday he had cut his daily training spins down to 'only' 10 miles, occasionally less. But he made up for the reduced mileage by getting out on his bike, sometimes solo, others long treks with friends. He did cycle marathons to Wales and also to Scotland, and was often accompanied by John Jewell, a research chemist who ran for South London Harriers. Newton sold his big black Hercules bike to Jewell for £1 and it would be used in Jewell's important road measuring exploits, which led to publication in 1961 of the seminal paper *Notes on the Measurement of Roads for Athletic Events*. Jewell and Newton had first met before the war and kept in touch while Jewell worked in the Persian Gulf and India, but by now he was back in the London area and a regular visitor to Ruislip.

Newton's old racing partner from their North American days, Pete Gavuzzi, also kept in touch with regular letters during and after the war years. Gavuzzi's athletics career had fizzled out soon after Newton's in the 1930s, even though he was the younger man by 22 years. For a while Gavuzzi showed promise as a coach, going to the 1938 Empire Games in Sydney to advise the Canadian marathon team. After quitting Canada, Gavuzzi moved to France to work, where he got caught up in the war and was interned until 1945 in a camp near Le Mans. He spent his time organizing sports for fellow prisoners and writing long wistful letters to Newton. Gavuzzi's letters from France were great long handwritten epistles that conveyed his unhappiness at not being part of a 'running scene' any more. In one, he talked of trying to emulate Newton by buying his first pipe, in which he smoked nosegay, but was promptly sick for the rest of the day. Approaching the age of 40, he'd let his own training slip, but was inspired by Newton's letters to resume running. Before long Gavuzzi would be back in Britain, joining the Ruislip 'tea, cake and running' club, and finding work as a caterer at the Northolt airbase and later as a school caretaker.

The early post-war years saw Newton encounter one or two health problems, particularly with regard to his eyes. For this he needed a corrective operation, although eyesight issues were to plague him for the rest of his life. He also recorded one attack of dizziness and sickness, and of another episode involving high blood pressure. Gavuzzi sympathised by letter: 'I know you quite well, and I know that so long as there's breath in your lungs you will always take it in good spirit. Grouse you will, don't we all, but some people just go on moaning instead of looking on the brighter side of things, and as you mention we must all bow down to old age. But no-one can stop us from thinking we're still young and full of pep can they?'

Gavuzzi was one of the few people in whom Newton could confide personal issues such as health and finances, and they often sympathised with each other's lot over such matters. Eventually Gavuzzi set up home in The Fairway in Ruislip, a mere half-a-mile from his old friend. The pair on one occasion cycled from London to Scotland together to see friend Bill Clark, who had moved there to work, and although the going was tough, the weather was far better than an earlier cycle marathon to Wales, which had been ruined by incessant rain.

A rather less strenuous outing on the bike would take Newton to Frieth in Buckinghamshire where he could visit sister Ursula, his niece Ann, and Ursula's grandchildren William and Linden. More than 50 years later the latter still recall their 'Uncle Tom' arriving on his bike from London, with a young runner accompanying him. Newton always kept in close touch with Ursula, but of the other Newton siblings, brothers Cyril and Ambrose had by now died. The former was killed in a huge explosion and fire which engulfed buildings in Port of Spain, Trinidad, where he worked as an accountant. Ambrose, a captain in the Merchant Navy, died of tuberculosis between the wars. Elder brother Henry had settled in Melbourne, where he became a key figure in the setting up of electric cable company BICC Australia. And the youngest sibling, Bernard, was now back in London after many years in India; his daughter Sally (now Mrs Galbraith, living in Wiltshire), recalls meeting Newton for the first time:

'He was definitely known within the family as 'Tom' and not Arthur. I only ever met him three times, and the first was in my first year at Barts as a medical student. I was told by my father [Bernard] that 'Tom' would like to meet me, so I went for tea at Ruislip. I knocked on the door and when it opened there stood an elongated version of my own father, an unassuming man, going blind due to glaucoma, which was an ailment that also affected other family members. I remember he peered at me and looked me up and down and seemed to approve, saying "You'll make a runner". This was not especially something I wanted to hear! When he made the tea, his failing eyesight meant he had to place his finger in the hot water to measure a proper cup of tea, but when teabags were introduced in the early 1950s this meant he no longer needed to do that. He was a very contained and undemonstrative man, very hospitable and seemed comfortable with his lot; he didn't grumble about going blind. He still got up around 5am in those days and went off for a 10-mile run even with his failing eyesight. I suppose he got so used to the area and the routine that he didn't need great eyesight to find his way around. I went to tea again the following year and remember seeing stacks of his own books on the staircase. He saw few of his relatives at Ruislip, but I know the neighbours were very kind to him. I didn't see him again until my wedding in 1958 [to the celebrated musician Prof Barry Tuckwell OBE]. This was at St Bartholomew the Great Church, near Barts Hospital where I was based. I recall my father painstakingly doing the seating plan as we were all sitting in the knave facing each other. Arthur, typically, sat very discreetly in the back row to allow a quick getaway without any fuss. He was an archetypal Victorian gentleman: dignified and quiet, and fond of phrases like "Upon my word" and "Perish the thought".'

Newton's third book emerged soon after the war, its contents based on his outspoken views on coaching, an athlete's lifestyle and the long-running debate on amateurism. It was an eminently readable, but slim volume of 75 pages called *Commonsense Athletics*. It would be followed in 1949 by his fourth and final book, *Races and Training*, (variant title *Racing and Training*) which is a mixture of his own race reminiscences and coaching advice. Reviewed in the very last issue of *Athletics* in December 1949, editor Jimmy Green said he enjoyed the self-published *R&T* better than Newton's earlier efforts, and praised the author's single-mindedness as a runner and his sincerity and keenness to help others since retiring. Commenting on Newton's controversial training views, Green added: 'An ounce of experience is worth a pound of theory and I would hesitate to question his ideas on training for the really long distances, for they are based on experience and sound commonsense. It is only when he leaves this realm of distance running and applies these principles to other events that I disagree with much of what then becomes mere theory.'

At one point Newton decided to go it alone, and took to reprinting and distributing his books himself, having contacted fellow coach Wilf

Richards in Manchester for advice about the world of publishing. Times were clearly hard and it appears the previous publishers were unwilling to reprint earlier editions, forcing Newton to take matters into his own hands. In return for his advice on self-publishing, Richards received from Newton a supply of suet and lard, which were presumably more plentiful in Ruislip than Manchester in those austere post-war days. Richards was certainly not the only one feeling the pinch: marathon runner Jack Holden had prepared for the 1948 Olympic marathon in London with the help of food parcels sent over by the South African Hardy Ballington.

Nutrition for runners was a subject Newton liked to discuss with the Harley Street specialist C R 'Ben' Woodard. The chief medical adviser at the 1948 London Olympics, Woodard wrote to tell Newton he enjoyed exchanging ideas 'with somebody intelligent for a change'. Woodard said he had recently been to the continent for the European Cycling Championships and had uncovered 'dope' and he despaired at how people refused to believe such things went on in sport. Woodard's Harley Street clinic was frequented by the likes of cycling stars Reg Harris and Wilf Waters and the rising middle-distance track star Gordon Pirie, and he was recognised as a forward thinker like Newton, being one of the first to identify the importance of psychological fitness and mental preparation in sport.

Newton was building up a motley crew of disciples from the world of running, with those living in or near London able to regularly enjoy the 'open house' policy at Ruislip, the remainder restricted mostly to communication by letter. Typical of the latter was Bert Hemsley, a Co-op shop worker from Gosforth, who was inspired by Newton to run fast marathons at an advanced age. Hemsley was a three-times winner of the Morpeth-Newcastle race who obediently followed Newton's radical training schedule of running twice a day, seven days a week. Hemsley just missed selection for the 1948 Olympics, won the Sheffield marathon twice, but was subsequently overshadowed by the emergence of Jim Peters.

In 1951, Newton was a driving force behind the staging of a revival of the London to Brighton run. Main organiser Ernest Neville joined forces with sponsors *The News Chronicle* to make the run part of the Festival of Britain. Acting on Newton's advice, Blackheath's Lewis Piper ran a perfectly even-paced run to win in 6:18.40, passing the less circumspect Crossley of Rochdale, who faded after a strong start. The race was a big success and the following year saw the formation of the Road Runners Club (Newton was made honorary coach), primarily to promote and organise an annual London-Brighton in the future. The major trophies for the race would be the Arthur Newton Cup for the individual winner, and the Len Hurst Belt for the winning team.

One of Newton's most regular and articulate correspondents by now was the Australian coach Percy Cerutty, a spiky extrovert who at first appeared to have little in common with the quietly spoken Newton, but the two were united in their view that athletics coaching needed a fresh approach and radical thinking. Cerutty, who would later coach fellow countryman Herb Elliott to world records and Olympic gold, credited Newton with changing his life. He said Newton's books had 'released my athletic genie out of the bottle after 25 years of sleep'.

In one letter, Cerutty said the news that Newton had bought himself a motorbike at the age of 60-plus, had caused shockwaves, but he congratulated the sheer enterprise of such a venture. Newton and Cerutty recognised in each other men who were deep, philosophical thinkers. In one letter, Newton told the livewire Aussie: 'I reckon the great majority of men haven't the time – they don't spend enough time alone for such a purpose – to do much constructive thinking and consequently they are apt to regard those who do as queer. But of course that doesn't worry us.'

Newton told Cerutty that in one week he had 28 different visitors to Ruislip from the running fraternity. This was above the average, but illustrated the success of his 'open house' outlook. Most visitors merely popped in for tea, cake and a chat about training or running in general, but some were visitors who stayed overnight, often when competing in a race in the London area. Newton always had one room put aside for his athletic visitors, but occasionally needed to call on friendly neighbour Mrs Burton at No 7 Cottingham Chase, who would make her own spare room available.

Cerutty was a great admirer of Newton's writing and ordered a quantity of his books, which were despatched to Australia to be passed on to various Melbourne-based runners. Cerutty was building a reputation over there as a maverick but perceptive coach himself, and during the 1950s would play a major role in the emergence of a number of world class performers.

In May 1952 Cerutty contacted Newton from aboard RMS *Orontes* as it approached Gibraltar, to warn him of his impending arrival at Tilbury, from where he would make his way to Ruislip. Cerutty was in high spirits, having been allowed to travel with the Australian Olympic squad heading to Europe for the Helsinki Olympics, but because of his professional status was an unofficial coach and could not be billeted with his countrymen, and would therefore head for the Newton 'bed and breakfast' in Ruislip. He said he would be bringing his rucksack and sleeping bag and would be 'happy to sleep on the village green' if Newton had other guests.

Hyperactive Cerutty was highly excited to be in London and to be meeting heroes such as Newton. He noted that Ruislip was handily placed for watching the Polytechnic marathon, which incorporated the AAA championship and whose winner was guaranteed to represent Britain at the Olympics. After they jogged down to the race's 15k point, Newton must have winced with embarrassment when Cerutty waited for race leader Jim Peters to reach them, and then started running alongside him. Peters' lurching and puffing style prompted Cerutty to brazenly order him to slow down as he was 'overcooking it'. Luckily Peters ignored the crazy Aussie, shrugging him off and recording a brilliant and unexpected world record of 2:20.42. At the finish, Cerutty claimed the course must be short and made enough fuss to prompt officials to re-measure it. It was found to be 60 yards over distance!

Cerutty proved a high-maintenance house guest, but he was generally respectful of Newton, whose lifestyle he found highly impressive. Cerutty would himself adopt the Newton regime of rising early before dawn to run, followed by a lengthy session at the typewriter, writing letters and essays while the mind was still uncluttered and refreshed following vigorous exercise.

Another house guest in 1952 was John Farrell, a marathoner from Glasgow, one of several runners from north of the border who corresponded regularly with Newton and followed his training advice. Scots such as Alex Kidd and Walter Ross would also stay in Ruislip when competing in the Polytechnic Marathon, the AAA championships and the Finchley 20. If the group got too large for Newton's house, there was always kindly Mrs Burton next door.

Towards the end of 1952, Mrs B was put on notice for a major invasion as Newton was arranging for a number of top South Africans to come over and attack the various ultra-distance records in 1953. Multi-Comrades winner Hardy Ballington was one, and he wrote to thank Newton and Mrs Burton in advance for all their trouble, but reassured them: 'I would be quite happy to sleep on a camp stretcher rather than a bed if necessary, for I have slept on the floor many times in my life and won't worry if I have to now.'

One of Newton's favourite South African disciples was marathoner Reg Allison, whose entertaining and carefully crafted letters were a source of great delight. On one occasion Allison wrote: 'The other evening I came home from work and like every other evening flopped into a snug armchair and sprawled my legs out. An electric heater burned brightly nearby, and all of a sudden one trouser leg seemed uncomfortably hot. Still ensconced in a lounge lizard attitude I pulled it up and gazed dreamily at one of the legs that has covered upwards of 13,000 miles. Little ripples were running up and down the leg at the slightest provocation and the calf muscles stood out defiantly. It was a leg, sir, that would have made half the girls in the world go across the Arctic regions to see. I continued to gaze at it through half-open eyelids and mused inwardly. The next instant I was out of the chair, clothes were flying in all directions and five minutes later I, now clad in shorts vest and tackies, and feeling like a cumbersome elephant, had hit the open road. Reg Allison the runner lived again. Reg Allison the lounge lizard is now non-existent!'

Newton enjoyed Allison's tales of running in the land he remembered so fondly: 'I put in a 32-mile training run to Eshowe and back to Nkwaleni. The sun was at blistering point and it was not long before I was tottering along, mouth agape, eyes agog, and a tongue like a strip o' kaffir blanket. The rivers had dried up owing to a drought but at last I espied an irrigation canal wherein some Zulus had previously been doing their week's washing. Never had I tasted such delicious water!'

Shortly before the planned arrival of his South African guests in 1953, Newton went to the Motspur Park track in South London to assist a 50-mile record attempt by 38-year-old Derek Reynolds of Blackheath Harriers. The lanky Londoner finally wiped out the 40-miles track mark set by Jimmy Fowler-Dixon (4:46.54) which was the oldest record on the books, having stood for 67 years and 350 days. Reynolds obliterated it with 4:19.20 and went on to break the 39-year-old track record for 50 miles (6:13.58) by running 5:30.22.

Reynolds' effort was just one among an array of fine performances at various distances around now, underlining how athletics was enjoying something of a renaissance in Britain. The likes of Roger Banister, Jim Peters and Gordon Pirie could attract bigger headlines than Reynolds, but the long-distance men were playing their part, and the busy traffic up and down Newton's garden path reflected the health of the sport. Appointments were never necessary, and a courteous welcome was assured at all hours. Athletics historian Dave Terry recalls coming home from an athletics meeting in the 1950s in a car driven by his coach, and dropping in unannounced on Newton. His coach had recently been inspired on a visit to the recent Olympics to take up the marathon for the first time. Over a steaming cuppa, Newton quickly sorted him out with a personalised training schedule.

Newton's writing continued to be prolific, occupying many hours and bringing him a small income. He was miffed, therefore, to find during

1952 that the AAA had introduced a new ruling that it would be necessary to get their permission to write and broadcast about athletics if payment was involved. Contravention of this would lead to official withdrawal of amateur status. Newton, of course, had long since lost his amateur status, but was still indignant about the ruling and dashed off his views to the *Daily Express*. 'You become a sort of moral leper,' he wrote, lambasting the AAA for their hypocrisy and cant.

Newton shared some of his frustrations with fellow writer and philosopher George Hackenschmidt who had settled in London, and had recently published books such as *Man and Cosmic Antagonism to Mind and Spirit*. It was highbrow stuff, but the two men would often correspond about more prosaic aspects of life, including wartime bomb damage to Hackenschmidt's West Norwood home, and the troubles he was having with his eyesight. Fellow-sufferer Newton was able to recommend and advise on the treatments available in London, recommending his own optician Harold Morris of Dalston Junction and Harley Street specialist R W Rycroft. He also offered the big Estonian consolation when a publisher demanded Hackenschmidt's autobiography be completely rewritten to make it more commercially viable. Another man who needed advice and reassurance at this time was Percy Cerutty, who since his return to Australia had evidently become disillusioned with life in general, and athletics officialdom in particular. He signed one lengthy epistle to Newton: 'Yours, Percy Cerutty, one time Olympic coach – what a mockery!'

The South African invasion of Newton's Ruislip home began in early 1953 when Hardy Ballington came to stay, followed later by a trio of talented distance men who would initially tackle the London to Brighton run in September. They were Wally Hayward, Fred Morrison and the up-and-coming Jackie Mekler, 22. Newton escorted them on his bike on long training runs down the country lanes, sometimes with a halfway stop at his sister's house in Buckinghamshire. To the amusement of passing motorists, the runners would picnic at the roadside, shovelling down the various goodies stashed in Newton's bulging saddlebags. Mekler's first contact with Newton had been when ordering one of his books in the mail. He recalls the period fondly:

'His home in Ruislip was open to all runners, at all times. The kettle was always left on the boil, for tea with cake, provided in case runners dropped in while he was out. His modesty was reflected at his home on Sunday afternoons with his lounge filled with visitors. Newton would sit quietly tugging away at his pipe, taking in what everyone else was saying and usually only responding when asked to. His living room had a desk with his battered old typewriter, and several comfortable chairs. This was surrounded with shelves, containing books of record and scrapbooks of his running achievements and memorabilia.

'I was in my early twenties and Newton by now aged 70, but in spite of this and in spite of his fame, he never made me feel uncomfortable. He was held in awe by everyone – not that he asked for it. In all the time I stayed with him I don't recall anyone calling him by his first name, except his brother Bernard. Not even Peter Gavuzzi, his racing partner and lifelong friend. It was always "Mr Newton", but not because he was a stuffy old gent, far from it. He was happy and contended and had sense of humour; he loved Spoonerisms. Soon I was known as "Mackie Jekler".

'They were very happy days. Whenever visitors arrived he used to shout "Slave!" and I would have to go and make the tea. He really enjoyed that. He used to accompany us on long runs on his bike and knew all the lovely country roads around places like Burnham Beeches, Beaconsfield and Chalfont St Peter. He had a pair of saddle bags strapped across the centre bar of his bike. On these jaunts he generally had on a lightweight jacket tie, and long trousers. However on long runs in the heat he would dispense with the jacket, tie and have on short trousers. Out in the country on one long run, Newton and Gavuzzi were on bikes, and Hayward, Morrison and I running. It was pouring with rain with not a semblance of shelter anywhere in sight and we were getting desperate for some tea. The best we could do was to simply sit down on the grass verge and drink our tea in the pouring rain. Along comes a double-decker bus filled with tourists. The bus stops, the hilarious tourists fetch their cameras to snap away at the mad hatters tea party!

'He used to get correspondence daily from all over the world and would reply promptly always. He was a keen stamp collector and loved classical music, especially piano concertos. He introduced me to his favourites, Greig and Schumann concertos, which he played every time I sat down to a meal. He was an avid reader, and always appeared to be fully occupied. His coaching ideas involved teaching a way of living, a holistic approach, mainly based on pure common sense. Perhaps controversial in some aspects, especially if applied to the shorter distances. In the main I took happily to his approach. He did modify his stance over speed training at a later stage, but perhaps not enough according to modern standards. He believed that running should be as natural and regular as eating and sleeping.

'He would help anyone he could and was genuinely pleased to help others break his own records. He was way ahead of his time and proud to be a professional. Why should runners not be paid? I remember sending for one of his books when I was aged 18, and writing to "The

Publisher at 9 Cottingham Chase, Ruislip". To my delight this turned out to be Newton himself and it launched a long series of correspondence. I asked if he thought I was too young to be contemplating running marathons and he replied: "Your airmail letter arrived this morning. Certainly there's no reason why you shouldn't run in any race, provided you don't half kill yourself at it, you'll be all the better physically and mentally for the experience . . ." This was at a time when the GB authorities forbade anyone under 21 to run more than 10 miles. I mentioned my own and Wally Hayward's interest in running the London-to-Brighton race and Newton invited us to stay with him.

'Newton is still revered here in South Africa. He remains one of the legends of the Comrades Marathon, run every year. It was said at the time that "Arthur Newton made the Comrades and the Comrades made Arthur Newton". That still remains true today. It is perfectly justified to call him the "Father of Ultra-Running" for in his time it was only really South Africa and England who practised ultra-distance marathons and this was largely due to Newton's influence. I remember in 1954 I was en route from South Africa to the British Empire and Commonwealth Games in Vancouver and the plane had a brief stop-over at Heathrow Airport. Newton, in spite of the heavy traffic and his own failing eye-sight, chose to ride the 20 miles each way on his bike, to meet me for a few hours' chat. What a joy that was.

'Back then I was apprenticed as a printer. After passing my practical examinations, I was given a year's remission and suddenly found myself qualified and free to travel, which was my aim. When Newton heard of this he didn't invite me to make my base at Ruislip, he insisted on it! Because Ruislip was virtually out in the country then, there were no printing works in the vicinity. The most suitable employment I could find which would allow me to carry on with my running was at Remington Rand at Park Royal. I found a lovely running route through Harrow–on-the-Hill, past Wembley stadium and into Park Royal, nine miles each way. Newton was never demanding or aggressive giving advice. If he wanted to demonstrate a point, he would do it in his own quiet way, which was just as effective.

'Before I left him he wanted to give me a gift of the Greig and Schumann concertos. This was not a simple exercise. On a Saturday morning we went into Harrods in central London. This was the era of the old 78 rpm records. After an hour-and-a-half of listening to find a scratch-free recording, Newton was eventually satisfied. After I returned, once a month I used to go to a tobacco store in the centre of Johannesburg on my way home from work where a kindly old English gentleman served behind the counter. He remembered Newton and his feats. He would wrap a parcel of tobacco with much reverence. From here I would cross the street to the Post Office and dispatch the parcel of "dried fruit" to Newton, giving the sender's false name and address, so that the sender could not be identified. There was always an immediate reply of thanks from Newton. The price of pipe tobacco in the UK at that time was eight times more than it cost in South Africa, you see.'

At the September 1953 staging of the London to Brighton run, inevitably it was Newton's house guests who grabbed all the glory and all the headlines. Representing the Germiston Callies Club, the trio romped to the team prize, with Wally Hayward winning in a sensational 5:29.40, smashing the course record by 22 minutes.

A month or so later, at Newton's insistence, 45-year-old Hayward went for his second world's best time, retracing Newton's footsteps along the 100 miles from Box to London accompanied by Jackie Mekler and Derek Reynolds. The run was preceded by controversy with the press pointing out the dangers of running on a busy road. Hayward admitted he was nervous, not because of the traffic but due to not having run 100 miles before. Newton warned them about 'hitting the wall' at 65 or 70 miles, but assured them if they relaxed it would all come right after that. Newton and Gavuzzi travelled the course by car as Hayward demolished Hardy Ballington's record (13:21.19) by a full hour, to win in 12:20.00 and catch officials on the hop with his early arrival in Knightsbridge. Mekler was second in 13:08.36 and Reynolds – only recently recovered from flu – third in 13:47.18

Immensely proud of his protégés, Newton was summoned by the BBC to give an interview for the radio show *Across The Line*. The segment concentrated on the achievements of the South Africans since their arrival in Britain and was broadcast to their home country the following day. Newton was paid four guineas for his trouble.

To make the most of Hayward's remarkable form, Newton persuaded him to stay on and try for a hat-trick of world records at a 24-hour race staged by the Road Runners Club on the Motspur Park track the following month. Hayward agreed, as did Derek Reynolds, although by now Mekler had returned home. Hayward had to attack Newton's 152 miles and 540 yards, set in Canada some 22 years earlier. It would mean circling the shale track in the chilly November conditions no fewer than 600 times. Hayward recalled clearly how his elderly mentor supported his attempt on that gruelling day:

'Newton gave me the odd cup of tea while my main second was Peter Gavuzzi. He kept me well supplied with tea, soup, custard – the eats I needed. All the hot drinks were prepared on a little stove. In the early hours I threw a major tantrum because my drinks were not hot, only to be told they had just come off the stove! Later I was to regret the scalding hot drinks. Both Newton and Gavuzzi told me before the race that after passing 100 miles I was to come off the track and have a massage – big mistake! I was feeling good and wanted to carry on but they insisted. I was in the changing room for about a half-hour and rigor mortis set in! Run? That was a joke, I could hardly walk I was so stiff and cold [after stopping]. Eventually I managed to jog on slowly and ultimately the record distance was within reach . . . I passed Newton's record in 22:41.21 but was so exhausted that in the last 80 minutes I could only move at about 5 m.p.h., and managed another seven miles to make a grand total of 159 miles and 562 yards which was 637 and a quarter laps [seven miles beyond Newton's record]. Derek Reynolds covered 154 miles and 1,226 yards, which was a new British domestic record. This type of race eventually gets very boring. Like a pig with its snout to the ground you circulate – lap after lap after lap – aarrgghh! I knew I should have gone home [earlier] with Mekler and Morrison!'

Hayward's new mark would stand unbeaten for 26 years until Ron Bentley came along in 1979. Including his sensational Comrades run earlier in 1953 (5:52.30), Hayward had now cracked four records at different ultra-distances in just six months. It had been a magnificent display, but things were to go a little sour later on. The cost of his trip to England had largely been met by his club Germiston Callies, who had permission to do so provided all monies were channelled through the South African AAA; later Hayward was accused of accepting funds directly from sponsors and declared a professional, thus banned from all amateur athletics. It was a development that disgusted both the runner and Newton too. Their protests got nowhere, and it would only be 21 years later, with Hayward by then in his sixties, that reinstatement was granted.

Hayward paid tribute to Newton later on: 'It must be said that Arthur Newton is undoubtedly the founder of ultra-distance running as we know it today. His influence during his lifetime on the sport is immeasurable . . . it was probably when he retired from active competition that his influence [really] came to the fore . . . Newton was an inspiration to distance running and was not only an exceptional athlete but also evolved training principles that influenced such coaching stalwarts as Arthur Lydiard and Percy Cerutty. Newton was an Englishman through and through. His house was always open to all and sundry, with the traditional cuppa for anyone who wanted it. Tea was supplied in tankards, never cups, which the runners considered too small!'

Chapter 18

Newtonian Laws of Motion

Newton's ideas on training and coaching evolved directly from his own experiences as an international runner between the wars. As we have seen, much of this running was done alone and without guidance, and at a time when published advice about long-distance work was scarce. As a result, his ideas were fresh, original and based on tried and tested methods. Importantly, immediately after quitting competitive running in 1935, Newton was able to spend most of the next 20 years of his life writing voraciously about his ideas, producing four books, dozens of articles in athletics periodicals and huge volumes of correspondence. A few of his theories caused upset, and one or two were even retracted, but broadly speaking his work gained recognition as essential reading for runners tackling the marathon and distances beyond.

Furthermore, with the benefit of hindsight, it is clear Newton was the first to describe in the English language a set of training ideas that modern experience has shown to be essentially correct.

In his definitive, 932-page work *Lore of Running*, the sports scientist Professor Tim Noakes points out that the only published training advice that preceded Newton came from Walter Thom (1813), Alfred Downer (1900), Harry Andrews (1903), Walter George (1902, 1908), Alf Shrubb (1908, 1910), James Sullivan (1909), J H Hardwick (1912), Sam Mussabini and C Ransom (1913) and Alec Nelson (1924). And none of these authors advised that training should be as frequent as Newton proposed, or that it should be practised all year round.

Professor Noakes says that Newton's legacy, besides his remarkable athletic achievements as an older man, was a body of work that can be condensed into nine aspects of long-distance training. Most of Newton's writing fell into one of these nine areas. The Newtonian 'laws', expressed in Newton's own words, were as follows:

Law 1: Train frequently, all year round

'What would happen to any animal which took a month's rest from hunting? If you want to be a good athlete, you must train all the year round, no matter what. What is really required is a little exercise, constantly, this will benefit you permanently to a far greater degree than single, heavy doses at long intervals'.

Law 2: Start gradually and train gently

'Nearly all of us dash into it, hoping for and expecting results which are quite unwarranted. Nature is unable to make a really first-class job of anything if she is hustled. To enhance our best, we need only, and should only, enhance our average. That is the basis we ought to work on, for it succeeds every time when the other fails. So, in running, it is essential to take to it kindly.'

Law 3: Train first for distance, only later for speed

'If you are going to contest a 26-mile event, you must at least be used to 100 miles a week . . . as it is always the speed, never the distance, that kills, so is it the distance, not the speed, that has to be acquired. In the early days of training you must endeavour only to manage as great a distance on each practised outing as you can cover without becoming abnormally tired . . . your aim throughout should be to avoid all maximum effort while you work with one purpose only, and that is to achieve a definite and sustained rise in the average speed at which you practise, for that is the secret of ultimate achievement . . . you must never, except for short temporary bursts, practise at racing speed.'

Law 4: Don't set your daily training schedule in stone

'Don't set yourself a daily schedule; it is far more sensible to run to a weekly one, because you can't tell what the temperature, the weather, or your own condition will be on any day.'

Law 5: Don't race when in training, or run at race pace for distances over 10 miles

'I decry such things as time-trials . . . I am convinced they are nothing more than a senseless waste of time and energy. They can't tell you any more than the race itself could . . . Racing, then, should be the only time-trial, and should only be run every two, or preferably three weeks apart – six weeks between events would be more suitable for a marathon runner, but once every two months is probably better.'

Law 6: Specialise

'Specialisation nowadays is a necessity. Modern exponents have raised the standards to such a height that nothing but intensive specialisation can put a fellow anywhere near the top. Before the 1914-18 war, the marathon was considered an event for only the favoured few, who had unusual toughness and stamina.'

Law 7: Prevent over-training

'Regulate your training so as to be sure of always being on the safe side. The least sign of overdose will surely lead to trouble. Go so for every day that the last mile or two becomes almost a desperate effort. So long as you are fit for another dose the following day, you are not over-doing it. But you must never permit yourself to approach real exhaustion; you must never become badly tired. A good way to judge whether you are over-doing it is by your appetite. A really fearsome thirst is a definite sign that either the speed or the distance has been too much. Not only are you unbearably thirsty, but your appetite disappears entirely, even for many hours after the event.'

Law 8: Train the mind

'When you begin training, you will find that the longest and most strenuous mental and physical exertions all come at the start . . . It seems to me that stamina is just as much a mental attribute as a physical one. Make your mind healthy and it will do the rest. If it is not normally healthy, you will never make a decent job of anything.'

Law 9: Rest before a big race

'Cut out all racing . . . during the last month of your training; you will need certainly three weeks to put the finishing touches to your stamina and reserve energy. When you consider what a vast amount of work you have already gone through, you will admit that a fortnight or so longer is a relatively trifling matter. Endeavour to keep all your spare time fully occupied with reading, writing, anything that will keep you still, anything to divert your mind from harping on the forthcoming event.'

Newton's writing would often be held up as being based on a common sense approach. There was always reasoning behind his verdicts. A 1955 letter to the South African marathoner Lawrence van Heerden typified this. Newton wrote: 'It's as well to get all the advice you can from any quarter, but then settle back and work out for yourself what appears to be common sense and probably useful, and discard the rest. You've got as good a head as the next man . . . We can only learn from nature, we cannot teach her anything. Nature knows how things can be done best and our business is to study her methods. Stick to the exercise which pleases you most because that is probably the one you are best built for - and don't ever be frightened by big names in the athletic world. They are just men like you and I.'

The solitary early years of teaching himself to run long distances along dusty and deserted roads in South Africa had seen Newton develop into a moral runner, one who sought to absorb pleasure and contentment from the purity of it. He was perhaps the first famous athlete who could be identified as a 'Zen runner'. He identified what would later be called 'runners high', the elevated sense of well-being when running comfortably. Achieving this state was far more important to him than seeking the thrill of beating other men. In his later years he would also express great distaste for 'tactical running', a practice he abhorred and thought was unethical and unsporting. He thought deliberately dogging the footsteps of an opponent, or deliberately slowing a race down from the front, was tantamount to cheating. He did eventually concede ground in this area, accepting that the hurly-burly of a middle-distance track race was a different world to that of the lonely ultra-runner.

Newton's friend John Jewell would later admit that Newton had 'peculiar Church of England views' about tactical running. The pair had lengthy, albeit friendly, arguments over the matter, Jewell pointing out to him that if physical running ability were the only factor, then all races might as well be reduced to time trials. Jimmy Green, editor of *Athletics* and later *Athletics Weekly*, agreed with Jewell, and sent Newton a stinging letter: 'Your ideas on tactics are a totally wrong conception. To talk about "wangling" is absolutely ridiculous and I can only assume that you have had no experience in middle-distance running.' Green was not afraid to take the great man to task, and also castigated Newton for his defence of professional athletes. Said Green: 'I have nothing against a man just because he was a pro, but I know what I am talking about when I say that when money comes in, sport flies out of the window. Ninety-nine per cent of pro running is sprinting and any pro sprinter will tell you that it is all one big wangle from start to finish. It is a case of trying to beat the book. Ever heard of a "light sting" or a "heavy sting"? These are the terms for dosing a runner with brandy or cognac or caffeine or strychnine. I have an article by Dai Stivens about pro running in Australia. Reeks with it. That's what I don't want to see in athletics.'

Marathon coaches of the eras that followed Newton were heavily influenced by him. In the early to mid-1960s the 'Arthur Lydiard system' would become established and would win almost universal praise. It was accepted many of New Zealander Lydiard's principles were founded on Newtonian philosophies. Neither Newton nor Lydiard placed value in such things as weight training, considering that core strength could be best improved in a more natural way, through sessions of hill running, for example.

There were, of course, some who were critical of Newton's insistence that stamina was the first and main requirement for all middle and long distance runners. Emphasis in the 1950s and earlier was very much on speed for all track men. It was a legacy of the days when Walter George managed to break the 10-mile world record despite very low training mileage. But Lydiard, with his 100 miles per week, and others who advocated LSD (long, slow distance) sessions, found almost universal support for the importance of stamina training. LSD was a concept invented by Newton that would became a staple part of all marathon training schedules. Club runners of all levels today, even those not attempting the marathon, appreciate the benefit of at least one LSD run per week as part of a balanced training programme.

It appears the only ideas that Newton ever took on board that didn't arise directly from his own experiences, were those gleaned from a handful of North American coaches in the mid to late-1930s. Newton wrote: 'At various times I had read much of American coaches and their methods and, of course, had seen some very definite results. So I was glad to get an opportunity at Hamilton [Canada] to observe one of their most notable experts at his work, J P Nicholson. By that time I had learnt a much needed lesson, viz. that England and the Dominions were hopelessly behindhand with regard to their handling of the interest and welfare of their athletes. I took careful note of the attitude of coach and pupils to each other; obviously mentality was in every single case taken into account as of primary importance . . . [Britain needs coaches] who have been expertly competent at their work, who have continued to make it their chief concern – like Capt F A M Webster for instance – and preferably, since nothing else can give them the requisite experience, men of middle age. Such men impart character and mental stability in addition to physical ability.'

The importance of re-fuelling properly during a long run was something Newton studied closely and at which he emerged as an innovator. As we have seen, the salt, sugar and lemonade concoction he developed in the 1920s became an important part of his race equipment, and gained great attention in the press, who coined it his 'magic drink'. Modified and enhanced in the years since, Newton's potion can be seen as the first primitive version of the electrolyte drinks of today. Of his eating and drinking habits, Newton wrote: 'Every time I went for a 30-50 mile training spin, or race, I had a good solid meal at the latest possible moment, and then started off quite casually to allow the digestion to call on what energy it needed until its primary demands were satisfied. For the first 20 miles or so I was running almost entirely on what was provided by this last-moment stock of vim. When that began to peter out, I had to think of re-victualling, and as only a very limited choice of foods was suitable for such an occasion, I had to restrict the menu severely. I found there were comparatively few items that could be relied on to furnish energy without a risk of digestive disturbance, and that quite the best of these was sugar.'

In his regular articles contributed to athletics magazines, Newton would occasionally stray into what a modern reader might consider dangerous and politically incorrect territory. As briefly mentioned in Chapter 17, the January 1950 edition of *Athletics Review* carried a piece by Newton that was critical of a radio broadcast which failed to resolve the question of why black athletes dominated sprinting, whereas white men were better at long distances. Newton suggested the answer was obvious: 'Those originally from Africa . . . have much thicker skulls than Europeans, and as their heads are approximately the same size, they must have some two ounces less brains inside.' He went on: 'You never heard of a native [African], however adept at it, able to outrun a well-trained European over a long distance. [This is because] the European has learnt how to use his brains to train himself, while the native never for a moment gave the matter of training a thought.'

Times and attitudes were very different in 1950, of course, but it is hard to digest such a view without wincing in horror. Was this really the same person described by his friends as the nicest, most tolerant man they had ever encountered? Perhaps we should consider the final sentence of Newton's article – in which he urges readers who disagree to pick up their pens and write in with all speed: 'Write to the editor and tell him where I'm wrong. It'll help all of us.' His skull-size theory sounds like racist nonsense today, but perhaps back then he was simply trying to provoke a debate?

Chapter 19

Genuflecting at Arthur's Seat

By the middle of 1955, Newton's failing health, and in particular his increasing blindness, was curtailing his running. After his 72nd birthday he was still able to get out for long walks, but was finding it difficult to maintain an early morning running regime that had lasted 33 years.

He found it all highly frustrating, but a constant stream of visitors kept him in good spirits and he was pleased to welcome Jackie Mekler from Johannesburg for a second stay at Ruislip. The pair of them were soon heading westwards for the 42-mile road race held between Bristol and Weston-super-Mare. Mekler accepted an invitation to run, and Newton agreed to be the guest of honour and official starter. The race would end just yards from the big townhouse in which Newton had been born.

Mekler recalls that soon after accepting the Bristol invite, he was contacted by organisers of the Edinburgh Highland Games Marathon, who wanted him at their race just a week later. They were highly persuasive and Mekler decided to cancel Bristol, as to run both events would surely be unwise. Newton was aghast and gave his house guest a rollicking: 'You've given an undertaking to the Bristol people and you've got to stick to it, he told me. So we made a compromise and I ran in both races!'

The Road Runners Club event in Somerset began early on an August morning near Bristol's Bedminster Bridge, the signal to start given by Newton. According to one local paper, he was visiting his town of birth for the first time since childhood. It was a hot day and 23 runners set off from Coronation Road, heading for the Grand Pier in Weston-super-Mare via the Clevedon road. Forty-five-year old Welshman Tom Richards, silver medallist at the 1948 Olympics, won in 4:17.18, and Mekler, representing Blackheath, came in second less than 14 minutes later. Mekler heeded Newton's advice on pacing, and was able to pass long-time leader Brian Ashwell in the closing stages. The heat led to half the field failing to complete the 42-mile journey.

By Christmas of 1955 Newton had decided his daily training regime would definitely have to come to an end, largely due to his failing eyesight. The end of the year would see him reach exactly 100,000 miles after 33 years in the sport, and he felt this was an appropriate point to call a halt. He felt he could get adequate exercise through walking, and the early morning runs would have to cease. Typically he didn't make a great fuss over this monumental decision, announcing his plans quietly in a letter to Mekler, although the news did later reach the *Johannesburg and Transvaal Sunday Times* on New Year's Day 1956.

After news of his situation spread among old friends in South Africa and Rhodesia, plans were soon drawn up to get him over there for a 'tour' featuring several weeks of receptions, banquets and speaking engagements. It would be a chance to honour his lifetime of achievements and for Newton, perhaps a final opportunity to visit his old haunts and meet old friends. Most of the cost was met by a special subscription fund, with Newton spending part of the time enjoying the hospitality of running pals such as Hayward and Mekler. In all, the trip would span some four months, covering his 73rd birthday in May 1956, and would involve some serious planning.

Newton asked to be kept up to date with the itinerary they were organising for him, and before sailing to Durban on the *MV Warwick Castle*, he scribbled down some of the key events on a sheet of paper. It would not amount to a complete list by any means, but gave an indication of what was in store, and ended up resembling the sort of schedule one might imagine a member of the Royal family might undertake, let alone a mild-mannered, half-blind 73-year-old man:

April:
Car from Bloemfontain to Jo'burg;
Press conference;
Banquet with Mayor and Mayoress at Springbok Hotel;
Dinner with the Meklers in Yeoville;
Receive honorary membership of Wanderers Club;
Inspection visit to Van Dyk mine;
Germiston Callies social events;
Radio broadcast with Wally Hayward – In Town Tonight;
Attend road races – present prizes, etc;
May:
Arrive Pietermaritzburg;
Give lectures and attend dinners;
Civic events involving Mayor;
Durban Press Club guest of honour;
Guest of honour of people of Harding;
Visit the Gunga Din Shellhole;
Plant ceremonial tree in Town Gardens of Harding;
Fly to Durban;
Attend start of Comrades Marathon;
Civic welcome, address schoolchildren;

Various scheduled stops along Comrades route;
Pietermaritzburg civic welcome at finish, present prizes;
   June:
Fly from Jo'burg to Bulawayo;
Various lectures, dinners and broadcasts;
Attend various races including Gwelo to Bulawayo 106-mile relay;
Get-together of Bulawayo Harriers;
Return flight to Jo'burg.

Newton enjoyed his trip down Memory Lane immensely and returned exhausted but happy. Back in Britain he soon found the social whirl was continuing, and he accepted an invitation to a Road Runners Club dinner at the House of Commons, staged to honour marathon runners from throughout the British Empire and Commonwealth.

In 1958 Newton made another nostalgic journey, this one to the Bear Inn at Box, to witness the finish of a 100-mile record attempt by 40-year-old Ron Hopcroft, who ran for Thames Valley Harriers and worked for the gas board. Hopcroft was running the route Newton knew so well, but in reverse, due to traffic issues. It meant he had to tackle the hilly sections at the end of his ordeal, but he still managed a fine new record of 12:18.16. Newton, of course, was never disappointed to see his old records beaten, and was delighted for the stocky Hopcroft.

By the late 1950s Newton was still walking up to 90 miles per week, small fry compared to previous years of course, and selecting his routes carefully so that his poor eyesight didn't hamper his progress too much. He still had plenty of visitors from near and far and one frequent caller was a local running enthusiast called Frank Perkin. Frank was desperate to own a copy of *Commonsense Athletics*, but as it was out of print, and Newton didn't have any spares, he had to call round with pen and notebook and transcribe the book's contents bit by bit, the author looking on and enquiring whether Frank required more tea?

During the summer of 1959 Newton encountered more health problems, suffering what was reported as a minor stroke at his home. Perkin and his other local acquaintances became very concerned over his condition, but when they urged him to seek help he refused as he didn't want to put anybody to any trouble. It would take several days of persuasion by friends, and by his doctor, before the stubborn old runner agreed to be taken to nearby Hillingdon Hospital. Perkin wrote to Jackie Mekler in South Africa to tell him Newton was insisting he didn't want any fuss, although during one moment of weakness had admitted he was now ready to die. Mekler today recalls the note well, and his sadness at receiving it: 'Remember Newton was a very proud man. He would have been horribly embarrassed to have people fussing about him, especially in the condition he was in. I'm certain he would not have wanted to survive under those conditions.'

On Monday, 7th September 1959, the man they thought was indestructible drew his final breath in Hillingdon Hospital, aged 76. Doctor H Savage recorded the cause of death as bronco-pneumonia and cerebral haemorrhage. For large parts of his life Newton had been a true loner, but his passing certainly left a hole in the lives of many acquaintances, particularly his running pals. He left behind a modest estate of £2,634 11s 7d, most of which was likely to have represented the value of his three-bedroomed house.

His niece Sally Galbraith can today clearly recall how she found out her famous uncle was seriously ill and dying. The message reached her during a car journey in the north of England with her then-husband, the celebrated French horn player Barry Tuckwell. They had been to the Edinburgh Festival where Tuckwell had performed, and then on to the opening of a new theatre near Whitehaven, where he and flautist Richard Adeney performed as soloists, alongside Dame Peggy Ashcroft. From here they had to drive across the Pennines to Durham for a third engagement. During this journey, Adeney felt unwell as their little VW Beetle trundled over the many hills. Spotting an AA roadside office, they stopped to ask the staff for a pill and some water to ease Adeney's discomfort. While this was going on, a staff member recognised their car as one they had been asked to look out for, in order to pass on an urgent message. This turned out to be notification that Newton was seriously ill and they should head for the hospital in west London urgently. They drove south and Sally's next task was to track down her father Bernard, who was travelling somewhere between Switzerland and Germany. Again messages were left and again, seemingly against the odds, reached the intended recipient, meaning members of the family were able to gather at Newton's bedside.

Newton was cremated at lunchtime on Thursday, 10th September at the Breakspear Crematorium in Ruislip. His ashes were scattered in the Gardens of Remembrance at a location known today simply as '43CC'. Sadly tree No 43 has now vanished, and all that remains to mark the spot is a small green marker peg. Newton is mentioned in the Book of Remembrance, however.

His passing escaped the attention of the Ruislip local papers in 1959, but the athletics press recorded tributes, as did *The Times*, whose correspondent wrote: 'Newton was quite the most generous man I have known. His hospitality was astonishing and at times quite embarrassing.

He gradually divested himself of his capital in the service of his friends and latterly literally gave them his sustenance. He was exceptionally modest and shy: the only time I knew him to boast was once when he spoke of the number of visitors he had had the week before.' Jimmy Green of *Athletics Weekly* wrote: 'Newton got people hot under the collar with some of his views, but to his credit had changed some of his radical beliefs in recent years which earned him even more respect.'

John Jewell paid tribute in the *Road Runners Club Newsletter*, saying Newton explored and preached new methods of training which became universal practice, and no detail was too insignificant for his study and attention: 'His adventurous life and amazing athletics career make fascinating reading. He never sought the limelight, yet never has any athlete been more universally admired and liked. His home in Ruislip became a Mecca for long distance runners. Often and long have we discussed the supremely exacting and fascinating sport of athletics there, with Newton asking if we had really enough sugar in the tea?'

There were few trophies or medals to be redistributed during the sad business of clearing Newton's home, for he had given most of them away years earlier. Some memorabilia was earmarked for his former club colleagues in Bulawayo, while a quantity of photos, papers, scrapbooks and correspondence would eventually find its way, via John Jewell, to the University of Birmingham where it would be carefully archived in the library's Special Collections department.

Just a week or two after his death, the staging of the ninth annual London to Brighton race saw the Arthur Newton Cup won by German-born 26-year old Fritz Madel of Durban AC. A touching tribute was paid to Newton by organiser Ernest Neville during the presentations. Not long after this, Jackie Mekler visited England again, but admits it was not a happy occasion without Newton to welcome him:

'It was very sad. His Ruislip house was my second home. I went to visit Peter Gavuzzi nearby and he looked after me, but it was all a haunting, empty experience. With the loss of Newton's house as a base, Arthur Whitehead of the Road Runners Club provided accommodation at Lauriston Cottage, but I did miss Newton not being around. I thought back to how he used to tease me in races, saying that I ran with "a dirty black look" on my face. His death was doubly sad really, firstly because he was gone and secondly because he had left me as one of the beneficiaries of his will.'

With thoughts of his mentor in the back of his mind, Mekler raced to victory in the 1960 London to Brighton race during this trip, creating a new event record of 5:25.26.

Meanwhile, back in South Africa, old Newton acquaintances organised the erection of a commemorative stone in Harding, beside the tree Newton planted during his 1956 visit. His old Harding friends wrote to the Road Runners Club to pass on news of the stone and to explain that its inscription mentioned Newton's Zulu name, Mantabeni, which translated as 'master of the mountains'. The stone also recognised the fact that Newton had been a retrospective winner of the American Helms Foundation's award as the Outstanding Sportsman of Africa of 1925. Newton had been a member of the Memorable Order of Tin Hats (war veterans) in Harding, and his stone would later be moved to their gardens to safeguard it against vandalism.

Late in the 1960s, the young New Zealand journalist Norman Harris joined forces with record-breaking athlete Ron Clarke to write *The Lonely Breed*, an acclaimed study of 21 distance runners. The chapter they called 'The Extraordinary Mr Newton' represented the first insightful work on Newton to be published. Reflecting on Newton all these years later, Harris agrees that of all their 21 subjects, Newton was probably 'the loneliest of that lonely breed.'

Outside of his immediate circle, Newton's name inevitably quickly faded from prominence after his death. There was an occasion, however, when he would grab the interest of the experts on the popular TV show, *Antiques Roadshow*. His brother Bernard's granddaughter paid the show a visit, taking along for inspection a chronometer used in his running days by Newton. The experts declared it was a fascinating timepiece with beautiful movement, but its value was not especially high due to its 'rather tawdry case'. In 2007 a silver salver presented to Newton to mark his 1934 record at 100 miles fared somewhat better. It went under the hammer at Bonham's auctioneers in Bath and caused considerable interest, eventually being snapped up athletics archivist Ian Champion.

In South Africa, Newton is nowadays sometimes referred to as 'Greatheart', in recognition of the way he used to donate his trophies to deserving causes. But he is best remembered there as a founding father of the Comrades Marathon, which remains a hugely popular annual event. At the race's halfway point, near Drummond, is a special landmark that many of the competitors look out for – Arthur's Seat. This is a niche cut into the bank of the cutting at the site of a 'Wall of Honour', and is reputed to have been a favourite resting spot of Newton, five times winner of the race. Legend has it that runners who pay tribute to Newton when they pass this point, by placing flowers in the niche and doffing their cap with the greeting 'Good morning Mr Newton', will enjoy a strong second half of the race.

A quick survey among modern day Comrades runners revealed that this tradition is indeed alive and well – and, more importantly, often seems to work!

South African Andy McKissock said: 'I've always dropped my floral tribute en route but have heard of many others tripping and getting injured shortly after passing this point. Needless to say in running lore the fallers were always the runners who had scorned the whole idea!'

Surrey-based 'Slow Duck' said: 'Nine runs. Nine stops at Arthur's Seat to pay my respects to Mr Newton. Nine finishes within the cut-off time.'

Cila from Namibia said: 'Last year I picked my flower early, ran with it in my hand, stopped at Arthur's Seat and gently put the flower down, and properly greeted the big man with a finger to my peak in a salute. I then finished my novice run in time and in good health and in good form. This year [2008] I was in a bus at Arthur's Seat and we were told "Just drop your flower somewhere here" and I did just that, being unable to get close, and in the rush didn't even say "hi" to Mr Newton. I did not finish the race. Enough said. Next time I'll do it properly.'

South African Caisa said: '2008 was my first Comrades. I saw the guy handing out the flowers, but he wasn't near where I was running and I was past him before I realised where we were. People ahead of me were just dropping the flowers on the road. No-one ahead of me stopped and I was past Arthur's Seat before I realised that the seat was on the left side, for I had been looking to the right. So I quickly looked back at the seat – it must have been prompted by my sub-conscious mind I guess – said a "Good morning Sir" to Arthur Newton in my head and kept going. No-one around me stopped, no-one else acknowledged the legend. I did finish, in 11:39, and had a really, really good day.'

Suren from South Africa: 'I did not stop at Arthur's Seat, but always had that silent respect for him in my mind when I passed that place.' Waco from South Africa: 'Yup two Comrades, two "Good Morning Sirs" and two very successful finishes.' Simon of South Africa pointed out: 'You will often find flowers at Arthur's Seat, any time from January onwards. Locals train on the route and try to suck up to Arthur before the big day, in the hope of gaining some advantage.'

The final word should go to runner 'Gobi One' from Britain: 'When I ran nobody was stopping, but there was a lot of very loud "Good Morning Arthurs" being shouted. I'm polite and I merely tip my hat as I go by. Has it helped me? I don't know, as my fortunes have been very mixed. But would I ever stop tipping my hat to the great man? Hell no, why risk upsetting him?'

Appendix

Although they were universally hailed at the time as 'world records' or 'world's bests', Arthur Newton's great runs on the road between 1922 and 1934 are today treated by athletics statisticians and experts rather more prosaically as 'Noteworthy Performances'.

The reason for this, explains ultra-running historian Andy Milroy, is that Newton's runs were generally solo, uncompetitive runs, performed on courses which were at best approximate. Meticulous and uncompromisingly accurate measurement of road courses, as we understand it today, was then many years away. Reportedly Newton himself measured the Comrades Marathon course using a surveyor's wheel in the late 1920s, but even this only gives an approximate distance and is not acceptable in today's high-tech terms.

Most of Newton's great runs were solo performances, which are not nowadays considered for record purposes because all those involved in the event are of course committed to the runner, and there would be no impartial, independent witnesses, i.e. opponents and their handlers.

It is interesting to note that in the 50 years since his death, Newton has been lauded more for his writing than his pioneering running. Milroy says: 'He provided a degree of continuity as a conduit between the late 19th century and the early 1950s, when the distance track records were revised. This was largely via his writing. It was as a pioneer and revivalist that Newton really came into his own, and we should recognise that for much of his running career he was operating in a virtual vacuum, so looked to be much better than he was.'

Distance running went through some very important stages of development during Newton's era. Perhaps the first major step forward in his lifetime came in 1896 when the first 'marathon' was held at the inaugural Olympic Games at Athens. The idea was speedily copied, but it took the heroic failure of Dorando Pietri in the 1908 London Olympic marathon to really capture the imagination of the sporting public. On a hot day the Italian dramatically collapsed and was helped over the finish line, thus not completing the 26 miles and 385 yards course under his own steam. The length of that course became the standard marathon distance in 1924. The great interest in 1908 encouraged promoters to stage professional races and the marathon craze was born.

Interest in racing from London to Brighton was revived by walkers and the first amateur running race (actually a 'go-as-you-please' contest) was won by Frank Randall in under seven hours in 1899. A professional race four years later resulted in an easy victory for Len Hurst, the outstanding British 'marathon' runner of the day. His record was to stand for over 20 years until Newton came along

Around the time of the 1914-18 War, we saw the gradual establishment of the 20km, 25km and 30km as recognised metric long-distance events, aided by the surge of interest created by the marathon craze. There was little activity in the ultra long distance events, however. In 1909 in the USA, Sydney Hatch ran close to 16 hours for 100 miles on the road, but Edgar Lloyd's new world record for 50 miles in 1913 was the only attack on the various track records set in the 1880s.

It was not until the 1920s that a new force came to stir this stagnation. Vic Clapham, a South African, remembering the route marches he made in the 1914-18 War, overcame opposition to organise a 54-mile race from Pietermaritzburg to Durban, and the Comrades Marathon was born in 1921. This was the race that piqued the interest of a certain local farmer, English-born Arthur Newton, who would go on to make the first concerted attack on the old 19th century standards.

In the early 1950s, with the help of Newton himself, by now in his sixties, the newly formed Road Runners Club dedicated itself to modernisation of the long-distance track records, some of which were nearly 70 years old. The time was ripe as there was an upsurge in long distance standards in the early 1950s, led by such runners as Emil Zatopek and Jim Peters. The records at 30, 40 and 50 miles were recognised by the Amateur Athletic Association from the 1880s, and many of these records survived up until the 1940s when the RRC staged its own events: for several of these, involving Wally Hayward and Gerald Walsh, Newton himself was a trackside helper.

Newton's training mileage, as published by him in mid-1935

	Walked	Run	Total	Daily average
1922	1,584	3,094	4,678	12
1923	1,688	7,480	9,168	25
1924	2,608	5,161	7,769	21
1925	2,609	3,949	6,558	17
1926	1,832	6,082	7,914	21
1927	1,552	5,383	6,935	19
1928	1,948	6,193	8,141	22
1929	2,249	5,214	7,463	20
1930	3,540	4,273	7,813	21
1931	1,899	6,866	8,765	24
1932	2,553	5,659	8,212	22
1933	1,989	5,419	7,408	20
1934	2,759	5,678	8,437	23
1935	823	2,651	3,474	19
Totals	29,633	73,102	102,735	20